THE
BEAR BOOK

THE

BEAR BOOK

Survive and Profit in Ferocious Markets

JOHN ROTHCHILD

JOHN WILEY & SONS, INC.

New York • Chichester • Weinheim • Brisbane • Singapore • Toronto

Published by John Wiley & Sons, Inc.

Published simultaneously in Canada.

This publication is designed to provide accurate and authoritative information in regard to the subject matter covered. It is sold with the understanding that the publisher is not engaged in rendering professional services. If professional advice or other expert assistance is required, the services of a competent professional person should be sought.

Library of Congress Cataloging-in-Publication Data:

Rothchild, John
    The bear book : survive and profit in ferocious markets / John
Rothchild.
      p.   cm.
    Includes bibliographical references and index.
    ISBN 0-471-19718-1 (alk. paper)
    1. Stock exchanges. I. Title.
HG4551.R67 1998
332.63'22—dc21   97-52583

Printed in the United States of America.

10 9 8 7 6 5 4 3 2 1

ACKNOWLEDGMENTS

AT JOHN WILEY & SONS, publisher Myles Thompson gave enthusiastic support for this project, thus overpowering all attempts by the author to procrastinate. Jennifer Pincott worked overtime to get the manuscript in shape, and in one late-night stint wrapped herself in a blanket when the office heating system had been turned off. Olga Moya helped with fact checking; Andrea Abbott pursued every angle from the marketing department; Laurie Thompson from the publicity department. Mary Daniello, associate managing editor at Wiley, along with Nancy Marcus Land and her staff at Publications Development Company of Texas, made a book out of chaos. Thanks also to Renea Perry, Myles Thompson's assistant, and thanks to David DeRosa, who provided expert feedback on the currency chapter.

Others who contributed time, effort, and useful advice are as follows:

At Morningstar: Annette Larson, who provided all the data on low-risk mutual funds, derived from Morningstar's Principia software program.

At the Zweig organization: Marty Zweig, Emma Lewis, Carol R. Whitehead.

At Standard & Poor's: Sam Stovall.

At InvesTech Research: Jim and Lisa Stack, Marianne Rosar.

At Elliott Wave International: Bob Prechter, Dave Allman, Sally Webb.

At Ned Davis Research: Ned Davis, Bill Hayes, Karen Tuttle.

At CNBC: Ron Insana, Jim Rogers.

At Holl International: Eric Fry.

ACKNOWLEDGMENTS

At Lipper Analytical: Anjela Traboulsi.

At Salomon/Smith Barney: Adam Carlin, Richard Bermont.

At the Leuthold Group: Jim Floyd.

From the short-sellers' camp: Jim Chanos, Bill Fleckenstein, the Feshbach brothers, Kathryn Staley, Bill McGarr.

Elizabeth Darhansoff, literary agent, a writer's best friend, and worthy adversary of the contract department at any publishing house.

Harry Strunk, who connects wealthy investors with money managers who make preservation of capital their number-one goal.

Jeff and Yale Hirsch at the Hirsch organization, which produces the *Stock Trader's Almanac*.

Michael O'Higgins, author of *Beating the Dow* and inventor of the "Dogs of the Dow" theory, currently at work on a sequel, *Beating the Dow with Bonds*.

John Waggoner, *USA Today* columnist, author of *Money Madness*.

Marc Faber, maverick investor; editor of the *Gloom, Boom & Doom Report*.

Jim Grant, *Grant's Interest Rate Observer*.

Nick Gulden, Victoria Hofstead at ING Barings.

George Martin, University of Massachusetts School of Management, Amherst.

Al Sindlinger, Sindlinger consumer research.

Richard Russell, publisher of the *Dow Theory Letter*.

John Dennis Brown, author of *Panic Profits*.

William O'Neil, John Schnieders at *Investor's Business Daily*.

Suzanne Wittebort, Moody's Investors Service.

Lynn Newman, New York Stock Exchange.

Nancy Smith, Securities and Exchange Commission.

Paul Stephens, Robertson Stephens, San Francisco.

Steve Norwitz, T. Rowe Price.

Rick Pucci, I/B/E/S International.

Mike Gmitter, Securities Research Company.

Robert Hagstrom, author of *The Warren Buffett Way*.

James Libera, publisher of the *Closed-End Country Fund Report*.

Harry Browne, enemy of the government hoodwink.

CONTENTS

CONTENTS

Contents

CONTENTS

Recent Signs of a Top

Love poems to the Dow appear in Bill Gates's on-line magazine, *Slate*.
Here's an example:

> In harmony with the Dow,
> Memory serves no purpose;
> Act with the day's momentum,
> Forgetting all history.
> '87 is but a pale shadow,
> '73 a warm breeze.
>
> The Dow is all-loving,
> That's why everyone loves it.

- Lou Harris poll (1996) shows 85 percent of respondents expect the stock market will be as good to them (or better) in the next decade as it was in the last; 41 percent don't anticipate even a minor correction.
- Headline on cover of *Barron's Magazine:* "Next Stop Dow 8,000?" followed by "When? How? Dow 10,000."
- Beardstown Ladies write third best-seller.
- Beardstown lady more concerned with sewing her son's Halloween costume than with Dow losing 554 points on big drop in October 1997.
- The Street.Com financial Website hosts a "mutual fund derby," to see which domestic fund managers can win, place, and show by end of latest quarter.
- Whitey Ford is seen signing autographs in a booth at a financial planning conference, as a promotional come-on. In another booth, Minnie Mouse offers photo ops.
- In a New York Stock Exchange survey, six out of ten respondents disagree or strongly disagree with the statement: "I think there will be a big stock market decline during 1997–1998."

These tidbits courtesy of Bob Prechter, Marty Zweig, Susan Antilla at the *New York Observer*, Kiplinger's, Jim Stack.

Recent Signs of a Top *(Continued)*

- One in three adults owns a mutual fund, whereas only one in four adults owns a car. In 1992, only one in six adults owned a mutual fund.
- Seat on the New York Stock Exchange costs a record $1.6 million, and the price doesn't include cushions.
- Egypt launches first mutual fund.
- New Jersey plans to cure shortfall in state pension system by borrowing money and investing it in stocks.
- Dean Witter, which once planted stockbrokers in Sears stores, merges with highbrow Morgan Stanley.
- Merrill Lynch announces plan to open "financial supermarket," where investors can choose from 1,000 funds.
- Bull with bicycle grips for horns appears in two-page full-color advertisement for life insurance company selling annuity tied to stock market.
- Average compensation of mutual fund portfolio managers rises 55 percent in single year, to $370,000. Last raise of this magnitude occurred near the stock market high of January 1973.
- *Business Week* reports three-quarters of the money in stock mutual funds was invested since 1990.
- Employment in brokerage industry breaks records, slightly below level reached at 1987 market top.
- Politicians in Washington consider allowing the Social Security system to invest in the stock market for the first time ever.
- National roster of investment clubs hits 32,000, up from 4,000 fifteen years ago.
- Never have bulls been attached to so many monitoring devices. Stock quotes are delivered by phone, computer, TV, pager, and satellite link. Investors are as close to the latest results as they are to the time of day.

INTRODUCTION

As of early 1998, 82 million Americans had become share-holders, mostly through mutual funds. At least half that number owned stocks for less than eight years. Their money had yet to make the acquaintance of a bear. Never in history was so much new wealth attached to stocks. Never before had so many investors avoided a bear's clutches for so long.

There was a Crash in 1987 and a mild bear market surfaced in 1990, but aside from these two cases of *taurus interruptus*, the bulls have had their way for a generation: long enough for children of investors to become investors, not to mention brokers, traders, fund managers, and analysts who write the bullish reports that push stocks higher. Stocks have gone up for so long that people have forgotten what a bear looks like and how to defend a portfolio from the havoc a bear can create.

That bear markets are inevitable there can be no doubt. Based on the standard definition—a 20 percent markdown in stock prices from the latest high—we see a bear market about as often as we elect a pres-ident—once every four years. Depending on who's counting, there have been twenty-four, twenty-five, or twenty-six bear markets in this century. Nasty bear markets happen every six and a half years. Smaller declines of 10 percent, called "corrections," happen every two years or so. Taken together, these minor and major setbacks have produced losses in thirty-three years out of the past one hundred, making in-vestors unhappy roughly one-third of the time.

Unlucky stockpickers often find themselves in a personal bear; their stocks go down when everybody else's stocks go up. This is harder to take than a general bear, where misery never lacks company. Even in a bull market, the average stock will fluctuate 50 percent from high to low in a typical year—for instance, rising from $10 to $12.50 and falling back to $7.50. The owners are subjected to constant revisions in net worth. These revisions are less drastic in mutual funds, where the paper gains and losses are smoothed out.

The bull lobby insists that future bear markets will be shorter and less vicious than their predecessors, for a variety of reasons, such as "Alan Greenspan won't let the bears get away with it." Greenspan is the chairman of the Federal Reserve Board (Fed), which acts as investors' Army Corps of Engineers. The Fed controls the nation's finances by pumping money into or out of the banks, the way the Corps controls the rivers and lakes by pumping water into and out of reservoirs. Bear markets have been relatively subdued in the modern era, but they still happen as frequently as they did in the days when the Fed was less adept at pumping. Since 1956, the market has fallen into a bear's clutches 14 times, or about every three years.

In the business and finance section of any library, it's easy to find advice on how to profit when stock prices are rising, but advice on how to profit (or at least to minimize losses) when prices are setting is much harder to come by. The "b" word is rarely seen in the title of an investment how-to book.

There's a regular supply of doomsday bestsellers, such as Ravi Batra's *The Great Depression of 1990* (Simon & Schuster, 1987), or Howard Ruff's *How to Prosper During the Coming Bad Years* (Warner Books, 1979), in which Ruff tells everybody to hoard canned spaghetti, join a barter group, and await the collapse of civilization. But when civilization doesn't collapse, as it didn't in 1979, the consumer of the doomsday best-seller is stuck with an oversupply of cans and still no clue as to how to handle the next stock market decline.

In fact, it's hard to think of a calamity for which the country is more poorly coached than the inevitable stock market setback. Brokerage houses and mutual fund companies offer occasional advice, but, like a parent talking to the kids about sex, the subject makes them nervous. Bear markets get a minimum of attention in the financial press for the same reason. Miami Beach was never zoned for a cemetery—why ruin the fun by dwelling on the negative?

It's no accident that the largest investment house in the world, Merrill Lynch, has a bull for a mascot, and took "Bullish on America" for its corporate motto. No investment house has dared adopt the slogan "Bearish on America," even during market declines when it might bring in extra business. After all, the United States is the country of origin for bullish phrases such as "Up, up, and away," "Have a nice day," "Can do," "Stairway to the stars," and "Everything's coming up roses."

Every hurricane season, Floridians are reminded to keep candles and flashlights at the ready, fill bathtubs with water, hang storm shutters, and seek higher ground, as conditions warrant. Every blizzard season, Minnesotans are told to replenish their heating oil, tune up their furnaces, sweep chimneys, install snow tires, spread salt on the walkways, and hang shovels near the entrance door. For an auto wreck or a slip on a frozen walkway, the entire nation is insured and prepared to file suit. But when a bear market happens, most investors are both unprepared and uninsured. That the next decline will be a surprise to many is shown in a recent Lou Harris survey: in which four out of ten respondents doubted that stocks would drop even 10 percent from now until the year 2007.

Should you sell stocks and hide out in cash? Should you sell certain stocks and buy others? Should you switch mutual funds? Should you wait it out? Should you do nothing and allow your assets to take a mauling? Should you cut your losses and escape to bonds, gold, or the money market? Should you switch from one stock to another, trade your small-stock mutual fund for a large-stock mutual fund, or your growth fund for a growth-and-income fund? These decisions are best pondered in advance, for the same reason that it's best to map an escape route before there's a fire in the house.

The purpose of this book is to fill the bearish information gap. Included is advice about how to cope with panics, crashes, corrections, or whatever the latest term for a kick in the portfolio. Most of the advice comes directly from investment advisers, strategists, and fund managers who've been expecting a bear market for some time. Many have suffered in the wallet and the ego; they've been held up to ridicule and criticized in print for crying bear too early. Sooner or later, and probably sooner, the market will prove them right.

A Good Word for Bearish Investors

Why and how two animals came to be associated with financial gain and loss nobody seems to know. It might as well have been a phoenix or a jackrabbit for the upside, and an ostrich or a burrowing mole for the downside. One theory dates these terms from the Middle Ages, when bull and bear fights attracted crowds to the local fairs. It's possible the same people who bet on the fights brought the bull–bear lingo into the traders' vocabulary.

In every trade, from bushels of wheat to barrels of oil, from the used car in the driveway to the cracked mirror in the flea market, there's a bull and a bear. The bull is the buyer of the merchandise, the bear is the seller. On Wall Street, a stock is worth only what somebody else will pay for it. This detail is often lost in rising markets, when investors assume rising prices are the natural order of things and a profitable outcome a foregone conclusion. Yet the profits can't continue unless the next buyer is willing to pay more than the last, and the buyer after that pays more than he does.

Meanwhile, a seller is willing to divest at a certain price because he thinks the cash he receives in the trade is more valuable than the merchandise. He's selling the merchandise because he's tired of looking at it, or perhaps because he expects today's buyer will be more generous than tomorrow's buyer. That means he expects the price will go lower rather than higher.

The seller's role is hidden in the popular vocabulary of finance. How often have you heard when you buy a stock, you're "putting money into the market?" That description leaves the impression money is injected into stocks like pecuniary fertilizer, enriching corporate blossoms. In fact, money isn't put into the market at all. It moves from the buyer's pocket into the seller's pocket, the same as money spent at any neighborhood garage sale.

This is why stocks can't go up forever. The higher the prices the merchandise will fetch, the more inclined the owners are to sell it. Then as prices begin to fall, owners who couldn't get top dollar will compete for the chance to sell for less than top dollar. A bear market is merely the sum total of millions of individual transactions, in which consenting adults are willing to make deals at progressively lower prices.

People who foresee a bear market are also called bears. To a chronic bear, something bad is always about to happen. The occasional bear sees trouble only in certain "bearish" situations. There are few if any chronic bears, as pessimists have a hard time making a living in America. Diehard pessimists can be found in apocalyptic cults, prairie militias, newspaper editorial offices, or college professorships. Academia is a preserve for bearish thought, from which dire predictions about global warming, Malthusian starvation (Malthus was a professor), plagues, pestilence, and nuclear winter emanate. Negative opinion is less tolerated in commercial establishments such as auto dealerships, ad agencies, shopping malls, corporate boardrooms, and Wall Street investment houses. Even occasional bears bristle at the suggestion they are bearish by nature. Robert Prechter and Charles Allmon, prominent newsletter publishers, have been temporarily bearish on U.S. stocks for more than a decade, but they remind their detractors that someday, when stocks fall to attractive prices, they will turn bullish again.

A glance at the cover of this book is prima facie evidence that bears are an oppressed minority. The painting, "The Bulls and Bears in the Market," was unveiled in 1879 by William H. Beard, a presumably frustrated investor. The two species are having it out on the street in front of the New York Stock Exchange. Bears are trampled on the cobblestones or tossed in the air like pizza dough. A lucky survivor has climbed a light pole to avoid the Pamplona below. As two bulls are wrestled to the ground by a cowpoking grizzly, another bull is being served for lunch. The street is littered with fur, rawhide, and stray limbs.

The full battle scene, only some of which appears on this cover, shows the bears outnumbered at least ten to one, and mostly confined to the edges of the canvas, while the bulls dominate the center, where they've gained the upper hoof. From the look of it, the bears are responsible for starting this rumble. Even 119 years ago, when Beard painted this, bears were depicted as troublemakers on the margins of capitalism, a second-class status they have held continuously since.

To be bearish in an optimistic society, even temporarily, requires a stubborn streak and a thick skin. Bears in a bear market are often accused of profiting from the misery of others. They bet on the cloud while others are betting on the silver lining. Sometimes, they even bet against the silver lining by "shorting" it, but this doesn't do any harm to investors on the long side of the lining. Short sellers perform a useful public service and become the saviors in a bear market, buying stocks at the bottom when nobody else is buying. (Further explanation appears on page 205.)

Bears in a bull market get called all kinds of names: insane, idiotic, dumb, stopped clocks, old fogies, reactionaries, alarmists, Chicken

Little, brain dead, old fools, and party poopers. In 1997, they were diagnosed as "equity-phobic" by *Washington Post* financial columnist James Glassman. The most popular tag to pin on a bear is "pessimist" or "hopeless pessimist," although bearish investors who expect things will get worse are relatively optimistic about the present.

Who could be more optimistic about the world financial system and its capacity for survival than practicing bears who bet against stocks, oil, gold, wheat, soybeans, bonds, lumber, or orange juice? A true pessimist wouldn't play the downside of these markets, because when the system collapsed, they'd never get paid by the losers who took the other side of the trades.

A bear has faith: faith that the banks and the brokerage houses will continue to transact business; faith that the debtors and the losers will make good on their losses; faith that in the bleakest of times for society at large, Wall Street will prevail. If that's not patriotism, what is?

Bears are pigheaded but not cocky, especially after they've missed the biggest gains from a fifteen-year bonanza in stocks. When bears get cocky, as some did after making big profits in the bear market of 1973–1974, a new bull market is about to begin. When bulls get cocky, as many have in the 1990s, a bear market is a distinct possibility.

PART ONE

~

BEARS WILL
RISE AGAIN

ARE STOCKS REALLY
THAT GREAT?

EVERY BROKERAGE HOUSE and most financial planners invite a new client—let's assume it's you—to fill out a questionnaire about your income, net worth, financial goals, and other intimacies you'd never share with your friends. Your answers are run through a computer and, in minutes, you get a printout of how much money you'll need in the future and the best way to accumulate it—most likely, by investing your seed capital 100 percent in stocks. This recommendation is based on the assumption that stocks will return 10 to 11 percent a year, as they have throughout the twentieth century.

Here's the catch that's often overlooked: stocks don't go up 10 to 11 percent *every year*. In fact, after several years of going up faster than 10 to 11 percent, they can be expected to go up slower than 10 to 11 percent, and perhaps they could even go down! At some point, they'll enter a bear market, where a stretch of losses will balance out the latest stretch of gains.

The 10 to 11 percent annual return from stocks is a twentieth-century phenomenon. Throughout the nineteenth century, stocks returned around 6 percent a year. If ancient history repeats itself, who's to say that stocks in the twenty-first century won't revert to their longer-term performance, throwing every financial plan out of whack? If that happens, all the planners, pension managers, and stockbrokers will have overestimated their clients' wealth at retirement by a wide margin. Instead of the condo in Lake Tahoe, tomorrow's retirees will get the trailer park on the prairie.

As of this writing, and after years of outsized gains, stock prices would have to drop in half, or undergo several years of subpar returns to bring them back into the normal range of 10 to 11 percent profitability. This would inconvenience many people who are relying on stocks to underwrite their retirement, but stocks don't care when anybody retires. They have their own schedule.

Scrape inflation off stocks, and much of the wealth they're credited with producing for investors disappears, even without a bear market. Bob Prechter insists stocks are overrated. Prechter operates out of Gainesville, Georgia, far from Wall Street. Many bearish commentators are camped in the hills where office rent is cheaper and they aren't surrounded by bulls.

Prechter's a Yale grad: opinionated, cogent, well-informed, unflappable. The kind of guy you like to see in an airplane cockpit. (See Bears' Hall of Fame, page 225.) He was a raging bull in 1982. The Dow was at 900; he said it would hit 3,900, and nobody believed him. When the Dow hit 8,000 in 1997 he said it would drop to below 3,000 eventually, and nobody believes him. He's been bearish far too long to hold an audience, but few pessimists are better informed on the subject of how stocks fail to live up to their reputations.

In terms of real purchasing power, Prechter notes, owning the Dow Jones Industrials since 1966 has resulted in zero gain through 1994! The Dow itself advanced from 1,000 to 3,978 in 1994, but the cash you received from selling a share in the Dow that year bought less merchandise than the cash you got from selling a share in the Dow at 1,000 twenty-eight years earlier.

The true Dow has been stuck in a rut in spite of Bill Gates, Sam Walton, and other innovators who have given America its competitive edge. "Consider," Prechter muses, "the implications of a stock market index that made no real progress in nearly three decades, and which is nevertheless historically overvalued."

Prechter argues stock market returns are overstated in other ways. The major averages don't reflect the damage done to smaller stocks in certain situations. The historic returns don't include the many companies that shut their doors and disappear from the listings. The typical portfolio in 1929 included names like Auburn, Cord, Missouri-Pacific, Pierce-Arrow, and Stutz, all of which landed on the trash heap of equities. These total losses surely would drag down the returns from owning stocks, because the owners of those particular shares ended up with zilch.

In any event, the much advertised 10 to 11 percent annual payoff is an imaginary return, from some other planet that has no taxes and no inflation.* For a less fanciful accounting of gains on earth, Marty Zweig has created the Deflated Dow Jones Industrials (Exhibit 1).

A successful market timer and chronic worrier who manages more than $4 billion with the primary goal of not losing a penny of it, Zweig started with the famous Dow average, then subtracted for inflation and adjusted for deflation. The result is the actual buying power of dollars invested in stocks over time.

Viewed in this harsher light, stocks have performed quite differently than the raw data suggest. In the 1920s, they enriched investors as advertised, because inflation was minimal in that decade.

---

* The real returns from competing investments such as bonds or savings accounts are also subverted by inflation, so stocks are not alone in this leaky boat.

Exhibit 1 Deflated Dow Jones Industrial Average

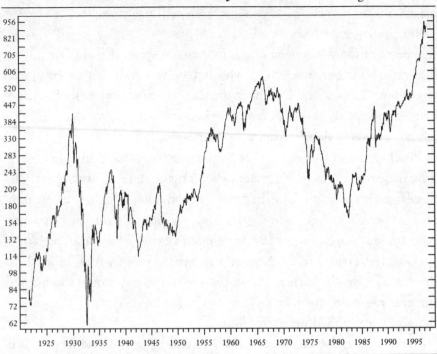

Source: Ned Davis Research.

Their rebound in the early 1930s was much more impressive than it looked; as stock prices went up in the rally from 1932–1937, the prices of everything else went down. The subsequent bear market from 1935–1942 was much worse than it looked, because a higher inflation rate in those years added to the losses. With inflation held in check from 1942–1968, stocks once again enriched investors as advertised.

The shocker on the Zweig chart comes from the 1970s. The raw Dow declined from Dow 1052 in 1973 to 777 in 1982, so on the surface, stocks lost 20 percent over that disappointing stretch. Adjusted for inflation, the actual decline was 75 percent, as shown on the chart. Government spending—on fighting poverty at home and the North

Vietnamese abroad—pushed inflation to its highest levels in the century: 9.25 percent annually per year for nine years.

Statistics are like prisoners under torture: with the proper tweaking, you can get them to confess to anything. Nevertheless, the numbers cited above lead to a few obvious conclusions:

- Periods of extreme inflation are lousy times to own stocks.
- Stocks aren't as profitable as most people think.
- If you accept the premise that stocks advance 10 to 11 percent over time, the recent fifteen years of exceptional gains won't be repeated in the next fifteen years.

The Case for
Cutting and Running

*"Buy and hold" have replaced "I love you" as the three most popular
words in the English language.*

Jim Grant

A NATIONAL PARK BROCHURE advises: "When you are
approached by a bear, try to look big. Be forceful but not aggressive.
Keep your pack on, wave your arms, talk loudly. Back away slowly, but
DO NOT RUN. If a bear attacks you, assume the fetal position and
protect your vital organs."

This is also the approved emergency plan for surviving a bear market: Assume the passive position and protect your vital assets, keep
your shirt on, play dead with the broker, complain loudly if you must,
but DON'T FLEE YOUR STOCKS OR ABANDON YOUR
MUTUAL FUNDS.

No doubt you've been fully briefed on the merits of buying
and holding. What investor hasn't? It's an article of faith that a

representative sample of stocks, if held for the long run, can't fail to pay off. Otherwise, how did the Dow get from 40.94 when Dow created it, to 8,000? It's another article of faith that being completely invested in stocks will result in greater profits than being partly invested or—perish the thought!—going stockless for extended periods.

Under the buy-and-hold regimen, the price you pay for a stock or mutual fund at any given moment is of minor importance. "No price is too high to pay for good stocks" was the theme of a brokerage house ad campaign. As long as you traffic in reputable companies, and give them time to "grow" their earnings (five years is the suggested minimum), you'll be able to sell your shares for more than whatever price you paid for them.

But how long is the long run? The answer may surprise you. It could be longer than a stockpicking Methuselah had bargained for. John Maynard Keynes, the brilliant economist who wasn't brilliant enough to avoid losing millions of dollars in the bear rout of 1929–1932, said of his unhappy experience: "In the long run, we'll all be dead."

It took acres of cemeteries to bury all the investors who died waiting for their stocks and mutual funds (then called "investment trusts") to come back from that Great Decline. Senior citizens who entered the market in 1929 expired before their heirs broke even. A forty-year-old who got in near the top and held on for the duration didn't see a hint of profit until he reached retirement age, in 1954. By then, his hairline had suffered a correction, his paunch advanced, his children had left home, and he qualified for the elderhostels. The long-term view had kept him in stocks through Herbert Hoover, Franklin Roosevelt (four terms), Harry Truman, and two years of Eisenhower, yet he had zero capital gains to show for it.

In fact, his breaking even after a quarter century was only an illusion, because the U.S. dollar lost two-thirds of its buying power over that stretch. Bring inflation into the equation, and his $10,000 portfolio of Dow Jones Industrials acquired at the top in 1929 was worth $3,333 in 1954. So much for the guaranteed rewards from patient investing in reputable companies that grow their earnings.

Although you may suspect you have a knack for it, the odds of buying at the top of any market cycle are quite low. What happened, then, if you bought Dow Jones Industrials at a lower peak in 1927, enjoyed two years of paper profits, and then held on for the Great Decline? In this case, better timing did you six years' worth of good. You broke even in 1948 instead of 1954.

So you're looking at nineteen years of losses from buying near a top of a Great Decline, and twenty-five years for buying at an absolute top, but these dreary prospects are admittedly far-fetched. Experts dismiss the 1929–1932 bear market as a financial fluke. It resulted, they say, from "margin investors" buying stocks at 10 percent down and playing them like horses; meanwhile, greenhorns at the Federal Reserve made rookie mistakes that paralyzed the economy. Because the modern stock-player can't buy stocks on 10 percent down—and the modern, sophisticated Federal Reserve is too smart and too experienced to make rookie mistakes—the Great Decline can never be repeated.

A bear's eye view of the Great Decline (see page 238) is less reassuring, but, for the moment, let's accept the notion that the investor who pays top prices for stocks will never again suffer an 89 percent markdown like the one that hit the Dow. How long, then, did you wait to break even if you bought stocks at or near the more recent peaks? Consider these examples:

- The Dow climbed to 194.40 in 1937. It sold for less 12 years later, in 1949.
- After topping out at 685.47 in 1959, the Dow sold for less 17 years later, in 1974.
- The Dow moved into record territory at 734.91 in 1961, and sold for exactly the same price in 1980, 19 years later.

- The Dow hit 995.15 in 1966 and sold for the same price nearly 17 years later, in late 1982.

Even in the best of these worst-case scenarios, if you invested in stocks or stock mutual funds near a peak, you bought yourself a decade, perhaps two decades, of red ink. Or, if you were clever (or lucky) enough to buy stocks in a valley, you doubled your money on the next rise, only to watch those gains disappear on the subsequent decline, leaving you no richer than you were at the outset. For example:

- The Dow hit a low of 42.15 in November 1903. It hit a lower low of 41.22 in July 1932—29 years later.
- The Dow fell to 72.94 in 1911. It sold for less in 1932—21 years later.
- The Dow bottomed at 566.05 in 1960. It sunk to 577.60 in 1974, gaining all of eleven points in 24 years!

The long run gets longer when the ill-timed investment in stocks is compared to an investment in Treasury bills, savings accounts, or money market funds that pay interest. Such a comparison is hardly unfair—money that isn't riding on stocks has to go somewhere. Jim Stack has crunched these numbers.

Stack's a character. With full beard, steely gaze, and ready grin, he looks like the bear that ate the salmon. He operates out of Whitefish, Montana, on the outskirts of Glacier National Park, where hikers carry cowbells to keep the grizzlies informed of their whereabouts. A giant wooden bear guards the entrance to Stack headquarters—a split-level on Whitefish Lake.

His relationship with sagging stocks goes back to 1973–1974, when his IBM pension plan (he was a young research engineer) had a quick 50 percent correction and planted a skeptical seed that sprouted later. He bought Colorado real estate, made a pile, then left IBM to return to Whitefish, and put the pile in the stock market in 1982. There was no broker's office or investment club in this outback, no place to watch the tickertape, nobody to compare gains and losses with. Out of loneliness, he started the InvesTech market letter: bullish in the 1980s, bearish since 1994. With the help of his wife, Lisa, and eight employees, he continues to issue bearish warnings from the first floor of his split-level, under the shadow of the wooden bear outside.

Stack figures it takes seven and a half years for stocks purchased at the onset of an average bear market to catch up to cash parked in Treasury bills—even if the stocks pay a dividend. In a worse-than-average bear market, the breakeven point is considerably delayed. The twin bear markets of 1969–1971 and 1973–1974 demanded exceptional patience in that regard. Money riding on the Dow Jones Industrials in 1966 didn't catch up to Treasury bills until 1986. Money riding on small stocks, in Value Line's small stock index in December 1968, still hasn't caught up to Treasury bills.

Buying and holding is far from the sure thing it's made out to be. It works in bull markets. It works if you invest regularly, in dribs and drabs, catching the ups and downs along the way. It works in mild bear markets, when the declines are quickly reversed. It may work if you've got ten to twenty years to wait for stocks to recover from a half-off sale. Otherwise, it's risky. It's very risky when you're holding stocks you bought at extravagant prices. It's extremely risky when your retirement depends on a positive result and you're planning to take up golf in a decade or less.

The most celebrated buyers and holders in recent memory, Warren Buffett and Peter Lynch, aren't wedded to stocks unconditionally. Both agree that companies that are carefully chosen and purchased at favorable prices can generate excellent profits down the line. Neither buys and holds "the market" with index funds, as many investors do today. And there's a point at which they'd sell.

In 1969, when prices reached the luxury box and Buffett could find nothing worth owning, he disbanded his limited partnership, sold everything in the portfolio, and gave his partners their money back. In financial circles, this was unprecedented—not the selling, but giving the money back. During the bear market that followed, Buffett was hiding in cash. He returned to stocks four years later, when they were cheap.

Unfortunates who got in near the top couldn't see a clear profit through four presidencies. Buffett got in near the bottom and became a billionaire on the way up. Today, his holding company (Berkshire Hathaway) is too big to be converted to cash, although Buffett may wish he still had that option. At the annual meeting in 1997, he told shareholders it was hard to find a stock worth buying—the first time since 1969 he had reached that bearish conclusion. Earlier, he even said his own Berkshire Hathaway wasn't worth buying at the high price of the moment.

Lynch steered the Fidelity Magellan fund to a record-breaking performance through good markets and bad. For most of the trip, his portfolio was loaded with stocks, but not always. At one point, his biggest position was bonds, even though as a general rule he shunned bonds. Now retired from Magellan and a devoted fund-raiser for charitable causes in Boston, Lynch keeps an eye out for the conditions that trigger the Lynch sell signal:

> When the yield on the thirty-year government bond exceeds the yield on the stocks in the S&P 500 Index by more than six percentage points, sell stocks and buy bonds.

If Peter Lynch has a selling point, and Warren Buffett once had a selling point, should you have a selling point? Buy stocks in the long run, yes, but what will you do on those occasions when it pays to be out of them? If you decide to hold on as prices begin their slide, can you summon the extraordinary courage required to stay fully invested all the way down and back up again? And do you have the time?

Buy, Hold, or Fold

An investor in a panicky market faces the same predicament as a moviegoer in a crowded theater after somebody shouts "Fire!" Staying put is the sensible thing to do, as long as everybody else stays put and stays calm. Otherwise, people who stay put run the risk of getting trampled, and people who rush to the nearest exit may have the best chance of escaping unhurt.

In a burning movie house, staying put is easier said than done; and in the deep woods, when a bear's bearing down on you, playing dead gets progressively more difficult. It's one thing to assume the passive position when the danger's a half-mile away, and quite another when it's at fifty yards and closing. Likewise, when a $100,000 portfolio turns into a $95,000 portfolio, almost anyone can summon the courage not to sell stocks; but when it becomes a $75,000 portfolio, and your investments are making you poorer by the day, you have to be either brave or oblivious to refrain from calling your broker with a sell order.

The very existence of bear markets proves that long-term investors become short-term investors. A bear can't materialize without large numbers of sellers, so a broad decline in stocks can mean only one thing: A crowd of former long-termers has been converted to cutting and running. No stock market on earth has produced a faithful constituency—not the United States in the late 1960s, or Japan in the late 1980s, even though Japan was touted as the island paradise of patriotic nest-egg producers.

In a bull market, the winners buy early and sell late; in a bear market, the winners sell early and buy late. Loyalty is punished with vanishing gains and mounting losses. Market timing is rewarded.

Coming over the top, stocks descend a wall of worry, beginning at the point of "What? Me worry?" when investors are hardly worried at all. Unless there's a crash, they'll have ample time to abandon stocks or mutual funds, raise cash, or take defensive positions. In eleven bear markets since the 1930s, the average loss in the Dow at the end of three months was 3 percent; after four months, it was 8 percent.

The sooner you take action, the more losses you'll avoid, but psychologically it's difficult to take quick action. The first drop in stock prices is trivialized by experts, who call it a "minor correction" and a "good buying opportunity." They remind you that stocks have a habit of rebounding from setbacks.

After the first drop, there's a sucker's rally (not to be confused with the serious rally that occurs after stock prices hit bottom). The suckers are buying too early, causing prices to rise, but only temporarily. This is a wonderful selling opportunity, but most people miss it. They're waiting for higher prices, in the hope that the rally will continue. It falters, and prices hit new lows.

Skittish shareholders promise themselves they'll unload at the slightest upturn, but the market doesn't turn upward. Lower prices beget more sellers, who produce even lower prices, which beget more sellers.

Along the trail of decline, you can spot a variety of winners and losers: big winners who sold near the top for a terrific gain; modest winners who sold a bit farther down the slope; people who sold at the breakeven point and escaped with their original investment; big losers who bought near the top; modest losers who bought halfway up or halfway down.

Because there's no way to know how low the market will go, the decision to stand pat or fold can never be clear-cut. The longer you wait, the less attractive folding becomes. With stocks 10 percent down, the decline has only begun, so a lot of money can be saved by folding. At 20 percent down, you're in bear market territory and have to wonder whether the worst is over. At 30 percent down, you're in a moderately severe bear market, and at 40 percent down (and below), the risk of missing a new bull market is greater than the reward from avoiding the tail end of the bear. Yet it's a common feature of many bear markets that the largest contingent of sellers exit at the point of maximum loss. Stocks hit bottom on huge volume in 1929, 1937, and 1974.

Here, a peculiar psychology is at work: the more stocks decline, the harder it is *NOT* to sell. This paradox has been the undoing of devoted investors who give up late in the decline, when they would have lost far less by selling at the outset. In 1968–1970 and 1973–1974, the market was obviously in severe trouble long before the bottom was reached, yet an ample supply of loyalists stayed to the end. Those who held on faithfully through the entire ordeal, only to get scared out near the bottom, lost the most. An instinct for capital preservation caused them to jump a floating ship.

Two other issues are pertinent here. First, if your stocks are down 50 percent, a 50 percent move won't bring them back up. It takes a 100 percent move to recover from a 50 percent decline, as when a $10 stock drops to $5 (the 50 percent decline) and crawls back to $10 (the 100 percent advance). This explains why a bear market may linger. Second, there's the tax quandry.

People often say, "I can't sell stocks because of the capital gains tax I'd pay. What's the point of getting out of a stock to avoid a bear market, when the tax is a bear market in itself?" This argument fails the math test. A 20 percent tax will cost you far less than a 20 percent decline in the value of your portfolio. Here's an example. You bought a stock for $50,000 that is worth $100,000 today. If you sell it to escape the oncoming bear, you'll lose $10,000 to the IRS (20 percent on the $50,000 gain), but you'll have $90,000 protected from the bear. If you hold onto the stock through the 20 percent decline, you'll have $80,000 to show for your persistence. You'll be $10,000 poorer than if you'd sold.

Of course you pay a commission when you sell, which you'd avoid if you held. And whether selling is a smart move in the long run depends on the fundamentals of the investment. But in severe bear markets, the losses far exceed what you saved on taxes by not selling.

Although a retirement account is generally regarded as the place to leave stocks alone, it is perfectly suited to bear-market maneuvering. When you get in and out stocks in a retirement account, the moves are tax-free.

IF YOU MAKE MONEY IN A DOWN MARKET, DON'T TELL THE NEIGHBORS

It's worse being a bear when you're right.
Michael Metz
Chief Portfolio Strategist
Oppenheimer and Company

OUTPERFORM YOUR PEERS in a bull market and you'll be applauded for your skill. Look at Warren Buffett—his popularity grows with his billions. Outperform your peers in a bear market—by turning a profit when they're nursing losses—and check your backside for darts, your rose bushes for poison, and your driveway for nails. On Wall Street, a winning bear in a bear market gets more cold shoulders than an SEC gumshoe.

This is where bears have a tough life. They're only tolerated when they're losing. Notorious bears are put on TV for public amusement. Take Jim Grant; Lou Rukeyser does. The witty publisher of *Grant's*

Interest Rate Observer, and a debunker of U.S. stocks since the Dow was at 2,000, has appeared on Rukeyser's TV show, where he gets bear-baited: "World's going to hell again, eh, Jim?"

Another Jim, Jim Rogers, a bow-tied pundit for CNBC and a globe-trotting author *(Investment Biker)*, was bearish on U.S. stocks, bonds, and the dollar in 1996–1997, when all three were rising. His foul-weather forecasts made Rogers the target of back-office banter and the occasional on-camera tweak.

This was mostly in good fun, but when the bear market proves Rogers right, he's prepared for chillier relations. He first learned the consequences in 1970, as a cub investor on Wall Street. At age 25, he landed a job in a small house run by Dick Gilder, a confirmed bull at the time. Gilder was so confident stocks were going up, he leased two top floors of the GM building, added dozens of new desks, and called in the decorators. Rogers, Gilder's youngest employee, promptly took his $5,000 life savings and bet against the market with "put options." Soon after he made this bet, stocks had their worst crash since 1937.

Large firms were forced out of business, and Gilder abandoned the GM building and retreated to cheaper digs with a skeleton staff. Rogers tripled his money, turning his $5,000 into $15,000 while the New York Stock Exchange turned $690 billion into $490 billion. He shared the good news with his boss.

"Gilder was miffed that a punk like me could had done this," Rogers recalls. "I got a lecture about how foolish it was to speculate in put options."*

In 1987, considerably wiser and wealthier after several years of working with George Soros, Rogers once again decided that a bear market was imminent. He made the mistake of telling the papers the "market would crash in October." A few days after the Dow shed 500

---

* Convinced he was the "next Bernard Baruch," Rogers proceeded to bet his entire $15,000 on the short side of six stocks. Rogers was too optimistically pessimistic. In nine months, the next Baruch had turned $15,000 into zero.

points, a follow-up story appeared in the *Wall Street Journal*, suggesting that Rogers had profited from the crash.

"I got hate calls," he says. "If there were faxes then, I'd have gotten hate faxes. The article was tacked to the bulletin board at Columbia University where I taught a class. Some angry investor ripped it down."

Long before faxes, two other investors who profited on the down side, Jesse Livermore and Ben Smith, got investors madder than that.

A farm boy with a nose for disaster, Livermore bet against the Union Pacific railroad just in time for the 1906 San Francisco earthquake and fire. He added to his fortune in the Panic of 1907 and in the postwar depression following World War I. He surrounded himself with yachts, limousines, gardens, oceanfront real estate, and elegant women. Because he made his millions in bear markets, he got worse publicity than Jack the Ripper.

"Isn't selling as legitimate a market transaction as buying?" Livermore once wondered aloud, after reading the latest editorial that lambasted his activities. "Without selling, could markets exist?"

For switching to the bear side at the last minute and making money in the Crash of 1929, Livermore was never forgiven. His phones were tapped. To avoid taunts and threats, he moved his operations to a secret suite of offices on Fifth Avenue and installed his own quote board, a bank of telephones, and a staff of clerks and statisticians who might as well have worked for the CIA. According to his biographer, "doormen and elevator operators denied the office existed, and the telephone company said his name wasn't listed."

Then there was Ben Smith, a Livermore contemporary, a temperamental Irishman, and no fan of stuffed shirts. Smith had more in common with H. L. Mencken and Will Rogers than with habitués of New York's fancy clubs and boardrooms. "His true attitude to the Morgans, the Kuhn, Loebs and the Mellons had always been to hell with them," a writer pointed out.

A relentless short seller in the 1920s, Smith made big bets against stocks before and during the famous Crash. He took enormous positions on the short side, and the more he sold short the more excited he became. One day, he rushed into his broker's office waving his arms and shouting, "Sell 'em all. They're not worth anything." Hence his nickname: Sell 'Em Ben Smith.

Like Livermore, Smith was heckled, harassed, stalked, pestered, and forced to travel incognito. He hired bodyguards to protect his two daughters. The press had nothing good to say about him, and Smith was the prime target of Congressional hearings called by politicians who decided short sellers had caused the Crash.

Sometime after the next crash, a national lynch mob will be formed, and squads of reporters will be dispatched to vilify the culprits. If prior bear markets are any guide, a new scapegoat will emerge. In the 1920s, it was evil bankers; in 1970, promoters of mutual funds; in 1987, program traders. But the perennial scapegoat is any bearish investor who profits from the decline.

Let this be a warning: When the market drops and you make money, don't tell the neighbors. They won't applaud your gains. More likely, they'll blame you for their losses. "If I ever make money being bearish again," says Jim Rogers, "I won't go on TV talking about it. I'll sit there and moan and groan like everybody else."

PART TWO

~

How to
Spot a Bear

THE URSA MAJORS

JUST AS PRICES IN A bull market often rise beyond the most imaginative projection of the optimist, in a bear market they may fall below the most imaginative projection of the pessimist. A few examples will suffice:

- 1637 bottom in Dutch Tulips: down 93 percent
- 1720 bottom in South Sea shares: down 84 percent
- 1721 bottom in French Mississippi shares: down 99 percent
- 1932 bottom in U.S. stocks: Dow down 89 percent
- 1974 bottom in Hong Kong stocks: down 92 percent
- 1982 bottom in Mexican stocks: down 73 percent
- 1986 bottom in Arab stocks (Kuwait): down 98 percent
- 1990 bottom in Taiwan stocks: down 80 percent
- 1990 bottom in Japanese stocks: down 63 percent

For a bear's-eye view of stocks, simply invert the standard chart. The ups then represent losses, and the downs represent gains. From this vantage, bear markets turn into mountains, which is how bearish investors like to imagine them. In a chart of the twentieth century, there are two dominant peaks: the Ursa Majors of the century, surrounded by Ursa Minors (Exhibit 2).

Ursa Minors may be easily overcome, but an Ursa Major is expensive to ignore. Around these twin peaks, investors were stalled for years, or even decades, of subpar returns. If you sent your money elsewhere while other people's money was stuck on these slopes, you did your net worth and your self-esteem a favor.

The Ursa Majors happened 40 years apart, a detail that Jim Stack finds significant. "It took that long," he said, "for one generation of big losers to pass the buck to another generation of big losers." The casualties from 1929 to 1932 swore they'd never own a share again, and most didn't. They taught their children that investing in stocks was no more reliable than investing in a pair of jacks. When the children reached adulthood and had money to lose—in the mid-1960s—the prosperous market lured them in, as it had lured their parents four decades earlier. They invested in stocks just in time for the next Ursa Major, and became the casualties from 1969 to 1973. Many swore they'd never own a share again.

Both Ursa Majors were interrupted by big rallies. Both proved equally damaging in the end. Both were presided over by Republican presidents with Quaker backgrounds (Nixon, Hoover). One ended with a Democrat in the White House (Roosevelt), the other with a Republican (Ford).

Exhibit 2 "Ursa Majors"

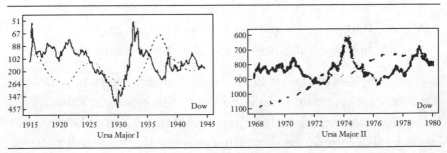

26

In both declines, the consensus opinion, the prevailing opinion, the educated opinion, the balance of opinion was bullish. Both happened during buoyant eras ("New Eras," they were called) when spirits were high, unemployment was low, business was terrific, inflation was benign, consumers were optimistic—and only a curmudgeon was despondent. A bear market? You couldn't see one coming by watching the economy, which is why most economists missed the call. Corporate profits in the late 1920s and the 1960s were at their all-time highest levels in memory: factories were running at full throttle, and fantastic new products were appearing on shelves and in showrooms.

The 1929–1932 bear followed eight years of rising stock prices—never before had stocks been so consistently rewarding. The 1968–1974 version followed nineteen years of rising prices that took the Dow from 200 to nearly 1,000. Investors in both periods were convinced by circumstantial evidence (rising prices) that stocks would never let them down. In both periods, buying and holding became a national pastime; loyal stockholders were celebrated as the prudent guardians of assets, and the market timer was dismissed as the reckless fool.

In the late 1920s, hardhats and bureaucrats, secretaries and actuaries, fashion plates and potentates all had brokerage accounts. People were reading *Common Stocks as Long-Term Investments*, a best-seller written by Edgar Lawrence Smith. In the late 1960s, the official tally of shareholders, as compiled by the New York Stock Exchange, had risen to 20 million (one out of six adults), up from just over eight and a half million (one out of twelve adults) in 1956. A larger group owned stocks indirectly through company pension plans. People were reading *The Money Game*, a best-seller written by a glib impersonator, "Adam Smith."

Both Ursa Majors happened when mutual funds were popular. (In the 1920s, they were called "investment trusts.") At the onset of both declines, stock prices were exceedingly expensive. On every measure of valuation—price to earnings, price to book value, price to dividends, price to output, price to Christmas bonus, price to spaces in the employee parking lot—stocks had broken all records for extravagance.

The first Ursa Major happened in peacetime, the second in wartime, but both led to extreme consequences: great depression and great inflation. In the Great Depression, bonds and cash were more valuable than things (stocks also had a huge rally from 1932 to 1937), because the price of things was dropping. In the Great Inflation, things (oil, gold, real estate, cashmere sweaters, etc.) were more valuable than cash, because the price of things was rising.

The two Ursa Majors appeared on the Dowscape when stocks were dear, mutual funds were in vogue, the economy was perky, the public was heavily invested, and a New Era had been declared. This will all sound familiar to investors in the 1990s. Are we looking at a third Ursa Major in the making?

DEFLATING BEARS, INFLATING BEARS

PERHAPS IT'S NO ACCIDENT that the Ursa Majors happened at economic extremes: one inflationary, the other deflationary. A listless economy can be bad for stocks, and a hyperactive economy with high inflation is worse. A listless economy with high inflation, called stagflation, doesn't do the shareholder much good, either.

That being the case, one way to manage a portfolio is to invest in stocks when inflation is low and the economy is doing OK, and get out of stocks when inflation is on the rise or when the economy is falling into a stupor.

If you exit stocks, how you fend off the next bear, depends on the type of bear you encounter. If you suspect deflation, where interest rates are falling, you're better off wrapping your money around a bond. In an inflationary scenario, where rates are rising, you're better off in cash (the money market yield will rise in sympathy) or in commodities. If you can't identify the bear, cash is your safest alternative.

A mild case of inflation doesn't hurt stocks, as the 1990s have proven. As long as costs can be passed along to consumers, a company doesn't mind paying extra for labor and raw materials, and mild inflation may give it an excuse to raise prices on its own products and squeeze some extra profit out of the deal.

A mild case of disinflation can do wonders for stocks. Disinflation is when the inflation rate is falling. You're still paying higher prices for things, but the prices aren't going up as fast as before. Deflation is when prices themselves (represented by the Consumer Price Index) are falling. The three greatest bull markets of the century (1921–1929, 1949–1968, and 1982–199?) happened during disinflation. The inflation rate was falling and interest rates went along for the ride.

Extremes of inflation and deflation produce severe bear markets, as the former did in the 1970s, and the latter did during the early and late 1930s. Investors have reason to worry about both. The problem is, they tend to worry about the wrong extreme at the wrong time.

In the first half of the twentieth century, the typical investor worried about deflation. Inflation had never been a problem in his lifetime. It hadn't been much of a problem in anybody's lifetime, going back to 1776. For 150 years, prices in the United States were stable, with brief spurts of inflation offset by deflation. It was during deflationary episodes, when the economy fell into recession or depression, that stocks had their biggest declines.

Therefore, market watchers were always on the lookout for signs of a sluggish economy, which might bring on another round of falling prices. Bad news for the economy was bad news for stocks. Among the bear markets of the prior century were numerous panics, shorter and more violent than the standard bear market and nearly always deflationary. This was another reason deflation was the U.S. stockholders' biggest fear from the 1800s and until the Great Depression ended. Panics produced deflation.

After a deflation watch that lasted several generations, the extreme inflation that appeared on the scene in the 1970s took investors by surprise. It wasn't extreme compared to the hyperinflation that brought Hitler to power in Germany, Mao to power in China, or martial law and death squads to countries in Latin America. But 6 percent to 15 percent inflation was extreme in the United States. Companies weren't prepared for it, and Wall Street analysts hadn't factored it into their projections. Earnings on the Dow Industrials more than doubled between 1970 and 1979, yet stock prices went down. The message from the market was clear: Earnings don't count for much when inflation eats the proceeds.

Inflation haunted Wall Street until 1982, when the Dow finally broke through the 1,000 level it had bumped up against sixteen years earlier. After 1982, disinflation returned, and the bulls took a ride on it. The Dow's earnings went nowhere, yet stocks more than doubled from 1980 to 1987, because falling inflation made earnings progressively more valuable.

The passing of nearly two decades of feeble inflation hasn't erased the memory of the 1970s. Monetary mugwumps from Alan Greenspan on down are on constant inflation alert, just as their predecessors were on constant deflation alert for four decades going into the 1970s. Good news for the economy was good news for stocks when investors were traumatized by deflation; bad news for the economy is good news for stocks today. Today's investor worries that a strong economy will rouse inflation from its doldrums.

Deflation hasn't been something to worry about, at least not until the talking heads took an interest in the subject after the Asian markets collapsed in the autumn of 1997. Inflation an investor worries about because the newspapers say that Alan Greenspan is worried about it, too. Maverick economists are sounding a different alarm: the Federal Reserve is fighting the wrong battle.

A staunch deflationist, Jim Stack, doubts the world economies are strong enough to take the shock of another crash like the one in 1987. What saved the financial system in that crisis, says Stack, was central banks' cutting interest rates in concert, giving the system a massive monetary jolt. Today, he argues, Japanese and European economies are weaker than they were in 1987, and Japanese interest rates are so low already, there's nothing left to cut. Japan's central bank has given its own economy a massive monetary jolt, and the economy hasn't responded.

Deciding whether the next bear market will be inflationary or deflationary is the first step in figuring out where to put your assets. In Marty Zweig's view, it pays to own stocks when the Consumer Price Index (the common measure of pricetags nationwide) doesn't stray far from the current reading. A sharp rise in commodity prices would signal inflation.

In an inflationary bear, money can be profitably deployed in the money market, Treasury bills, or savings accounts, all of which will capture the continuous rise in interest rates. A more aggressive investor will buy gold, commodities, real estate, and other such tangibles. If it's too heavy to carry, it's worth owning in an inflationary situation. Avoid long-term bonds, which lose value as interest rates rise. Avoid most stocks.

In a deflationary bear, long-term government bonds are your best bet, and "zero coupon bonds" are the most profitable. Don't buy corporate bonds; when the economy falters, companies are more likely to default on their payments. With long-term government bonds, you "lock in" a rate of return that becomes more favorable as interest rates continue to fall.

Cash is less attractive than bonds in a deflationary bear because as interest rates decline, the yield on a money market or savings account will also decline. However, making a modest return on cash is preferable to big losses in stocks, real estate, and/or commodities. If it's unclear whether the economy is headed for deflation or inflation, you can't go too far wrong with cash.

ARE EARNINGS
OVERRATED?

THAT STOCKS RISE AND fall on corporate earnings is a much ballyhooed misconception. The price investors will pay for earnings varies from hour to hour, week to week, year to year, depending on the inclinations of the buyers and the sellers. Stock prices can move on interest rates, financial gossip, and other factors that make stocks more or less valuable to holders and beholders.

No subject gets more scrutiny on Wall Street than earnings, where an army of analysts is deployed to do reconnaissance on next quarter's "number." There are "earnings disappointments" and "earnings surprises," "official earnings" and "rumored earnings," also known as "whisper earnings." These all cause stocks to fluctuate.

Being congenitally optimistic, Wall Street rates stocks on next year's earnings. Since next year's earnings are expected to be better than last year's, this futuristic approach gives investors an excuse to pay higher prices. Last year's earnings, or so called "trailing earnings," provide a more conservative benchmark: what really happened as opposed to what might.

In any event, if a company can double its earnings, other things being equal, its stock price should double. Triple the earnings, and the stock should triple, and so on. The flaw in this formula is: Other things aren't equal—namely, the different prices investors are inclined to pay for earnings at different junctures.

For instance, National Presto Industries, a small appliance company, earned exactly $2 a share in 1996. The recent stock price was $40. At that price, a buyer was paying twenty times Presto's earnings ($40 divided by $2). This price–earnings ratio, or p/e for short, is subject to constant change. P/e ratios always are. Buyers won't always pay twenty times Presto's earnings to own Presto's stock, any more than they'll pay twenty-three times earnings (the going rate as of this writing) to own the Dow Jones Industrials.

In this sense, a share of stock is no different than a baseball trading card. The price of a Ken Griffey Jr. card—to mention a slugger for the Seattle Mariners—may rise and fall according to Griffey's home run output, based on the price-to-home-run ratio. Then again, it may not. If baseball is in disfavor, as it was during the players' strike in 1994, cardholders will pay less for cards in general, including the Griffey card, no matter how many homers Griffey hits in a season.

Likewise, if stocks are in disfavor, investors will pay less for Motorola, Disney, or McDonald's, no matter how much money those companies earn this season. Exhibit 3 shows the fickle relationship between the earnings on the Dow Industrials and the pricetag on that accomplished group of thirty stocks. There doesn't seem to be much relationship. Along the way, the price–earnings ratio has oscillated from a high of 29.89 set in 1991 to a low of 6.44 set in September 1979—only slightly lower than the 6.99 recorded in 1949, perhaps the best and most obvious buying opportunity of the century. Since 1961, the mainstream p/e is 15.

Dow earnings fell from the previous year's earnings no less than seventeen times, and on twelve of those seventeen occasions, stock

Exhibit 3 Dow Prices versus Earnings

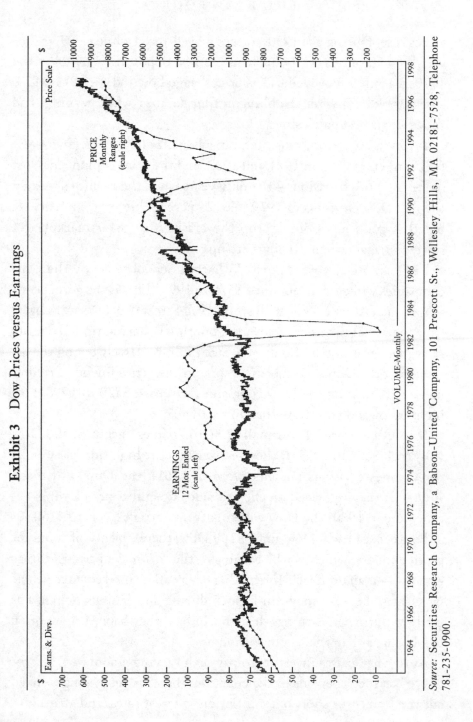

Source: Securities Research Company, a Babson-United Company, 101 Prescott St., Wellesley Hills, MA 02181-7528, Telephone 781-235-0900.

35

prices rose. During the 1950s, prices moved ahead while earnings wavered but stayed basically unchanged. The opposite occurred in the 1970s: earnings moved ahead as prices lagged behind. In 1973–1974, stocks took their worst drubbing in four decades, while earnings had shown their best gains since 1962.

1975 was an earnings disaster, but a bonanza for stocks. Two great bull markets started in 1921 and 1932, and the Dow components lost money on both occasions—the only years when the earnings were in the red. Dow earnings in 1929 were 25 percent higher than in 1928, but that good news didn't stop the crash. Most bear markets get started in years when earnings are up.

Let's say a clairvoyant at the Wharton School tells you the Dow companies will earn a combined $520 in 1998. This is the actual consensus guess-timate from analysts on Wall Street. Analysts work overtime to predict earnings in advance, but this Wharton tip is ironclad. How much is it worth? Could you parlay it into a timely bet on the direction of the Dow, and capture a spot on the *Forbes* lineup of richest humans? Knowing the Dow companies will earn $520 in 1998, how high, or low, do you think the Dow will go?

If stocks are priced "normally," at 16.7 times earnings, the Dow will reach 8684 in 1998. If they're priced on the high side, at twenty-three times earnings (as they were in 1961), the Dow will reach 11,960. If they're priced on the low side, at eight times earnings (as they were in 1980) the Dow will sink from current levels to 4160.

Between a 11,960 Dow and a 4160 Dow, there's plenty of room for profit and loss, which is why earnings—the "e" in the price–earnings equation—is an unreliable forecasting device. Bear markets take people by surprise because they can happen during an earnings bonanza as easily as during an earnings drought. In fact, they happen more often in a bonanza than they do in a drought.

As to what causes investors to pay such varying amounts of "p" for the "e" on the other side of the equation, there are many long-winded answers and three short ones: inflation, interest rates, and attitude.

Price–earnings ratios were quite stingy in the 1940s and early 1950s, because investors lacked faith in future prosperity. In his book, *The Money Masters*, John Train describes how inhabitants of that era grew up hearing "A depression always follows a major war," so they expected a depression to follow World War II. With Japan and Europe in a shambles, the United States had a virtual monopoly on world production—a bullish scenario for stocks if ever there was one. But investors weren't focusing on that prospect. They were stuck on the idea that the economy would falter after the gun makers, khaki producers, iron mongers, etc. lost their biggest customer— Uncle Sam.

By 1953, when it became obvious a depression hadn't materialized, investors began to pay more for stocks. The "e" was on the rise and so was the "p," creating the basic double play that makes a great bull market. (In a bear market, the double play works in reverse: the "e" and the "p" fall together, resulting in big losses.) This 1950s bull ended when Vietnam and high inflation caused investors to lose faith in future prosperity all over again. They got stingy with the "p," and a bear market broke out. When earnings go nowhere and the p/e ratio is reduced from 20 to 10, stock prices are cut in half.

Rattled by inflation, investors in the 1970s ignored the excellent profits turned in by corporate America and focused instead on two unpleasant prospects: (1) the Fed would raise interest rates to quell inflation and scuttle the gravy boat, or (2) inflation would go unchecked and would outdistance the gravy boat. Either way, investors began to doubt the gravy boat and insisted on paying less for the gravy. The lesson from all this? Strong earnings lead to higher stock prices, but only when the buyers want them to.

Having won its fight with inflation (and having caused a recession in the process), the Federal Reserve reversed a ten-year trend and lowered interest rates in the 1980s. This was a bullish development that changed the p/e equation and investors' attitudes all at once. Lower rates excited the economy, leading to more "e"; they also coaxed investors out of bonds (where yields were declining) and into stocks. This renewed demand for stocks gave a boost to the "p."

The trend of the 1980s—lower interest rates, higher earnings, higher stock prices—has continued into the 1990s, and from this double play, stocks are up fourfold. Enjoy it while it lasts, but high earnings/high prices aren't forever. It's impossible to know how long this perfect outcome will persist—already it has gone on far longer than p/e watchers would have expected.

THE SELL AT 19 METHOD

"Twenty times earnings, history shows, is too rich a price for the Dow," says John Dennis Brown, in his book, *Panic Profits*. A simple approach to timing the market is to take defensive action whenever the p/e passes 19. "Sell at 19" got you out of stocks a few months before the Crash of 1987, but in other cases it has moved you in and out too early to be of much value.

In 1991, the Dow's p/e was pushing 30, and you were sorry to sell then. In this latest bull market, sell at 19 has produced only disappointment; market timers who acted on that signal have left huge sums on Wall Street's table. A surge in earnings in 1992 caused the "e" to rise and brought the p/e ratio back into a safer range.

A more sophisticated rating system for earnings is called "earnings yield." You get the earnings yield by turning the p/e ratio on its head, dividing the earnings by the stock price instead of the other way around. This becomes an e/p ratio. Using our National Presto example, the $2 earnings divided by the $40 stock price produces an "earnings yield" of 5 percent.

Earnings yield gives you an easy way to tell whether stocks are expensive or cheap versus the most popular competing investment, bonds. Exhibit 4 plots the earnings yield on the S&P 500 stocks against the

Exhibit 4 Stock Earnings Yield versus Bond Yield

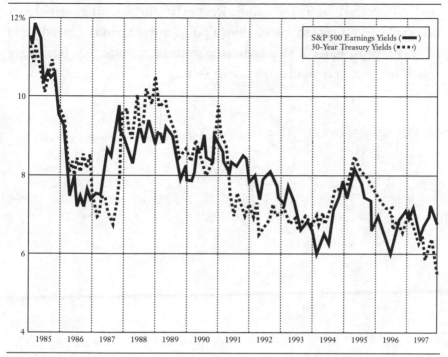

S&P 500 Earnings Yields (▬)
30-Year Treasury Yields (▪ ▪ ▪)

Source: I/B/E/S International.

yield on a thirty-year Treasury bond. You can see how this relationship changes as bonds and stocks become more or less attractive.

The bond yield is fixed in advance and guaranteed by the government; the earnings yield is speculative and subject to disappointment.
For this reason, among others, stocks are riskier than bonds. That
being the case, you'd expect to be rewarded for the extra risk with a
higher earnings yield on stocks than the yield you get from a bond.

There are times when the earnings yield *is* higher than the bond
yield, suggesting that stockholders are properly rewarded and stocks
are fairly valued. There are other times (1989, 1995–1996) when
the bond yield is higher, suggesting that stocks are overvalued. As

Exhibit 4 indicates, stocks can be overvalued for a while, but eventually they fall back into line. Recently, the earnings yield has dropped to 4.5 percent, more than a point lower than the bond yield of 5.8 percent. Fans of this indicator would conclude that bonds are worth buying, and stocks are worth selling.

Pulling the Trigger

Bear markets happen for a simple reason. The owners of the merchandise can't get their asking price. The shortage of buyers forces them to lower the fare, until a buyer can be coaxed into making a deal. It's a common occurrence in retail. Stores have a bear market after every Christmas rush.

There's no Christmas rush on Wall Street, and for stocks to have a 20, 30, 40, or 50 percent off sale, public confidence must be shaken. Conditions once seen as favorable—a strong economy, for instance, or low inflation—are now perceived as having changed for the worse. Investors no longer focus on the good news that gave them a reason to buy stocks. They focus on the bad news that gives them an excuse to sell stocks. Meanwhile, smart shoppers are holding out for the bigger discounts that are likely to develop, because other would-be shoppers are delaying their purchases for the same reason.

How long the sale lasts and how low the discounts go will depend on when the crowds return to the store. This psychological element makes bear markets hard to negotiate.

The Bear Market Trigger

Once the general outlook turns negative, all that's needed to start the decline is a "trigger"—some shocking development or sudden calamity that scares away buyers and causes sellers to agree to sell for less. Numerous bear markets in the twentieth century have been triggered or helped along by a recognizable event or events.

In 1990, it was Saddam Hussein's march into Kuwait. In 1893, the failure of the Erie Railroad. In 1899–1900, a Boer War in Africa, a Boxer Rebellion in China, and insurrection in the Philippines. In 1890, Argentina went into default, which nearly collapsed London's Barings Bank. (Barings finally did collapse 100 years later, due to misguided billion-dollar currency bet made by a greenhorn trader in the Singapore office. At that point, however, Baring's stature was so diminished, the markets hardly noticed.)

Some declines have multiple triggers. In 1956–1957, there were three: (1) war in Suez, (2) Soviet tanks in Budapest, and (3) a Soviet satellite in outer space. A slump in U.S. auto sales and high inflation provided the gloom. In 1973–1974, there were five: (1) Watergate, (2) the Spiro Agnew scandal, (3) the Arab oil embargo, (4) the Yom Kippur War, and (5) Nixon's resignation. A sick dollar and rising inflation added gloom. The shooting of four students at Kent State University pushed stocks to the bottom.

Occasionally, the obvious trigger doesn't rouse a bear. The day after the Japanese attacked Pearl Harbor, the Dow lost only four points, and less than 10 percent was lost in the weeks that followed. When Iran took American hostages in 1979, the Dow barely noticed. President Eisenhower's heart attack on the golf course prompted a mild correction—it's a mistake to assume a bear would have appeared at his funeral had he died.

Four Presidents died by assassination, and stocks rose all four times. Lincoln was shot April 15, 1865; the market closed for a week, then stocks inched higher on the opening. Garfield was shot September 19, 1881; stocks went up the next day. Stocks advanced after McKinley was shot, because Wall Street expected his wealthier replacement, Teddy Roosevelt, to be a more reliable capitalist tool. Roosevelt wasn't. He triggered a bear market by forcing the breakup of J. P. Morgan's pet conglomerate, U.S. Steel, then slapping a huge fine on J. D. Rockefeller's Standard Oil.

A half century later, President Kennedy triggered a bear market by imposing price controls on the same steel industry Roosevelt had dismembered. Maybe that's why stocks rallied after Kennedy was shot in Dallas on Friday, November 22, 1963. Heavy selling was expected on the Monday following the assassination, but that was the day of the funeral, and the New York Stock Exchange canceled the session. To the NYSE's amazement, when trading resumed on Tuesday, stocks posted their second highest one-day gain in twenty-four years. Two weeks later, the Dow hit a record high. Wall Street was telling the world it preferred Lyndon Johnson.

So far, we know this much: Presidential assassinations can be bullish; nonfatal Presidential heart attacks, mildly bearish; and Presidential attacks on big business, extremely bearish.

SELLING ON THE SOUND OF CANNONS

Since a nineteenth-century Rothschild (no relation, alas) uttered his famous remark, "Buy to the sound of cannons," generations of investors have grown up thinking that war is bullish. An armchair review of important wars shoots this theory full of holes. Buying on the sound of cannons is so consistently unprofitable, it's a wonder the Rothschilds can afford to pay the upkeep on their estates. Cannons are the most reliable triggers for bear markets, and selling on the sound of them has been a winning strategy.

A skirmish or a police action—such as U.S. troops being sent to Panama to extract General Noriega, to Haiti to restore democracy, or to Somalia to deliver food and disarm the attack jeeps—does no harm to stocks, as long as costs and casualties are low. A longer and deadlier conflict almost never fails to produce an unpleasant slide on the world bourses. Bear markets accompanied the Spanish–American War (1898); the Boer War and Boxer Rebellion, as mentioned above; the Balkan War of 1912; World War I (when the Dow, erasing earlier gains, dropped 40 percent by December 1917); the Japanese attack on U.S. and British ships in the harbor of Nanking, China (1937); Hitler's invasion of Czechoslovakia (1938, when stocks rose briefly on the sound of coos at a Munich peace conference, then fell), and the defeat of the Allies at Dunkerque (1940).

World War II put stocks in a holding pattern after a mid-war bounce in 1942. War in South Korea in 1950–1952 inspired a 12 percent decline. The Vietnam War gave stocks their worst drubbing since 1937; investors who took the third part of Timothy Leary's advice—"Turn on, tune in, drop out"—were saved from ruin. If Leary had said "Turn on, tune in, sell short," hippies would have made the Forbes 400.

The conflicts involving British troops in the Falklands and Israelis in Lebanon downed stocks in 1981. Saddam's invasion of Kuwait (1990) did the same, although the sound of smart bombs falling on Iraqi installations put an end to the bear on Wall Street. Not in Japan, where the Gulf War triggered Ursa Nikkei.

While wars create jobs, which is bullish, they also destroy factories, roads, bridges, retail outlets, and shoppers, which is bearish. They result in trade barriers, which stifle competition, also bearish. They're expensive and are usually paid for with a printing press, which puts more cash into circulation. This produces higher interest rates and higher inflation. The Consumer Price Index escalated during the Revolutionary War, the War of 1812, the Civil War, the two World Wars, and the Vietnam War. This was bad for stocks. The

Gulf War didn't produce this side effect because other countries picked up part of the tab.

The second half of the Rothschild maxim, "Sell to the sound of trumpets" (meaning after peace has broken out), is also misguided. Peace is bullish, by and large. It was good for stocks from 1920 to 1928 (post World War I), 1946–1950 (when peace was interrupted by Korea), 1954–1966 (pre-Vietnam), and 1982–1990. Investors who abandon stocks in a war have cash on hand to reacquire them at lower prices.

Tops, Bear Bottoms, and Rallies in Between

The safest time to buy stocks is when people are afraid to be in the market, as they were in 1974, 1982, and after the crash of 1987. The most dangerous time to buy stocks is when people are afraid not to be in the market, as they are in 1997.

Robert Prechter

A BULL MARKET CREATES unrealistic expectations, whether it's in stocks or in neighborhood real estate. Joe Doaks puts his house up for sale for $250,000, the highest asking price in recent memory. This creates joy up and down the block, as the neighbors tell themselves: "Doaks has a tiny backyard, so if his house is worth $250,000, ours must be worth more!"

But then the Doaks' residence sits unsold for several months, along with two others that have gone on the market. Doaks gets restless, and drops his price several notches. A buyer shows up at $175,000 and a desperate Doaks makes a sale. There's no joy in Doakville because the net worth of the neighborhood has dropped $75,000 per dwelling, the distance between Doak's original asking price and what he took, in the end.

The same scene is played out on Wall Street, where the price of a stock makes a new high and causes jubilation among all the owners worldwide, who deem their shares are equally valuable, and make upward revisions in their families' net worth. However, a high price is only as reliable as the next buyer's willingness to pay it. Otherwise, it can drop like Doak's house.

The key advantage of houses over stocks in a bear market is that people live in their houses and are less inclined to sell the roof over their heads, but they have no live-in attachment the pieces of paper that aren't waterproof. Moreover, the prices of houses in the neighborhood aren't paraded across the bottom of TV screens, so the owners aren't reminded constantly of their losses.

You've heard that stocks must climb a "wall of worry." In 1982, with the Dow at 800, there were more worriers than shareholders as stocks were thought to be too risky for prudent investors. That was near the bottom of the wall. In 1997, with the Dow at 8,000, shareholders far outnumber worriers, and stocks are thought to be safe for adults and children alike—so we were a lot closer to the top of the wall.

The change in sentiment from top to bottom is reflected in the prices paid for well-known companies. What else could explain why investors in 1969 were happy to buy McDonald's at $50 a share; but by 1973, many were unwilling to pay $6, $5, $4, or even $3, making the stock cheaper than a fast-food lunch? McDonald's made the same hamburgers, and customers were eating them at the same rate. The company was ringing up more sales and higher profits, but at the bottom of that wall of worry, people were too worried about inflation, oil shortages, and the collapse of civilization to focus on positive news from the front line of hamburgers. More than these other worries, they worried about the seemingly endless slide in stock prices caused by other worriers selling their holdings to get a jump on the crowd.

Tops are always hard to pick, and no top has been picked prematurely more often by more experts than on the recent high-altitude adventure in stocks. Joe Granville called a top in 1982, fifteen years and 7,000 Dow points too early. Others saw a top at Dow 2,000, 3,000, 4,000, 5,000, 6,000, 7,000, 8,000. It was seen as a sign of a top when the 1000th, 2000th, 3000th, 4000th, and 5000th stock mutual fund opened a mailbox.

People said a top was near when Warren Buffett bought his corporate jet, the Indefensible; when the road to East Hampton, Long Island, became impassable in the summer; when cigars made their comeback; when employment in the brokerage houses reached an all-time high. Reporters called a top when Peter Lynch left the Fidelity Magellan fund in 1990.

Short seller David Rocker saw a top in December 1993, and said so in *Barron's:* "The anecdotal evidence is growing that we are rapidly approaching the end of this investment cycle." He was joined in this premature exhortation by Jim Finucane, a prominent money manager, who dumped his entire stock portfolio in 1993. "I expect the market averages to drop as much as 40 percent over the next couple of years," Finucane told *Barron's* (December 20, 1993).

Hasty top callers who shed stocks early watch their friends and neighbors celebrate further increases in net worth. The higher stocks go, the more convinced they become they'll be right in the end.

In 1994, Merrill Lynch strategist Robert Farrell predicted we'd see a top in 1995–1996. At Dow 4,000, Marty Zweig's human database, Ned Davis, said of the coming bear market, "I think it is going to be pretty quick." In 1994, Jim Stack was worried about "breadth deterioration and distribution" and the Dow utility average hitting a yearly low while the industrials hit a yearly high.

Charles Minter of Comstock Partners, bearish since 1991, tells *Barron's* he "feels terrible about what's taken place" but knows he'll be right eventually. David Shulman, market strategist at Salomon Brothers, an off-and-on bear since 1994, notes the "hoof marks all over my back." Barton Biggs, at Morgan Stanley, expected a 10 to 30 percent drop "pretty soon," in December 1996; Byron Wien, another off-and-on bear at the same firm, stayed bearish in the August rally of 1996, then threw in the bear towel before the market hanged him with it.

Laugh if you want, but these latter-day top callers may well turn out to be right in the end.

Chart watchers note the steeple tops in 1919, 1929, and 1973; the triple top in 1956–1957, when the Dow bumped up against 520 three times; the double tops of 1937 and 1946; the stretched top of 1906. What do these tops tell us? Tops of markets don't follow any set design, any more than tops of mountains do.

Some tops are reached in a trading frenzy, when stocks are bought and sold at a furious pace. But these "high-volume" tops are unusual. Some tops are reached with one type of company selling at obviously ridiculous prices. In 1901–1902, the conglomerates, or "trusts." In 1919, the oils. In 1968, new issues, mostly high-tech. In 1973, the Nifty Fifty. (All of the above are courtesy of John Dennis Brown.)

Folk tales about tops can keep you in stocks too long, or get you out of stocks too early. These include:

- "No top can be reached until the last bearish forecaster capitulates" (there have been bearish forecasts at every top).
- "No top can be reached unless 80 percent of investors are in the bull's camp" (in 1996 , only 50 percent were bullish).
- "No top until money begins to flow out of mutual funds" (in 1969–1970, the outflow began after the bear market was two-thirds over).

- "No top unless the country's in a recession" (several bear markets didn't involve recessions; or, if there was a recession, the bear market usually started several months before it arrived).

Marty Zweig observes that tops happen when "optimism is king, speculation is running wild, stocks carry high p/e ratios, and liquidity has evaporated." But optimism and speculation are subjective and difficult to measure. You could easily have concluded that optimism was king in the U.S. market in 1992, with speculation running wild since 1996. Price–earnings ratios looked dangerously high in 1994, until a surge in corporate profits brought them down and pushed stocks higher.

Although there's no sure way to call a top, in many bear markets, you don't need perfect timing to make a profitable escape. In the 1981 bear, the S&P 500 peaked on November 28, 1980, at 140, but six months later, in June 1981, had dropped only 10 points, to 130. The small-stock-oriented Russell 2,000 didn't peak until that June. The real damage came later, as it did in the Ursa Major of 1973.

In that one, the S&P 500 peaked on January 11, and nine months later was down less than eight percent. Two-thirds of a typical bear's decline happens in the last third of the episode.

THE BEAR MARKET RALLY

A bear market may be interrupted by an exciting and unexpected rally. As most investors sit on their assets, hamstrung as Hamlet, bargain hunters move in to make a buck. The rally breaks out on encouraging developments: lower interest rates from the Fed, a truce in a major war, economic revival. Stock prices move up quickly, and some stocks may reach new highs, but many fail in the attempt. The rally fizzles, and another big drop takes stocks down again.

There were more bear rallies in the 1930s than in all the decades since. Seven rallies since 1956 produced gains of 10 percent plus. This includes a spectacular advance that interrupted the twin bears of 1968–1970 and 1973–1974. It carried the Dow from 631 to 1051, recovering all the prior losses and then some. (Purists see this rebound as a new, abbreviated bull market, but whatever it's called, it was an enriching experience.)

The ten-year period from 1968 through 1977 was the most confusing and exhausting yin-yang in the annals of U.S. equities. At the end of the 1970s, the Dow was only 30 points higher than it had been ten years earlier. During this period, buying and holding was a waste of time and money, because stocks—even stocks that paid a dividend—failed to keep up with inflation. This era was useless for the patient investors, but it gave market timers and rally players a wonderful chance to test their skills.

How do you decide when to reenter a falling market, to take advantage of a rally? Whenever stocks decline 10 percent—a correction but not yet a bear market—Marty Zweig sees a potential buying opportunity. His research shows that when stocks are down 10 percent, there's a reasonable chance a "rally is due." This assumes the market has no strikes against it. (See "Three Strikes," page 64). Zweig never invests in any market without a careful review of his key indicators. He learned that lesson the hard way in 1974.

Two years earlier, in 1972, Zweig had turned bearish with uncanny timing. He shorted the market near the top, making a nice profit for his clients, but in June 1974, as stocks were coming back, he convinced himself the rally would continue. Ignoring the indicators that told him otherwise, he stocked up on stocks just in time to lose two years' worth of gains in three months.

"I could argue that I wasn't wrong, just 'early,'" Zweig recalled in his book, *Winning on Wall Street*. "These are all common rationalizations for those who err. . . . The weight of the evidence was still bearish and I blew it.

My main mistake then was in ignoring the very bearish monetary conditions that prevailed. . . . Determined not to go that route again, I then constructed several new monetary indicators that have since served me well. . . . I made one more major mistake a year and a half later, in January 1976 . . . since those days I absolutely and utterly refuse to fight a major trend in the market."

HITTING BEAR BOTTOM

A bear market is a bull in gestation.
Anonymous

After the final plunge in stock prices that heralds the bear's demise, you're presented with a buying opportunity, perhaps the opportunity of a lifetime. You need two things to take advantage: ready cash and a tin ear. The latter is necessary to drown out the drone of doomsaying that's sure to accompany stocks at the bottom of the Wall of Worry, where doubters are preeminent. They've been disappointed too often to believe the next turnaround is for real.

Capitalizing on these opportunities is easier said than done. Those who sold already are sitting on a pile of cash, reminding themselves never to gamble in stocks again. When the new bull market begins, they don't benefit. Those who haven't sold already are obvious candidates to sell into the next rally.

An excellent example was the Great Depression bull market of 1932–1937, a happy interlude lost in the gloom of the day. People who bought stocks near the Dow's low of 41.22 in 1932 nearly quintupled their money as the Dow advanced to 194.40 in five years. They got a quicker payoff in the S&P 500—up 154 percent in three years. Such gains are always uncommon, but in the 1930s, with one out of four adults lacking a paycheck, they were nothing short of fantastic.

How could you sense it was time to jump on stocks at their nadir in 1932? Not from the newspapers. They were spreading despair headline by headline: banks going bankrupt, companies closing their doors, one out of four workers out of work. Not from expert commentators, none of whom was calling for a rally. Not from your broker, if you still had a broker in 1932. Brokers with clients were more fearful of stocks than the clients were. Groucho Marx's broker was gloomier than Groucho, as Groucho himself reported:

Groucho: Aren't you the fella who said nothing could go wrong . . . that we were in a world market?
Broker: I guess I made a mistake.
Groucho: No, I'm the one who made a mistake. I listened to you.
Broker: I lost all my money, too.
Groucho: Well, buck up. Don't let it get you down. Just remember—twenty years from now you'll be looking back on these as the good old days.

This, on the eve of the most profitable advance for stocks in any five-year period before or since! To take part in this bonanza, you had to ignore prevailing opinion and rely on the obvious fact: stocks were incredibly cheap. By the end of 1931, Dow stocks were throwing off nearly 11 percent in annual dividends. No matter what happened to the market going forward, you could be reasonably confident of collecting that huge yield, made more attractive with inflation in remission and long-term bonds paying 5–6 percent.

Stock prices might have sunk lower, to be sure. Anything was possible, but with the Dow down 89 percent already, you had to figure there was an upside, unless Wall Street was forced out of business and bankers returned to hunting and gathering. Meanwhile, the Federal

Reserve was cutting interest rates furiously—seven times in 1930 alone, shrinking the key prime rate from 6 percent to a very accommodating 3.5 percent. It was no secret, even then, that lower short-term rates were healthy for stocks.

You didn't need perfect timing to take advantage of this bear market rally. Maybe you waited until stocks rebounded from Dow 41 to Dow 100 before you got up the courage to buy. Still, you nearly doubled your money in three years. After that, the rally failed and your profits turned to losses by 1939, so if you bought and held at Dow 100, you were temporarily out of pocket. Nevertheless, buying cheap in 1932 and then holding was far more rewarding in the long run than buying dear in 1929 and then holding.

You had another chance to pick up bargains off the bottom in 1974, when the Dow Industrials sold for less than six times record earnings of that year, and many wonderful companies sold for three times earnings. If you missed that one, or were too young to take advantage, the Crash of 1987 gave you another rare buying opportunity.

Again, it was difficult to take advantage. Brokers, analysts, and well-known experts were advising caution, which always translates as "Buy later." Look what eight Wall Street all-stars were telling each other at the roundtable sponsored by *Barron's* Magazine in January 1988, four months after the crash, at the start of a record-breaking bull run.

"Wails of anguish," observed *Barron's* in the introduction to this annual exchange of views, "reverberated through the canyons of the financial district as year-end bonuses were cut or eliminated. Tuitions to Hotchkiss and house payments in the Hamptons hang in the balance. Not even New York's homeless have received as poignant press coverage as the beleagured suspenders crowd struggling to maintain its standard of living" (*Barron's*, January 25, 1988).

Here are a few sample forecasts from four of the eight participants:

Feliz Zulauf: The honeymoon, from 1982 to 1987, is over. The world changed in the fall of 1987. A bear market started that will probably last several years. We have had the first down leg.

Oscar Schafer: I just think that stocks are basically trending down.

Jim Rogers: Most stock markets around the world are going to go up dramatically, maybe for another six days, six weeks, six months—but no longer than six months. At which point, we are going to have a real bear market. I am talking about a bear market that is just going to wipe out most people in the financial community, most investors around the world.

   And in fact there are many markets that I would short but which I will not be short, because I think they will probably close them down.

Paul Tudor Jones: The questions, to me, are not so much Will the stock market make new lows? Will we go into recession? Will we have a bear market?—but will we be able to avert a worldwide depression like we saw in the early Thirties?

That three of the other four participants were tepidly bullish and one stayed on the fence hardly neutralizes the scary scenarios evoked above, and any reader who cared about protecting capital would swallow hard before buying stocks when four all-stars were so profoundly pessimistic—one predicting another Great Depression and another, a worldwide financial collapse. That's not to say these men took their own advice (Rogers insisted later he hadn't). But it shows how widespread and deep the fear was.

"The experts will still be saying, 'Uh oh, the economy's started to slow down,' or 'XYZ Co. just went bankrupt,' or 'Boy, things are really bad,'" says William O'Neil, publisher of *Investor's Business Daily*. "So the news is bad, and all the advisers are scared. And you've gone through six, eight, nine months of a poor period, so everybody's now accepted the fact that it's pretty terrible. Nobody's got the nerve to buy anything. So you're sitting there frozen, licking old wounds because you've been kicked around for six, eight, nine months. You haven't got the guts to go in there and buy the next Microsoft or Cisco."

This is the bear's double whammy—you wait too long to sell stocks on the way down, then exit at unfavorable prices. Then you wait too long to buy them on the way up, and watch while others prosper. But again, if the headlines don't tell you the market has turned and it's time to buy stocks, how do you know?

Perhaps a disturbing event will produce the selling climax that sends stocks to the bottom, e.g., the Kent State massacre of 1970 or the Soviet launch of Sputnik in 1957. More likely, they hit bottom for no particular reason, which makes it nearly impossible to determine when the worst will be over. How then, can you separate a minor bear market, with stocks down 20 percent, from the more devastating variety, with stocks down 40 percent or more? You need some hard evidence something has changed for the better.

You probably won't get any clues from corporate earnings at this point, especially if the bear market has been accompanied by a recession. Stocks will likely record their best gains off the bottom while corporations are struggling to make money. That's why the price–earnings ratios of the major market averages at these key turning points seem too high to warrant buying stocks—the earnings are lousy.

You may get a valuable clue from declining interest rates. Lower rates help stocks in two ways: (1) they tend to revive the economy, which eventually restores corporate prosperity, and (2) they make stocks more attractive to investors who might otherwise prefer bonds.

To save a dying economy, the Federal Reserve Board leads the charge, cutting short-term rates. Banks return the favor by passing the lower rates along to customers. This easier credit leads to more borrowing, which leads to more spending, which leads to more corporate prosperity, which leads to higher stock prices.

A Fed action of this kind is particularly notable after a series of rate increases, such as occurred numerous times during the late 1970s and into 1982. Paul Volcker, Fed chairman at the time, fought inflation by raising short-term rates repeatedly, a therapy that weakened the economy and hurt stocks, so his relaxation of rates was a momentous reversal.

Another sign of a turn in the market is a sharp rally on huge volume. William O'Neil says this is easy enough to spot: "After stock prices have turned higher, a sharp advance on heavy volume serves as a confirmation the recovery is for real. This momentous trading session usually happens in the first few days of the upturn, when the averages surge and some new stocks jump up six or eight points—just as Cisco Systems, PeopleSoft, and Acend did, coming off the bottom of the last bear market . . ."

Such a jump can only occur when a crowd of buyers has entered the market, which tells you the gloom is beginning to lift and trend-setting investors have decided stocks are too cheap to pass up.

EARLY WARNING SYSTEMS

Some disappointment may be felt by the reader at this point because no infallible rule for calling the turn on the major movements of the stock market has been suggested. A moment's thought will show, however, that if there were any infallible technical method of forecasting the major swings of the stock market, there could be no major swings. If every trader knew or could discover by a half hour's investigation that the stock market was about to go down, there would be no buyers.

Phil Carret
The Art of Speculation

SINCE STOCKS WERE INVENTED, stockpickers have sought a formula that will tell them when a bear is in the neighborhood. Tape readers have studied the charts of the market's ups and downs, looking for telltale patterns (head-and-shoulders, double tops, double bottoms) in the wiggles on the page. In the 1920s, Colonel Leonard Ayres, vice president at the Cleveland Trust Company, noticed a telling connection between aluminum prices and stock prices. Others noticed a connection between leather prices and stock prices,

prices of a seat on the stock exchange and stock prices, livestock prices and stock prices.

The same Ayres who made the aluminum connection also observed that stocks declined whenever short-term interest rates rose higher than long-term rates—the "inverted yield curve" sell signal, which he issued in January 1929. Another indicator, Coppock's Curve, was developed by Edwin Coppock, who measured investor sentiment with an "emotional barometer."

In the Babson charts popularized by economist Roger Babson, a statistical landscape with black mountains and valleys was crossed by "growth lines." Every economic action supposedly led to an equal and opposite reaction—the communist dialectic applied to capitalism. A "composite forecaster" advanced by Dr. Willford King, of New York University, rolled forty-four different statistics into one indicator. At the far end of the century, Elaine Garzarelli developed her own composite forecaster with fourteen key statistics.

No chart, formula, or composite forecaster has proven infallible, and few have proven remotely reliable. (This tells you something: The most accurate market timer in the recent era is Wall Street astrologer Arch Crawford, who says the market is controlled by the planets.) Nevertheless, here's a sample of bear-spotting systems that have attracted a loyal following:

THE DOW THEORY

If the Dow theory confuses you, there's a good reason. The Dow theory isn't really a theory. It's a batch of suppositions harvested from 252 *Wall Street Journal* editorials written by William Hamilton from 1907–1930. Hamilton was a disciple and employee of the original Charles Dow, the father of the Rails (now Transports) and the Industrials. Dow wrote very little about the Dow, so Hamilton played Plato to Dow's Socrates, and put to paper what he thought Dow had in mind. He produced a book on the subject, *The Stock Market Barometer*, in 1922.

Hamilton was a frequent trader and market timer who looked for key turning points on the path of the two Dow averages. He tried to find a way to separate the momentary advance or retreat from a long march that carried stock prices in one direction for a meaningful stretch. A long march, he believed, could only occur if the averages were headed in the same direction together, and therefore "confirmed" each other's ups or downs. If the Industrials reached a new high and the Transports faltered, it put the future forward progress of both indexes in doubt.

Soon after writing an obituary for the bull market on October 25, 1929, Hamilton generated his own obituary by dying. Ever since, the Dow theory has been alternately embellished and debunked. Two camps of followers appeared on the scene: the literal Dowists who reduced Hamilton's teachings to a formula, and the poetic Dowists who said 252 editorials couldn't be reduced to a formula.

In the 1930s, an academic named Alfred Coles convinced a lot of people the Dow theory (whatever it was) was a flop. This didn't discourage an ailing investor named Robert Rhea. Stricken with tuberculosis, Rhea managed to make a nice living from his bed trading stocks along Hamiltonian lines. Rhea launched an advisory service and promptly called the exact bottom of the market in 1932. "Rhea's early letters were written during the depths of the greatest depression in American history," says contemporary Dow theorist Richard Russell, from whom much of the information in this section derives. "So you can imagine the skepticism with which his almost shocking bullish reports are greeted. Rhea also called the turn (to the downside) in 1937, and this feat made him a household name on Wall Street."

Rhea died in 1939, leaving the Dow theory without a champion until an Indiana stockbroker, E. George Schaefer, used it to forecast a new bull market five days before the bear turned tail on June 19, 1949. Schaefer based his interpretation on Charles Dow's original opinions, which apparently had stocks moving up or down more on whether they were overvalued or undervalued, and less on the alignment of the Industrials versus the Transports. "The philosophy of Charles Dow," wrote Schaefer, "always gave first consideration to values, then to economic conditions and third to the action of . . . the averages."

Schaefer rode the bull until 1966, when he turned bearish just in time for the Dow to summit at 995.15. He remained bearish until he committed suicide in 1974. Meanwhile, Schaefer's work caught Richard Russell's attention in late 1957. When other Dow theorists predicted worse times ahead, based on a coordinated decline in both averages, Russell disagreed. Valuation and other factors convinced Russell stocks were still on a long march uphill, and he said so in the inaugural edition of his Dow Theory Letter. He quickly developed a following. Subscribers kept subscribing and Russell kept rewarding them with profitable advice. He got his readers out of stocks in 1973, and back in in January 1975, just in time to join the big rally. He got them out two months before the Crash of 1987. Forty years since his first edition, he's still forecasting. Russell's is the oldest continuously-published stock market newsletter in existence.

Russell pays close attention to the interplay between the Industrials and Transports, but he doesn't necessarily reach the same conclusion as other Dow watchers, as the Dow theory is an inscrutable today as it was in Hamilton's day.

In a recent attempt to clarify the Dow theory, three academics asked a computer to study Hamilton's buy and sell recommendations over the years he wrote his editorials. Once the computer was trained to invest like Hamilton, the scholarly trio devised a simulation in which the computer invested like Hamilton through all the Dow's up and downs from 1929 to the present. One of the three,

Will Goetzmann at the Yale School of Management, describes this process as "neuralnet estimation using genetic algorhythms to train the neuralnet."

The results, says Goetzmann, are an "astounding vindication" of Hamilton's methods. The computer couldn't reduce the Dow theory to a formula, but its simulated trades a la Hamilton were consistently on the money through decades of gyrations.

It's interesting what the Dow theory is telling Richard Russell these days. It's kept him bullish since the fall of 1987, but ten years later, he notes a worrisome development. Neither the Industrials nor the Transports has made a new high in four months. He also notes the high valuations. He hadn't issued a sell signal yet, but he suspects a major top is in the making.

CONTRARIANISM

When investors are overly bullish, it's bearish for whatever they're bullish about, and whenever they're bearish, it's bullish. On this topsy-turvy premise, contrariansim rests. It turns out contrarians are organized—a contradiction in itself. They hold an annual meeting every October at a frumpy resort in Vermont—the kind that has a nautical museum and a library but no TV in the rooms. New England in the leaf season is an oddly popular destination for this crowd.

Twice a day, after breakfast and lunch, a man in a top hat appears at the door of the dining room, beeps an air horn, and leads the procession to a nearby lecture hall. This is James Fraser, regarded as the nation's leading contrarian. Fraser has a small publishing house, where he keeps the movement alive by reprinting various classics of the genre, beginning with *The Art of Contrary Thinking*, written by Humphrey B. Neill, Fraser's mentor and fellow citizen of Vermont. Along with books, Fraser publishes a monthly newsletter and various buttons with antithetical messages, such as "Doubt All Before Believing Anything" or "Buy Suntan Oil in January."

"Go where the crowd just came from," tycoon and contrarian hero Bernard Baruch once said. The contrarian is never loyal to any particular class of investment, the way the gold bug is loyal to gold. He acquires stocks, bonds, gold, or pork bellies whenever they're out of style, and sells them at a profit when they're in style. He likes what is disliked, and dislikes what is liked, so a contrarian in 1982 was buying stocks when the public shunned them, and in the 1990s he's shunning stocks when the public can't get enough of them.

As in all matters financial, the devil is in the when and not the what. More often than not, stocks, bonds, gold, pork bellies, etc., are neither wildly popular nor wildly unpopular at any particular moment, so it's hard to tell when the crowd gets crowded enough to oppose.

Just because a certain asset is out of favor at the moment doesn't guarantee it will turn a profit anytime soon. Gold has been so unpopular for so long it was the star attraction at contrarian conferences dating back to the mid 1980s, when a fervent gold bug lost control of himself, jumped on a chair and hollered "gold! gold! gold!" At some point gold became so widely ostracized even gold bugs wouldn't buy it. There wasn't a better contrarian play on the planet, unless it was mad cow patties, and still the price of gold didn't rise.

Various sentiment indicators and market timing services report on the bullishness or bearishness of Wall Street traders, options players, fund managers, financial advisors, and the general public. These figures are often pored over for clues as to what the crowd is doing. Marty Zweig reports that in three out of four cases where bears outnumber bulls in a sentiment survey, stocks rise 3.5 percent in 90 days or less.

This sort of information may be useful for frequent traders who make repeated entrances and exits in and out of stocks. But it doesn't help the average investor who's looking for long-term trends. Mistimed contrarianism kept people out of stocks from 1992–1997, when stocks already were too popular to pass the suntan oil in January test.

In another contrarian twist, leading contrarian James Fraser confides that the father of the movement, Humphrey Neill, admitted he made his fortune in the stock market buying Xerox, a very popular holding in his day.

ZWEIG'S THREE STRIKES

Marty Zweig, in his *Winning on Wall Street* (Warner Books, 1986), says the bear markets of his acquaintance share at least one of three key characteristics: (1) extreme deflation, (2) extra-vagant multiples, and (3) an inverted yield curve.

Extreme Deflation. Things are getting cheaper, and the Consumer Price Index (Zweig keeps his eye on this barometer) is falling fast. Whenever consumer prices have dropped 10 percent over six months, Zweig goes on bear market alert.

Extreme deflation was the big factor in the painful declines of 1919–1921, 1929–1932, and 1937–1938. Then it disappeared from the scene for sixty years, before recent events have suggested that it might return. Many investors still aren't aware of the damage it can do.

Extravagant Multiples. When stock prices reach the point where the Dow or the S&P 500 is selling for twenty times earnings, a setback is a likely prospect. This only applies to a perky economy, when companies are healthy and their earnings are robust. In a recession, when earnings are subpar, the fact that stocks are selling for a high multiple is no cause for alarm.

Extravagant multiples have been detected in eight bear markets (Zweig, p. 35) since 1919. In 1962, says Zweig, the economy was perky, inflation was no problem, and the only thing wrong with stocks was the high pricetag (the Dow sold for twenty-three times earnings). That was enough to bring down the market.

Inverted Yield Curve.   Normally, long-term interest rates are higher than short-term rates, but once in a while, you get the odd situation where short-term rates are higher. This usually means the Federal Reserve is trying to throttle a zealous economy. A temporarily inverted yield curve may not threaten stocks, but if it lingers, or if the curve becomes more inverted, stocks will disappoint. Inversion was a factor in nine of the past thirteen serious declines.

As shown in Exhibit 5, only one bear market had three strikes against it: the 1929–1932 market. Four others had two strikes, including three

Exhibit 5   Zweig's Three Strikes

Bear Markets	Extreme Deflation	Very High P/E Ratio	Inverted Yield Curve	% Decline in Dow Industrials
1919–1921	Yes		Yes	−47.6
1923			Yes	−18.6
1929–1932	Yes	Yes	Yes	−89.2
1933	Yes			−37.2
1937–1938	Yes			−49.1
1939–1942		Yes		−41.3
1946–1949		Yes		−24.0
1956–1957			Yes	−19.4
1962		Yes		−27.1
1966		Yes	Yes	−25.2
1969–1970		Yes	Yes	−36.1
1973–1974		Yes	Yes	−45.1
1978–1980			Yes	−16.4
1981–1982			Yes	−24.1
1987		Yes		−36.1

Source: Marty Zweig, *Winning on Wall Street* (Warner Books, 1986).

doozies: 1919–1921, 1969–1970, and 1973–1974. Every bear since 1929 has had at least one strike.

THE Q RATIO

Q is the brainchild of economist James Tobin of Yale. If your house had a Q ratio, here's how you'd find it. First, you'd estimate how much it would cost to replace the house and its contents, if the house suddenly was obliterated. Then you'd compare the replacement cost of the house to the price the house and its contents would fetch in today's market. Divide the market price into the replacement cost and you get the Q ratio.

Tobin took this brainchild several steps further and figured the cost of replacing all the public companies in America (land, buildings, machinery, inventory, fixtures, and so on). This was far from a precise number, but once he came up with a ballpark figure for this replacement cost for American business, he divided by the latest market value of all shares of public companies traded on U.S. stock exchanges. This gave him a national Q ratio.

Naturally, the Q ratio varies with the price of stocks and the replacement costs of corporate assets. Whenever the ratio falls below 1, it's cheaper to buy stock in public companies than to build new companies from scratch. This means stocks are undervalued relative to the underlying assets. When the ratio exceeds 1, it's cheaper to build new companies than to buy stock. In that case, stocks are overvalued relative to the underlying assets. Exhibit 6, a map of the Q ratio going back to 1960, appears on page 67.

After the Q rose above 1 in the 1960s, stocks sold off. In fact, Q is three-for-three at calling the major market tops in this century: 1929, 1935, 1968. Tobin's indicator wasn't invented in 1929 and 1935, but if he'd been born earlier, Q might have saved many investors from ruin. Lately, Q hasn't done investors any favors; a Tobin devotee would have

Exhibit 6 Tobin's Q (S&P 500/Corporate Asset Replacement Costs)

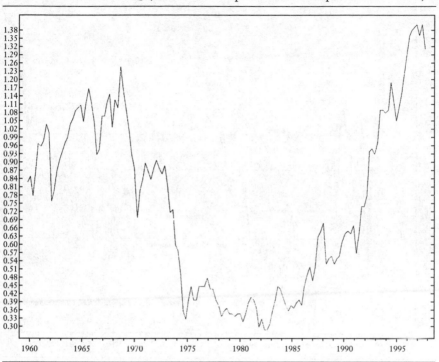

Source: Ned Davis Research.

left the stock market in 1993 when Q crossed above the 1 line. It remains to be seen whether this early exit, 3,000 Dow points below the 1997 scenic overlook, will look smart in retrospect.

THE 75 PERCENT RATIO

In this close relative of Q, the total market value of publicly traded stocks is compared to the entire U.S. economic output, or gross domestic product (GDP). The record shows that whenever stocks are worth more than 75 percent of the U.S. economy, stocks go into decline (Exhibit 7). This ratio has called the last two severe bear markets,

Exhibit 7   Stock Market Capitalization as a Percentage of GDP

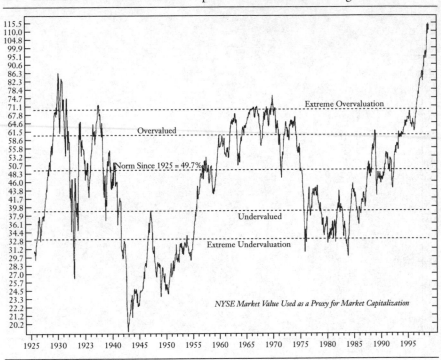

Source: Ned Davis Research.

but this time around, it's been was too early. In 1997, for the first time since this data has been collected, stocks are selling for 100 percent of U.S. economic output.

REVERSION TO THE MEAN (RTM)

RTM groupies believe prices of anything and everything will occasionally run away with themselves, but eventually they return to their normal interrelationships. The problem with this theory is that prices often run away much farther and stay away much longer than people expect. Also, it's hard to pick the mean that prices are supposed to revert to. Gold has been in a bear market since 1980, but, nearly twenty years later, nobody knows where the mean is. Silver overshot the mean and ran from $4 to $49.93 an ounce in 1980. Investors who think they know where the mean is, and who buy or sell when it's reached, are likely to miss big gains on the upside and catch big losses on the downside.

Here's what RTM tells us about how far stock prices must fall before they return to the mean, based on earnings, book value, and dividends.

At present, the S&P 500 companies are selling at 20 times earnings, when the normal pricetag in this century is 13.6 times earnings. To get back to normal, the price of the S&P 500 index must drop from current levels (950) to 640.

Meanwhile, the companies in that index pay a combined annual dividend of less than 2 percent. If investors demanded a "normal" dividend of 4.4 percent, the S&P 500 would fall in half.

Stocks in today's market are priced at more than four times the book value of the companies to which they're attached. The last time they were this expensive on book value was 1929. In the past, bear markets have arrived when stock prices reached two times the book value.

THE SAN JUAN HILL THEORY

Hong Kong pundit Marc Faber says stocks reach the top when the generals (large stocks) are charging up the hill while the troops (small stocks) lag behind. It's not uncommon, says Faber, for the generals to plant the flag nine months after the troops have retreated.

How can you tell when generals and troops have parted company? The big stocks in the Dow or the S&P 500 will be rising while the smaller stocks, in the Russell 2,000 or other small stock indexes, are declining.

Near the top of the Nikkei average in 1990, the troops already had retreated, so the San Juan Hill theory worked in Japan. In the United States, the troops began to lag the generals in 1996. Large stocks advanced while a third of the small stocks traded on NASDAQ were down 40 percent or more.

THE ADVANCE–DECLINE LINE

Chart readers pay close attention to the number of stocks going up or down on any given day. They believe a market is healthy when the majority of stocks rise together, and unhealthy when the risers are outnumbered by the decliners. The daily tally of risers and decliners is reflected in the advance–decline line that's featured in a variety of financial publications. In the U.S. market, the ranks of the decliners have grown, and the advancers have been less prevalent.

In April 1997, Jim Stack noticed that a huge number of former advancers on NASDAQ had become decliners, a sharp reversal of fortune that told him the "NASDAQ has bear market written all over it."

PART THREE

~

WHO'S CRYING BEAR?

THE FULLY-MISINFORMED
INVESTOR

A Barron's *headline of January 1973, "Not a Bear Among Them,"*
summed up the learned opinion of institutional investors at the onset of
the biggest bear market in thirty-six years.

Bob Prechter

UNLESS YOU LIVE IN A cave with no mailbox and no cable,
you aren't investing alone. Experts are telling you what to do from
the morning paper to the nightly news. Round the clock financial advice didn't exist when there were three TV networks and no Lou
Dobbs, Lou Rukeyser, Dan Dorfman, or Maria Bartiromo; no *Money,
Worth, Smart Money, Bloomberg, Inc.,* or *Investor's Daily.*

Is being fully informed an advantage or a liability? Jim and Lisa
Stack and their staff on the lower floor of the Stacks' split-level in
Whitefish have tried to answer this question. They put in long hours
culling articles, headlines, and advice columns that appeared around
the bear markets, going back to the 1920s. This tedious effort
produced fascinating results. When they are predicting anything

that involves money, economists, prominent investors, and the reporters who quote them haven't been wrong on occasion. They've been unerringly errant.

Financial reporters and editors are just as emotional as their readers. They cry and laugh at the same scenes in the movies, and they take the same cues from real life. When things are going well for others, things are also going well for them, and they write stories with happy endings. And when things are going so well for everyone that the happy ending becomes prevailing opinion, the prevailing opinion is mistaken. Here is a sample of what the media were saying when stocks were at the market top, heading for disaster:

The long-term outlook for stocks is bullish.
U.S. News & World Report, October 28, 1968

Stocks can potentially appreciate in value over the next 10 years by an average of 8 to 10 percent a year.
U.S. News & World Report, November 11, 1968

An increasingly bullish mood among investors points to a stronger stock market in 1981.
U.S. News & World Report, April 20, 1981

Don't Climb Off the Bull Yet: The ride isn't over. Despite their recent run-up, stocks should rise as profits improve and foreigners buy more.
Fortune, August 3, 1987

Why Greenspan Is Bullish.
Fortune, October 26, 1987 (The issue was postdated; it hit the stands a few days before the Oct. 19 crash.)

In the months before the 1987 crash, the same bullish chorus was singing the same wrong song in other magazines, and the Stacks have the quotes to prove it. Their files go back as far as September 28, 1929, when the *New York Times* offered this soothing commentary a few weeks before the Great Decline:

Even in such markets as those of the last few days—unless he is operating in particularly volatile stocks, the customer with a 50 percent margin has little to worry about.

If you're tempted to wait for the media to ring the bell that rings out the bull market, take a tip from Stack: Don't wait. When the time is right, the hired pens and talking heads will reassure you that now's not the time. Your instincts or your indicators might tell you to sell stocks, but prevailing opinion never will—unless, of course, it's time to buy.

The same misguided advice you get near the top of a market is distributed in larger amounts at the bottom. Dire predictions about the fall of stocks are made after stocks already have fallen. Stack sets the scene. You're ten years from retirement and your future is tied up in a growth stock mutual fund. You bought and you've held, which hasn't been easy because the fund is down 46 percent from its high. With your faith in stocks badly shaken, you pick up the latest issue of *Forbes* and find the following: "In the last analysis there is no floor to equity prices, except at such a low level that it becomes ludicrous to dwell on it."

Checking other financial magazines for second opinions, you encounter these headlines:

"The Gray Mood May Last All Year"

"Stocks Will Sell Permanently Lower"

"Wall Street Won't Be the Same Again"

"Gone Are the Go-Go Days"

"Statistics Refuse to Signal Any Short-Term Hope"

"Unrelieved Gloom Clouds the Business Horizon"

If you ignore these nerve-wracking summations and manage to stay invested in stocks, you're more pigheaded than most. After what you've just read, you wouldn't think of buying more. Let's say you're pigheaded enough to keep your portfolio intact for three more years, through an intervening rally and into another bear market. Now you're seven years from retirement, and you're looking at big losses on paper with stocks at their lowest levels in 11 years. You pick up the latest issue of *Business Week* and read: "Many analysts feel stocks have a lot farther to fall for fundamental reasons. The statistics say the downturn is only beginning."

Checking further for second opinions, you run across these headlines:

"Now Even Nations Are in Danger of Default"

"A Runaway Federal Deficit"

"The Telltale Signs of a Deepening Recession"

"A Case for Gloom About Stocks"

"The Real Recession Is Yet to Come"

"Economic Woes Still Scare the Professionals"

"The Coming Dividend Crisis"

Stack didn't make this up. The first string of headlines appeared in the press from May to July, 1970, near the bottom of the worst bear market since the 1930s—a fine time to buy stocks, and a terrible time to sell them. The second string appeared at the bottom of what some regard as the continuation of that worst bear market, 1973–1974. This was another fine time to buy and a terrible time to sell.

In 1981, you reach retirement age, and your portfolio has the same face value it had in 1969. You remind yourself it could have been worse. You could have acted on expert advice and sold stocks near one or both bear bottoms when the press was hopeless. A lot of people did, and their portfolios lost face value.

After stocks have gone nowhere for ten years, you're wondering whether you should add to your positions, to give your portfolio a value lift. Near the bottom in 1982, the buying opportunity of a generation, you pick up the December 27 issue of *Business Week* and read: "The easy part of the rally is over. . . . Almost no one expects interest rates to drop far enough or fast enough to power stocks . . . to their next plateau . . . ."

This doesn't put you in a holiday stockpicking mood, and neither do the second opinions you find at the newsstand:

Go slow. That's the watchword for investors from experts.

U.S. News & World Report, July 12, 1982

The only thing that seems to pay off these days is that bundle of cash deposited in a money market fund, an investment neither daring nor original, just profitable.

The big concern is cutting losses and protecting capital, because if your capital erodes, you have greatly diminished any chances of breaking even or making a profit.

Business Week, July 5, 1982

Every file drawer in Stack's office leads to the same conclusion: the media aren't going to help you at the key turning points. The stock market is the one place in modern life where the better informed you are, the harder it is to make the right decision.

The very idea of financial news contradicts the first lesson investors are taught in the features sections of the financial press: it's the long term that matters, and the latest gyrations shouldn't count. Yet, every day, reporters must explain the ups and downs even when no sensible explanation exists. On top of reporting the gyrations, they search their Wall Street Rolodexes for informed sources willing to predict tomorrow's ups and downs, for predictions must be embedded in each market recap. There's never a lack of predictors, nor a reluctance to reuse them; nobody bothers to check on the accuracy of their prior statements.

As in all news reporting, financial news must be made to sound dramatic—otherwise, it wouldn't be newsworthy. The need for drama leads to headlines like this one, on the front page of the *New York Times*, on Tuesday, April 1, 1997: "Stock Plummet, Dow Loses 157.11." "Plummet" is the favorite word, second only to "plunge," whenever a declining Dow makes front-page news. In a sidebar to the plummet story, columnist Floyd Norris described the plunge as "wide and deep," never explaining how a plunge could be "wide," unless a grand piano was being tossed from a rooftop.

"Stock prices plunged for a second consecutive session yesterday," echoed *Times* reporter David Barboza, "feeding growing concerns about whether the bull market could sustain itself after two years of double-digit returns." He failed to mention how his own newspaper was doing the feeding. Millions of readers woke up to plummeting and plunging, when stocks had dropped a measly 2 percent.

On that same April Fool's Day that brought the 2 percent drop, *USA Today* published an "advice box," intended as a tranquilizer for readers who may have been unsettled by news of the plummet. Under the headline "Experts Urge Calm in Times of Crazy Stocks," readers were given two suggestions:

1. Don't sell any stocks ("in five or ten years this won't even be a blip," a financial planner from Atlanta reassured).
2. Don't buy any stocks ("don't jump into the stock market now, experts say").

This advice was logically incompatible. If you shouldn't buy stocks, it means prices are headed lower, and if prices are headed lower, what's wrong with selling?

If a 2 percent drop inspires "plunging" headlines and a .7 percent drop, as ocurred on Monday, July 29, 1996, can be recounted in the *Wall Street Journal* as "A Shaken Wall Street Reaches for the History Books," you can be sure that a 10 to 30 percent drop will inspire apocalyptic references. The same publications that coaxed you into buying stocks with articles such as "20 Winning Investments for 1997," or "Stocks You Can Sleep On," will try to scare you out. The same commentators who passed along the undiluted optimism (a New Era for equities; inflation permanently neutralized; the Federal Reserve masters the art of economic yin-yang) will not dilute the pessimism.

It happened in the Crash of 1987, which took the Dow down 1,000 points in two months, and then 500 more points in a single day, Black Monday. On Black Monday evening, anybody with a portfolio was staring at the TV set, looking for clues as to what to do next. The cameras focused on John Phelan, the head of the New York Stock Exchange, who looked like a man who had just got a fatal diagnosis, or a politician subpoenaed by a grand jury. Phelan said some encouraging words while looking quite discouraged. The morning after the *New York Times* headline read: "Does 1987 Equal 1929?" The article implied it wouldn't, but a companion piece raised "fear of a recession."

Reliable sources appeared or were quoted on TV, predicting bigger losses to come, and a global financial meltdown. Few encouraging words were heard. A record 604 million shares had changed hands on the New York Stock Exchange. A lot of believers in buying and holding had quickly converted to cutting and running.

Experts said a deep recession was inevitable; a brief rally would fail, and bigger losses would follow. The Federal Reserve would flood the banks with money in a valiant but futile effort to ward off a depression. The Federal Reserve did flood the banks with money and the effort succeeded. None of the other dire predictions came true.

No doubt things could have gone the other way, but, typically, the news is gloomiest when stocks are already down 30 or 40 percent, as they were in 1987—when they are perched on an extravagant multiple, set up for a fall.

To avoid making fully informed investment decisions that will put you into and out of stocks at the least profitable moments, the best thing to do at key-turning points is watch the Simpsons, docudramas, or whales breaching on the Discovery channel; or, read the sports pages, the style pages, or the classifieds, but under no circumstances take in the nightly or the daily news.

THE CASSANDRAS

IT'S A MISTAKE TO THINK bear markets only happen when the last bearish forecaster has died or turned bullish—an old saw that still gets passed around. Bearish forecasters were alive and forecasting in 1929 (Roger Babson being the most famous), in 1987 (Elaine Garzarelli, Marty Zweig, Richard Russell, and Jack Stack to mention a few), and at the opening of every decline before or since. Stack advised readers to "take profits" through summer, and recommended a 100 percent cash position in time for the crash.

Babson issued his famous sell signal in the fall of 1929: "There's a Crash coming and it may be a terrific one." This put Babson in the history books after the fact, but he'd cried bear too often for people to act on his warning. The problem is that by the time these alarmists get it right, nobody believes them anymore.

"Nobody was listening to Babson," says Phil Carret, who was on the scene and is still around to tell the tale. "That's because he'd issued the same warning in 1927 and 1928. In fact, he prefaced his 1929 warning with the statement 'I'm about to repeat what I said at this time last year and the year before.'"

Elaine Garzarelli, Marty Zweig, and John Kenneth Galbraith all cried bear in 1987, but have you ever heard of anybody who liquidated a portfolio prior to the Big Drop because they took Garzarelli's, Zweig's, or Galbraith's word for it? Bearish forecasters suffer from the Cassandra syndrome. At the very point they should be taken seriously, they aren't.

Cassandra is not a partner at Goldman, Sachs. She was the daughter of Priam and Hecuba of ancient Troy. She dated the Sun God, Apollo. In their courtship phase and with no jewelry store in sight, Apollo gave Cassandra the gift of prophecy. Now she could see what was coming next, so she rejected his advances. Apollo got mad, then got even. He fixed it so nobody would believe Cassandra's predictions.

Her brilliant calls ("Greeks in the Trojan Horse! Troy will be destroyed!") fell on deaf ears, just as Babson's did. Prominent bearish forecasters from Prechter to Jim Grant and Jim Stack will be right sooner or later, but they won't be taken seriously. Premature bearish forecasts will already have cost them their audience.

Bears have been ribbed by Rukeyser. They've been chided in print—"Bears will be right someday, just you watch!" a *Wall Street Journal* reporter snickered in a July 17, 1997, analysis. "So they missed 5,000 points. It's no reason they ought to stop prognosticating." Occasionally, they've received backhanded compliments. A Chicago money manager compared Jim Grant's newsletter to the Marquis de Sade: ". . . interesting reading as long as you don't try it."

Bears lose credibility with the investing public and with clients. They lose clients, especially the short sellers and the newsletter writers. They get hate faxes. They're psychoanalyzed at investment conferences. "I'm going to tell you what your problem is," an annoyed conferee told Morgan Stanley's Byron Wien in 1977: "The problem with you is that you went through [the bear markets of] 1973 and 1974 and those scars are still healing."

Fed chairman Alan Greenspan found out how hard it is to stand up to the bear baiters when he mentioned that an "irrational exuberance" had carried stocks to Dow 7,000. Even this hint of a warning, investors couldn't tolerate. From the reaction he got for his remarks in December 1996, you'd have thought Greenspan had torched Old Glory.

On page 1 of the *Wall Street Journal*, he was called "Yellowspan" by the chief investment strategist of Wheat First Butcher Singer Securities. On the floor of Congress, he was read the riot act by Representative Jim Bunning of Kentucky, a former major league pitcher with a former 92-mph fastball. Bunning was furious because the Fed chairman had "meddled" in the market. He blamed Greenspan for the Dow's dropping .3 percent—hardly an antidote for irrational exuberance. The tiny drop only showed that Greenspan's remark was widely overlooked.

"Somebody's got to tell that guy to stop talking," tax attorney Rich Curtin was quoted as saying in the *Journal*. Imagine the abuse that would have been heaped on the Fed chairman if investors had sold on the warning and the Dow had dropped 10 percent instead of .3 percent. The fact that his remark didn't cause a selloff ensures that his next warning (if he's brave enough to issue one) will be ignored like Cassandra's.

Forecasters and Economists

In other professions from plumbing to heart surgery, the expert can foretell and forestall disaster. Yet in market forecasting, knowledge of whatever kind does not necessarily lead to any ability to foresee the future. That's not entirely the forecaster's fault.

A market forecaster has a much harder job than, say, a weather forecaster. If the clouds gather and rainy conditions develop in the atmosphere, the weather forecaster can predict rainfall and be confident the rain will fall. But if bear market conditions (high stock prices, rising interest rates) develop on Wall Street, the market forecaster can't be confident stocks will fall. That depends on the whims of the audience.

If investors aren't selling their shares, then stocks won't drop, no matter what the market conditions. It's as if rain won't come if the audience of a weather forecast leaves their umbrellas at home. That's exactly the situation that foils the market forecaster. The audience gets in the way of the forecast.

Are trained economists more adept at forecasting than pundits with shaky credentials? Apparently not. Exhibit A in this case is Irving

Fisher of Yale. Fourteen days before Black Tuesday, 1929, he said: "In a few months I expect to see the stock market much higher than it is today." He followed that remark with: "Stocks are now at what looks like a permanently high plateau." Fisher put his money where his forecast was and lost the equivalent of $140 million in today's dollars. The Great Decline took away almost everything he had gained from the index card system he had sold to Remington Rand, according to the biography written by his son, Irving II.

On the other side of the Atlantic, John Maynard Keynes of Cambridge lost 1 million pounds in the same Great Decline—in spite of his uncontested brilliance as an economic thinker.

A few days after Black Tuesday, the Harvard Economic Society assured its members that "a severe depression . . . is outside the range of probability. We are not facing a protracted liquidation." According to Phil Carret, the Harvard Economic Society was liquidated in 1932.

Thus, notable economists from Yale and Cambridge (Keynes was regarded as the greatest in the world), and a group of renowned economists from Harvard, all failed to foresee, or even to comprehend, the writing on the tickertape.

This failure in the history of economic forecasting doesn't necessarily tell us much about modern economic forecasting, where the tools are sharper and the operatives are more sophisticated. Or does it? In 1997, three economists with nothing better to do fed all the data available to economists in 1929 into a new high-powered computer. Based on these data, they asked the computer: Is a Great Depression coming our way? Using the most advanced economic models, the computer checked and crosschecked every conceivable angle. It concluded there was zero chance that a Great Depression was about to happen in 1929. (From Friedberg's *Commodity & Currency Comments*, March 16, 1997.)

Out in Whitefish, Jim Stack provides further incriminating evidence. Trained economists, he concludes, are no more adept at predicting recessions that cause bear markets than market forecasters are adept at predicting bear markets. He bases that conclusion on the consensus of economists around three major recessions (1969, 1973–1974, and 1981) all of which were accompanied by bear markets.

Selling stocks at the onset of a recession has proven profitable 100 percent of the time. The catch is a recession is likely to be well underway before anybody notices, and economists may be the last to know. The official scorekeeper of recessions is the National Bureau of Economic Research, but its pronouncements are often made many months after the fact. By that time, the stock market has usually had its decline.

Recessions have always caused stocks to drop, but a drop in stocks doesn't necessarily cause a recession. Economists cried "Recession!" in 1987 after the Crash in October, but the recession didn't show up. In 1962, after the Steel Bear market, they did the same, and recession again failed to materialize. Thus, the saying: "The stock market has predicted two of the last eighteen recessions."

In any event, here's Stack's scorecard on recessionary forecasts:

1969–1970 Recession

- The year 1969 is going to be a good one for U.S. business, probably the best ever, in the opinion of most of the country's investment bankers.

  U.S. News & World Report, December 16, 1968

- Most economists agree that there will be no recession this year.

  Business Week, March 8, 1969

- Now with three more months of statistics under its belt, the Wharton computer confidently sticks to its guns and predicts no major recession for 1970.

  Business Week, February 21, 1970

1973–1974 Recession

- 1973 will be an excellent year for the economy. That is the clear consensus of the vast majority of economists, the economic consulting companies and all the widely known econometric models.

  Business Week, December 23, 1972

- Slower growth, yes; recession, no.

  Fortune headline, July 1973

- An easier money policy on the part of the Federal Reserve . . . is the major reason many economists no longer fear that there will be a recession next year.

  Newsweek, October 22, 1973

1981–1982 Recession

- After another quarter or two of decline, real GNP should begin a sustained recovery.

  Fortune, January 12, 1981

- . . . Recent forecasts show the economy, after a dip in coming months, strengthening.

  U.S. News & World Report, April 20, 1981

- No recession worth mentioning could occur without a drop in capital goods purchases. And no such drop seems ahead.

  Fortune, November 2, 1981

1990 Recession

- Outlook for the New Year Is Cheery.

  Wall Street Journal, January 2, 1990

- None of its 19 economists [referring to the Business Council] expects a recession this year or next.

  Wall Street Journal, May 14, 1990

- The Old Inventory Demon Won't Trigger a Recession This Time.
  Fortune, March 12, 1990

Stack says that by the time each of the past four recessions was recognized by the media, the stock market had already experienced 70 percent of its losses. Thus, informed investors who track the consensus of opinion among leading economists were unprepared for multiple recessions and costly bear markets over four decades.

In addition to what they learned from economists about recessions, those same informed investors learned that inflation would taper off in the late 1970s (it doubled) and would remain in double digits through the mid-1980s (it fell to single digits).

The Doomsday
Best-Seller

EVERY FEW YEARS, a gloom-and-doom book crawls to the top of the best-seller list. The author, sometimes an academic but more likely self-employed, makes a persuasive case for the coming deflation, depression, hyperinflation, currency collapse, or whatever else he thinks will wreck a portfolio. The masculine pronoun fits here because, to date, these books have been written exclusively by males. Does that mean women are less depressed than men? Does it pay to act when these books appear? Here are six prominent best-sellers, in chronological order, with summaries of their predictions and advice, and the actual results that occurred in the U.S. economy:

1. **Book:** *How You Can Profit From the Coming Devaluation.*
   Author: Harry Browne.
   Credentials: None in particular. Investment adviser, public speaker, opera enthusiast, Libertarian candidate for president, 1996.

Publication Date: 1970.

Prediction: Dollar will crash, precious metals will soar, stocks and bonds will lose big, as "traditional investments will fail to keep up with the changes."

Advice: Sell stocks and bonds, buy the metals.

Result: Dollar crashed, precious metals soared. Stocks and bonds lost big, traditional investments failed to keep up with changes. Browne was right!

2. **Book:** *You Can Profit From a Monetary Crisis.*

Author: Harry Browne again.

Publication Date: 1974.

Prediction: Economy in trouble. Runaway inflation, leading to depression: "A depression is 100 percent inevitable because of what's already happened." Dollar will nosedive. Stocks, bonds, mutual funds, real estate, and fixed-dollar investments big losers; gold a big winner. Gold could reach $300–$500 an ounce, silver to $10 or more.

Advice: Sell stocks and bonds, buy metals.

Result: Runaway inflation. Dollar nosedives. Fixed-dollar investments are losers. Gold and silver big winners. Browne was right about inflation, bonds, and precious metals; wrong about the inevitable depression.

3. **Book:** *How to Prosper During the Coming Bad Years.*

Author: Howard Ruff.

Credentials: Speed-reading franchiser, TV host, showman, actor, singer, stockbroker, food supplement promoter, newsletter writer.

Publication Date: 1979.

Prediction: Recession will cause government to crank up "the money and spending machine," leading to inflationary spiral and then to a depression that will be "remembered with a shudder for generations." Runaway inflation, collapse of Social Security and other pension programs, international monetary holocaust. Government forced to impose price controls.

Advice: Buy tools, seeds, and survival gear, plus enough food for one year. Hoard basic items that will be in short supply after price controls are imposed. Invest in one bag of junk silver coins for each family member, plus a like amount of gold coins. Sell all big-city and suburban real estate and buy small-town income property. Join a barter group. Avoid Wall Street-type investments.

Result: Federal Reserve puts brakes on economy to slow inflation. Short but severe recession in 1982 is followed by decade of prosperity. Price controls never imposed. Silver and gold enter long bear market, stocks and bonds generate record profits. Ruff was wrong.

4. **Book:** *The Great Depression of 1990.*

   Author: Ravi Batra.

   Credentials: Professor, Southern Methodist University.

   Publication Date: 1987. Six weeks on *New York Times* bestseller list, jumped to number four in summer, 1987.

   Prediction: Another Great Depression. "It will occur in 1990 and plague the world through at least 1996." Sees parallels between Roaring Twenties and Soaring Eighties. Big culprit: concentration of wealth. Lower and middle classes must borrow and become overextended. Heavy risk on banks that lend them money. Financial house of cards will topple, stock market will crash, banking system will collapse.

   Result: Stock market soars, banks in good shape, America prospers. Batra was wrong.

5. **Book:** *The Economic Time Bomb.*

   Author: Harry Browne, yet again.

   Publication Date: 1989.

   Prediction: Severe recession in 1989 or 1990; banking crisis, followed by Fed rescue that will result in "Nicaraguan-style inflation." Interest rates could rise to 20 percent, causing the Dow to fall in half. "You might not survive the 1990s if you're invested wholly in stocks or mutual funds."

Advice: Invest in Browne's "permanent portfolio," divided into four equal parts: 25 percent each in bonds, cash, gold, and stocks.

Result: Mild recession in 1990, followed by Fed's easing and decline in inflation. Banks make stunning recovery, become huge winners in stock market. Interest rates fall, Dow triples in value in seven years. "Permanent portfolio" gives poor returns: gold, silver, and cash underperform.

6. **Book:** *Bankruptcy, 1995: The Coming Collapse of America and How to Stop It.*

   Author: Harry Figgie.

   Credentials: CEO Figgie International, small player in leveraged buyouts.

   Publication Date: 1992. Twenty-six weeks on *Publisher's Weekly* best-seller list.

   Prediction: Deficit spending will bankrupt the country. Eighty-five percent of all personal and corporate income taxes will go to paying the interest on national debt. Interest rates, inflation will soar. "By 1995, the United States as we know it will most likely be dead."

   Result: Lowest inflation in 30 years, lowest unemployment in 23 years, widespread prosperity, first gain in real wages in two decades. Figgie International loses money; Figgie ousted as CEO.

Harry Browne started out well enough, but faltered on the third try. Others were off base from start to finish. This performance overall offers no compelling reason to spend money on the next gloom-and-doom best-seller.

BEWARE THE NEW ERA

EVERY GENERATION OR SO, there's talk of a "New Era"—a financial Camelot where the economic climate is forever balmy, inflation is kept outside the walls, and companies bask in a garden of prosperity, watered by the frequent brainstorms coming out of corporate research. A perfect time for stocks to thrive? Sounds like it from the following descriptions.*

First New Era

- For five years at least, American business has been in the grip of an apocalyptic, holy-rolling exaltation over the unparalleled prosperity of the "new era."

  Business Week, September 27, 1929

- It seemed to be taken for granted in speculative circles that this is a market of "manifest destiny," and that the destiny is to go continuously forward.

  New York Times, September 1929

---

* All quotes courtesy of Jim Stack, president of *InvesTech Research*, Whitefish, Montana.

Second New Era

- ... There seems to be a consensus that the present is something of a "new era" ... a number of conservative economists and businessmen now accept the idea that business expansion can go on indefinitely. ...

  U.S. News & World Report, November 15, 1965

- At least two members of the Federal Reserve Board now are saying that prosperity can go on and on, that what goes up does not necessarily have to come down. ... The present is something of a "new era" in which serious depressions ... are things of the past.

  U.S. News & World Report, November 15, 1965

- Backers of the "new economics" think Government now can keep the boom going indefinitely.

  U.S. News & World Report, November 15, 1965

Third New Era

- ... Market watchers, whom some call the New Era group, divine a new period that is defined by low inflation and the public's keen attraction to stock mutual funds. When old standards for valuing stocks are adjusted for these factors, they assert, stock prices look either perfectly reasonable or at worst, modestly high.

  New York Times, February 11, 1997

- Is the market crazy? Hardly. Underlying the equity boom is the emergence of a New Economy, built on the foundation of global markets and the Information Revolution.

  Business Week, December 30, 1996

The First New Era was the 1920s, when the phrase entered the financial vocabulary. Leading economists of the day said that the

United States had reached a permanent plateau of prosperity, thanks to American ingenuity, of which the mass-produced motor car was an obvious example. Reporters at *Business Week* noted the "amazing increase in man-hour production . . . [where] new industries rise like rockets. . . ."

The Second New Era was declared forty years later, when a new generation of economists rediscovered the permanent plateau of prosperity. This time around, American ingenuity had put a man on the moon, color TV in the house, and built giant computers that could do the work of thousands of file clerks. Affected by the ambient optimism, the nation's leaders elected to fight a war on communism abroad and a war on poverty at home.

The Third New Era was declared thirty years after the Second New Era, as the Dow approached 7,000 and another generation of economists had re-rediscovered the permanent plateau. American ingenuity had stored all human knowledge on a microchip and helped to clone a sheep. Coca-Cola was about to surpass water as the world's most popular drink.

The three New Eras share several characteristics:

1. A strong economy and weak-to-moderate inflation.
2. A belief that the government can ban recession and make the ban stick, to wit:

   Plan just right, be prepared to act at the first sign of trouble, and recessions can be prevented.

   U.S. News & World Report, February 15, 1965

   Recessions no longer seem as inevitable.
   The Washington Post, December 2, 1996

3. Mutual funds gaining or regaining popularity after a long period when they were unknown, disparaged, or avoided.

4. Stock prices off the charts of normal valuation, creating the need to find excuses why these unreasonable prices are reasonable, to wit:

Apparently there has been a fundamental change in the criteria for judging security values. Widespread education of the public in the worth of equity securities has created a new demand.
   The Outlook & Independent Magazine, May 15, 1929 (First New Era)

The United States has entered a new investment era to which the old guidelines no longer apply.
                    Barron's, February 3, 1969 (Second New Era)

Leading analysts on Wall Street are counseling that the old rules no longer apply when judging whether the stock market has soared beyond reason.
               New York Times, February 11, 1997 (Third New Era)

5. American technological know-how and overall brilliancy widely praised.
6. Only geezers from the previous New Era remember they've heard all this before.
7. The first two New Eras ended badly. The fate of the third hangs in the balance.

The Bearish Newsletter

ARE THERE STOCK MARKET newsletters of the bearish persuasion that can provide solace and good advice when the worst finally happens? Mark Hulbert, a one-man tracking service for such publications, finds few consistently bearish voices in the stack that regularly arrives in his mailbox.

Newsletters don't reveal their count of paid subscribers, so it's difficult to know how many readers they actually have. Many owe their survival to desktop publishing, which keeps costs to a minimum, and to Wall Street institutions that support oddball commentary on the off chance they'll glean an idea from it.

Hulbert notes that the typical newsletter can't be pigeonholed as bullish or bearish. Most publishers take a nimble approach, changing their betting advice (known as "asset allocation") from issue to issue. Otherwise, they'd have nothing new to tout for months or years on end, and might lose subscribers who get bored with the steady diet.

Having followed this self-publishing industry since 1980, Hulbert has noticed a high dropout rate. Only eighteen of the 160 newsletters tracked by Hulbert in 1997 go back as far as his own

Hulbert's Financial Digest, launched in 1980. This is one case where the reviewer has outlasted most of the performers.

Of those eighteen newsletters that survived since 1980, only three have beaten the stock market averages over time, which tells you that the vast majority aren't worth the price of a subscription. As Hulbert recently observed, in an article written for the American Association of Individual Investors, the three winning newsletters beat the market in very risky fashion, usually by advising subscribers to buy stocks with borrowed money (a.k.a. leverage). They've been exceptionally profitable to date, but these market beaters will no doubt become exceptionally unprofitable when the market reverses itself. "Newsletters that win with excessive risk are prime candidates to lose a lot when [the] market declines," Hulbert says.

In a related article in *Forbes,* Hulbert observed that the average letter has kept its readers only slightly more than half invested in equities since 1980, which means most letters have missed a heap of gains. Nevertheless, a handful of letters "earn their keep by cutting risk without causing a commensurate erosion in your return." Hulbert gives high marks to only two letters that have delivered gratifying returns at low risk in both bull and bear markets:

- *The No-Load Fund Investor,* published continuously since 1979 by Sheldon Jacobs. Once an analyst for television's Neilsen ratings, Jacobs turned his attention on stocks. He tracks no-load mutual funds and recommends various top performers. (Subscription $129 annually, phone (800) 252-2042.)
- *Value Line Convertibles Survey.* Along with stocks, the editors also recommended convertible bonds (the kind that pay interest the same as a standard bond, and can be converted into stock at prearranged prices). This letter will be most useful to wealthy investors who can afford to buy convertible bonds in quantity. (Subscription $625 annually, phone (800) 634-3583.)

Hulbert also has identified several outstanding performers whose advice may have lagged the market on the upside, but who are good at protecting assets in down markets:

- *FXC Investors*, subscription $190, phone (718) 417-1330.
- *Growth Stock Outlook*, subscription $235, phone (301) 654-5205.
- *Investor's Guide to Closed-End Funds*, subscription $365, phone (305) 271-1900.
- *LaLoggia's Special Situation Report*, subscription $230, phone (716) 232-1240.
- *Market Logic*, subscription $179, phone (800) 327-6720.
- Finally, Jim Stack's *InvesTech Mutual Fund Advisor* got kudos from Hulbert in a 1995 Forbes recap: "It lags the market in rallies . . . but it also appears more or less impervious to declines . . . InvesTech has been ahead of the market for significant periods—not merely after the 1987 crash but also very quickly during the brief 1990–1991 decline." Subscription $160, phone (800) 955-8500.

Growth Stock Outlook is the mouthpiece of Charles Allmon, who ran a mutual fund by that name until he sold it. *The Wall Street Journal* calls him "contrarian chicken." Allmon started his career a long way from Wall Street, working on rubber plantations in West Africa, then as a photographer and reporter. He started buying stocks in the early 1950s, and successful trades led him to start a fund. A saavy stockpicker with a keen eye for small growth companies, Allmon has been bearish for at least ten years—his fund was 50 percent in cash for most of the decade, and he advised the readers of his newsletter to keep 50 percent in cash as well. Given that stance, the 12.5 annual return on his fund and his advice over the ten-year stretch is remarkable.

Allmon, now 77 years old, continues to publish the newsletter. At present, he's telling investors to keep 90 percent in cash, 10 percent in stocks. He's been called a "stopped clock bear" and a "brain dead bear" but he's never let the hecklers change his mind.

A popular amateur investor's resource, the *Value Line Investment Survey*, provides regular updates on 1,700 stocks and also advises readers on asset allocation. Bullish as a rule, the editors took a bearish stance (45–55 percent stocks, the rest cash) during 1997. Recently, they changed the recommendation to 60–70 percent stocks and 30 percent cash. Their latest advice can be found in the Selection and Opinion section of *Value Line*, which is updated every week. Copies are readily available in most libraries. For subscription information, phone (800) 833-0046.

Fed Watching:
A Profitable Pastime

The monetary climate—primarily the trend in interest rates and Federal Reserve policy—is the dominant factor in determining the stock market's major direction.

Marty Zweig

FED WATCHING (AND LISTENING) has become a national pastime, and not just for economists and policy wonks. For non-Fed watchers, "Fed" is shorthand for the Federal Reserve Board.

The Fed serves as a bank for the bankers. Hundreds of banks around the country do their banking at one of the twelve Fed branches, the way you do yours at the nearest branch of Citicorp, NationsBank, etc. These banks keep cash on account at a Fed branch. When they need extra cash, they borrow it from the Fed. By raising or lowering the interest rates on these loans, the Fed can use the banking system to influence the economy.

A shadowy cabal of Fed governors, known as the Open Market Committee, meets eight times yearly behind closed doors in a Greek temple in Washington. Journalists are dispatched to snoop around the pillars, picking up hints as to what the Deceptive Dozen will do to help or hurt the investing public.

The current chairman of the Fed governors, Alan Greenspan, is a recognizable character in the TV pantheon of talking heads (his is bald). His testimony to Congress and his incidental speeches are scrutinized like a coded message intercepted across enemy lines. What was he saying? What was he REALLY saying? Did he mean it? Is this a trick? Will there be a preemptive strike? Not even the Pope or a psychiatrist in the paranoia ward has to choose words more carefully than the Fed chairman does. Billions of investor dollars are riding on every turn of phrase.

Say what you want about how the three branches of government make laws and wars; the Fed can make or break the national prosperity. Through its network of branches, the Fed can launch a new bull market or conjure a bear. Hence, Marty Zweig's motto to invest by: "Don't fight the Fed."

When the Fed was established in 1913, it gave the banking authorities a new purpose in life: tinkering with the money supply and interest rates, to goad or subdue the economy as conditions warranted. Prior to this debut of modern central banking (the Fed now has its equivalent in other countries worldwide), the economy ran free and often ran amok, as booms turned to busts and then back to booms again. The Fed tries to moderate these extremes by pumping or siphoning money into and out of the banks, or by raising and lowering interest rates.

When the Fed raises rates, also called "tightening," the banks pay more to borrow money, a cost they will surely pass along to their customers. This discourages borrowing and causes businesses to cut back on their plans for new factories and homeowners to delay buying new houses. The economy slows down, which means less inflation and less stimulation, which is what the Fed had in mind when it tightened in the first place.

When the Fed lowers rates, known as "loosening," the banks pay less to borrow money, which encourages borrowing and causes businesses to expand and homeowners to buy houses. The economy speeds up, which may jolt the country out of recession—exactly what the Fed had in mind when it loosened in the first place.

Conventional wisdom says a single Fed tightening, the preemptive strike mentioned above, will benefit stockholders by nipping inflation before it has a chance to bud. Convinced of this result, Fed watchers are inclined to buy stocks after a preemptive strike. Is this smart? Data crunchers at Ryan Laboratories in New York studied six such strikes, and found that stocks had gained 15 percent, on average, a year later. This average includes the two instances when stocks lost money, and also the huge 1986 advance, later undone by the 1987 Crash.

After five out of six of these strikes, cash did worse than stocks (Treasury bills returned 5 percent) and bonds did worse than cash (long-term Treasuries lost some of their face value and returned only two percent).*

Nevertheless, after the Fed tightens, the benefits from stocks is often short-lived. That's because one tightening leads to another. The postman always rings twice, and the Fed rarely tightens once. *Barron's* pointed this out on February 14, 1994, in an intriguing article by Randall Forsyth, "Tightening's Impact: History's Lessons for the Year

---

* A Fed tightening often marks a turning point where stocks will outperform bonds. Confirmed bondholders can't stand prosperity, at least not the kind that arouses inflation and higher interest rates. They're much happier in a recession, when rates are falling and the bonds become more valuable by the day.

Bonds did particularly badly after the Fed tightening in 1958. Long-term rates rose from 3 percent to 4.5 percent. An initial tightening in 1994 was enough to send the bond market crashing to its worst loss in the twentieth century.

After the Fed Moves." Forsyth showed that it takes several strikes to stun the economy and slow it down, and during these multiple attempts at stunning, inflation runs riot and stocks and bonds sell off.

That's why investing in stocks after an initial Fed tightening is temporarily profitable but may soon become the opposite. The staff at *Economic Week*, a Citibank newsletter, studied tightenings back to World War II and found that when the Fed continued to tighten over periods ranging from 18 months to 8 years, it sent interest rates 6 ¾ percent higher (on average) than they were at the outset.

A long inflationary uptrend lasted from the end of World War II into the 1980s, in spite of numerous Fed attempts to reverse it. Several of those attempts produced bearish side effects in the stock and bond markets.*

The Fed tightened repeatedly in 1962, causing a big drop in stocks that's usually blamed on President Kennedy's showdowns with the steel industry over steel prices and with the Soviets over missiles in Cuba. According to Hugh Johnson, chief economist for First Albany Securities, the brunt of the drop happened before the two showdowns and after the Fed had tightened. This bear market had more to do with the Fed than with steel magnates and Soviet potentates.

The Fed also tightened in the early 1970s after the dollar was devalued and inflation erupted. In the mid-1970s, inflation erupted again, the dollar took another dive, and the Fed tightened more. Paul Volcker, the cigar-chomping Fed chairman at the time, called inflation "public enemy number one" and devoted himself to wiping it out, even if he had to strangle the economy in the process. He didn't stop strangling until short-term interest rates hit 20 percent in 1981. Stocks reacted badly in the bear market in 1973–1974, and then went nowhere for the balance of the decade.

---

* The entire period, 1947 through 1981, was disastrous for bonds: long-term interest rates rose, right along with short-term rates.

When Volcker raised rates in 1983, his opponents argued that the economy was too weak to stand another tightening. Stocks dropped 10 percent in sympathy. Soon, Volcker reversed himself; instead of tightening, he loosened. Other nations did the same, reducing short-term rates in an effort to enliven a sluggish world economy. Stocks rallied, but when Volcker's loosening gave inflation a lift, he tightened decisively in the spring of 1987. His successor at the Fed, Alan Greenspan, tightened once again for good measure. The result was the October Crash, the latest in a string of declines that serial tightenings have been known to produce.

Six months later, after Greenspan had surveyed the damage and saw no evidence of another Great Depression, he tightened again, and the tightening continued into 1989. As inflation was squeezed into submission, interest rates declined. Stocks and bonds rallied, as they have (with occasional intermissions) to this day.

Marty Zweig reports that the second Fed tightening is more damaging to stocks than the initial one. He reviewed the record back to 1928, and found that a second Fed tightening signaled trouble ahead for stocks. Paul Warburg, Fed governor at the time, issued his own warning about irrational exuberance, which the Fed already was doing something about. (This contrasts with Alan Greenspan's 1996 warning about irrational exuberance, which the Fed was doing nothing about. It's Fed action, more than Fed rhetoric, that separates the bulls from the bears.)

The Dow fell 60 percent in nine months, after a second tightening in October 1931. Second tightenings in 1969, 1973, and 1980 all led to bear markets. In 1948, 1955, 1958, and 1977, they produced delayed declines or so-so performance. Second strikes of November 1964 and August 1988 were exceptions. They didn't hurt stocks at all.

Customarily, it takes eighteen months after a second tightening for stocks to react adversely, and prices often rise in the interim. Second tightenings aren't very useful as short-term timing indicators, but they lead to lower prices down the road. In any event, Zweig's research shows that buying stocks while the Fed tightens is more risky than rewarding.

A Fed loosening, on the other hand, is more rewarding than risky. By reducing short-term interest rates, the Fed makes stocks more attractive and gives investors a reason to believe the economy will shake its doldrums, which makes stocks doubly attractive. Meanwhile, when the Fed pumps money into the system through the banks, bankers tend to buy stocks with it. This gives stock prices a third boost.

It's no wonder, then, that after the Fed loosens and short-term interest rates drop 20 percent, stocks advance at a spectacular clip: 29.3 percent a year. Fed watchers who practice what Zweig preaches— "Don't Fight the Fed"—will lighten up on stocks when the Fed is tightening, and go shopping for stocks when the Fed is loosening.

Besides the Fed's tightening and loosening, the government can also manipulate the economy through the printing press, although that method of creating money has gone out of style. Today, when it wants to add money to the system, the government simply buys Treasury bonds from one of several commercial banks that serve as bond dealers. It "pays" for the bonds by crediting the bank with millions if not billions of dollars in its cash account at a Fed branch. With a few strokes of a computer keyboard, the bonds in the bank's portfolio become government property, and the bank has a heap of new dollars with which to make loans. This is real money, even though it appeared out of nowhere.

A decade ago, money supply watching was as popular as Fed watching, and the latest figures on M1, M2, or M3, the various categories of money, were celebrities on the nightly news. A sharp rise in the money supply as occurred in 1985 and 1986 was a harbinger of higher inflation and lower stock prices, as Fed watchers expected the Fed to fight the incipient inflation by raising interest rates.

It's a fascinating spectacle when one government body works against the other, as when the Fed takes action to undo the damage caused by an increase in the money supply orchestrated by the Treasury Department, or an increase in government spending orchestrated by the White House. On occasion, the Fed tightens its grip on the banks at the same time the White House is loosening its grip on the budgetary purse strings.

Marty Zweig keeps a constant watch on the broadest definition of money, known as M-3, noting a potentially dangerous rise in March, 1997. "The Fed hasn't been paying great attention to money supply in recent years," Zweig told his subscribers, "but if (the money supply) heats up enough, it could ignite inflation and prompt the Fed to tighten." He checked the data going back to 1959 and discovered when M3 grows by less than 10 percent in a year, stocks rise by 10.3 percent, and when M3 grows by 10 percent or more, stocks hardly rise at all.

Though not all economists agree the rapid increase in money leads to inflation, a long-standing connection between the two was established by economists Milton Friedman and Anna Schwartz years ago.

THE COVER JINX

IN MID-1996, MARTY ZWEIG was wearing a sweatshirt in his office, and looking worried as usual. His worry of the moment was the cover of *Time* magazine, which showed Ned Johnson, the head of Fidelity, spinning the globe on his hand as if Ned owned the planet. This cover was similar to the cover on Donald Trump's second book, *Surviving at the Top*, which showed Trump spinning the Big Apple in his hand as if he owned New York. It was published at the exact point when Trump was in deep hock with his bankers. As Trump signed copies at a Manhattan bookstore, creditors were lining up to serve him dunning papers. His net worth was reported as below zero.

This time around, Zweig said, Ned Johnson on the cover was a bad omen for mutual funds and maybe stocks in general. It reminded him (things always remind Marty of something else) of a *Time* cover featuring a mutual fund company called MIT, now known as Mass Financial, or MFS. This "glowing eight-page article" appeared in June 1959, after which MFS stock lurched forward and keeled over.

Zweig was right about Johnson as the *Time* coverboy. The Fidelity cover was followed by months of Fidelity purges, defections, and carping from angry fundholders tired of that firm's sagging performance. Fidelity is a private company, or else Zweig could have shorted it.

In his cover watching, Zweig ignores financial magazines, which deal in financial topics as a matter of course. He takes note when a general-interest magazine runs a cover that carries a subtle or not so subtle bearish or bullish message. More often than not, this means the opposite is about to happen.

Like many other indicators, the magazine cover indicator works in reverse. A bear on a cover is bullish for stocks, a bull is bearish. Zweig and his crony Paul Montgomery at Legg Mason Wood Walker have gone back into the stacks of *Time* and *Newsweek* and found the Wall Street equivalent of the famous *Sports Illustrated* jinx: companies, or stocks in general, run into problems after they get admired on a front page.

Zweig remembers how Ivar Kreuger, the Andrew Carnegie of matches, got his mug on a *Time* cover the week after the Crash of 1929, and Samuel Insull, the holding company magnate, showed up for the prior week. Two bullish financial covers with the Crash in between.

He remembers that a *Newsweek* cover on the slump in the housing market—a house turned upside down—preceded a revival in the housing market. An April, 1994 *Time* cover, "Is It All Over For Smokers?" featured a hapless smoker with 14 guns aimed at his head. A year later, Philip Morris stock was up 67 percent, on its way to a triple by 1997. General Motors stock was up 50 percent in the months after *Time* published its "Can GM Survive?" cover in 1994. A later cover, "Detroit Shifting Into High Gear," was followed by GM's stock falling 50 percent.

One of his favorites was the January 13, 1992, *Time* cover. A man was selling apples on the street, under the headline "How Bad Is It?"—referring to the recession that ended soon thereafter. Usually, says Zweig, it takes a month or two for the cover jinx to take effect. Other Zweig finds:

- Kiplinger put a bull on its cover in July 1996, and the market took a tumble.
- After a bearish *Business Week* cover titled "Jitters!" appeared at the end of July 1996, the market recovered.
- The July 15, 1995, *U.S. News & World Report* cover, "Time to Bail Out," was an excellent buy signal.
- The May 11, 1996, *Business Week* cover, "Economic Anxiety," was a sure sign of good times ahead.

Zweig's partner in cover watching, Paul Montgomery, says he often restructures his portfolio based on what he sees on the newsstand, and a persuasive cover can cause him to trade 40 percent of the value of his holdings. He once thought cover watching had become too popular for the indicator to be of much use, but now he's convinced people know about it but don't take it seriously. "That's why it still works."

"*Time* magazine is my favorite research tool," he says. "Take the GM cover, 'Can GM Survive?' When that one appeared, every person who'd been thinking about selling sold. The last marginal sellers abandoned GM, so the stock was a buy."

"If the market drops 2,000 points and people bail out of their mutual funds," says Zweig, "I can see the cover now: 'How Mutual Funds Killed the Stock Market for Good.' What a buy signal."

What a sell signal was seen on the cover of *Reader's Digest* in 1997. The headline read: "How to Make a Million." The article claimed that "striking it rich in America is within everybody's grasp." It bore a striking resemblance to a *Ladies' Home Journal* cover story in August 1929, entitled "Everybody Ought to Be Rich," in which author John Jacob Raskob explained how anybody could get rich investing $15 a month in stocks. Raskob figured the money would compound at 24 percent annually for the next twenty years, based on recent performance. Does that sound familiar? In fact, stocks returned about 2 percent a year for twenty years. So says Marty Zweig.

PART FOUR

~

IT'S A BEAR'S WORLD, AFTER ALL

There's Always a Bear
Market Someplace

THE UPSIDE TO BEARS abroad is obvious to Ed Bozaan, a Wall Street arriviste who parlayed the Shining Path in Peru into an expensive apartment in New York. In 1991, when tourists were avoiding Lima because a paramilitary group had spooked the nation, Bozaan traveled there to pick up shares of Peru's finest companies, which he says were "tossed out of portfolios like trash." He bought a representative sample at trashy prices, stored them in his own portfolio until the Shining Path had a correction, and in four years his profit reached 1,000 percent. He can thank the Andean revolutionaries for seed capital and his pleasant upper Manhattan view.

Bozaan's coup in Peru made him aware of other investable crises in countries faced with civil unrest, palace revolts, ministerial scandals, or monetary turbulence. He reviewed 60 emerging bear markets going back 20 years, in which stock prices declined at least 40 percent. The standard rebound was 70 to 80 percent in 12 months and 100 percent or better in 18 months. Notable examples include China after the

Tiananmen Square massacre and Greece after the repressive rule of Papandreau, once foreign investors returned with the money they'd pulled out in fear and loathing.

As mentioned earlier, the investor who gets in at the top and suffers 50 percent decline makes no profit on a 100 percent rebound. He only breaks even. Bozaan tries to avoid this result by entering these markets in what he calls the "crisis/value zone," where losses already exceed 50 percent. He doesn't expect to pick bottoms, and he spreads his money around several debacles at once. Every year brings new opportunity. Mexico, Argentina, Turkey, Hungary, Russia, and Venezuela all fell more than 50 percent in 1995, and all produced 100 to 700 percent gains by 1997. In 1997, some of Asia's finest companies are being tossed in the trash along with Bangladesh (down 85 percent). "Retail investors are demonstrating in the streets there," Bozaan recalls. "The crises we are seeing today—Malaysia, Sri Lanka, Thailand—may bring very high returns in 1998 and 1999."

To that end, Bozaan has put together the Global Stabilization and Recovery Fund, which he could just as well have named the Global Mayhem and Panic Opportunity Fund. The minimum investment in this nascent venture (in operation since 1996) is $250,000. George Soros has taken a modest stake. The entire fund (valued at $20 million in late 1997) would be a modest stake for Soros. Interested parties can call (212) 980-9000 for details.

Other cultures may be more receptive to bearish thinking than ours is. In Latin America, where fatalism pervades art and literature, the worst is routinely anticipated, even celebrated. The Mexicans have a day of the dead *(dia del difunto)*, which they consecrate by dressing up as skeletons and drinking purple punch. The triumphant novel, *One Hundred Years of Solitude*, is based on the notion that life is a wheel of fortune and what goes up will always come down. What better preparation for grasping the concept of the economic cycle?

Limitless horizons stretch before the practicing bear. For every country that's waxing, another is waning. In the emerging markets, waxers and waners operate simultaneously. For instance, in the first nine months of 1997, stocks in Russian had waxed to a huge gain, as had those in Turkish stocks, and Brazilian stocks. Over the same span, Thailand, the Philippines, and Indonesia, had waned.

Russia had an entire bull market. The three Asian losers went through what was, in U.S. terms, the second worst bear of the century—all in the time it takes a seed to grow into a tomato. Over the past decade, an investor in the U.S. market tripled his money; an investor in the Japanese market was poorer by two-thirds. It's fashionable to describe the world's bourses as "linked," or part of the "global marketplace," but the results, being quite unlinked, create opportunity for the speculating globetrotter.

Stock exchanges are open for business in more than 60 countries. In the early 1980s, only a handful of emerging markets were prepared to accommodate foreign investors, but today, there are more than 30 such markets operating in exotic settings. A contrarian bear marketeer or a stockpicking ambulance chaser can find a continuous supply of calamities with upside potential.

Free markets are far from free because wherever you invest, the government has a huge say in the outcome. Stocks in good companies have been subverted for years when those companies happen to be located in countries where the government overspends (as in Turkey or Thailand today), fails to respond to a financial crisis (Japan, Korea, Malaysia), closes its doors to free trade and free flow of capital, overtaxes, restricts foreign investing, or moves interest rates in the wrong direction. To say government doesn't matter to the fundamental health of a company or a stock market is the same as saying the life expectancy of a soldier in a foxhole has nothing to do with the plans hatched at headquarters.

Thanks to modern financial engineering, if you don't like what Romans do, you can short the Italy Fund. If you have unpleasant encounters with supercilious Parisians, you can short France. There are multiple chances to play the long and the short side of the world atlas: foreign stocks sold on domestic exchanges, country funds, regional funds, and index funds with foreign accents, called WEBS (World Equity Benchmark Shares).

Many country funds are the closed-end variety. They differ from normal mutual funds in that they trade on the stock exchanges like individual stocks. Closed-end funds are an excellent way to invest globally. Some specialize in a single country (the Turkey Fund, the Korea Fund, etc.); others are regional (the Asia-Pacific Fund, the Latin American Discovery Fund, for example). Country funds often sell at a wide discount to the value of the stocks in the portfolio, giving patient investors an extra bonus when the discount narrows or disappears.

One way to profit from global misfortune is to sell country funds or foreign stocks short—that is, bet against them. But short selling is best left to the masochists. (For amplification, see page 205.) A more promising strategy is to buy country funds in countries that have already had their calamity.

Third world markets (some emerging, some emerged) are far more volatile than the seasoned markets of the United States and western Europe. This has something to do with the fact that third world capitalism resembles U.S. capitalism in the nineteenth century: economies lurching from boom to bust; heavy indebtedness to foreign investors, which puts a shaky foundation under prosperity; governments on the take; incomplete and/or unreliable financial reporting; legalized insider trading; a weak excuse for an SEC, which lacks the authority and/or the gumption to police the pits, the trading desks, and the boardrooms.

The damage done by U.S. bears in the past half-century is nothing compared to the grizzly declines seen abroad: Peru as mentioned earlier, Mexican stocks down 73 percent in thirty months, in 1978–1981; Taiwan down 80 percent in twelve months, in 1990; Japan down 63 percent, in fifty-four months. The Dow Industrials hasn't been down 50 percent in sixty-six years, but in an emerging bear market, half off doesn't necessarily get you close to the bottom of things. In the Hong Kong bear of 1974, if you bought at 80 percent off, you brought 12 percent too early. The final loss was 92 percent!

Domestic investors are taught to "buy on dips," but buying on dips abroad is an extreme sport. Some dips are cavernous, and large fortunes disappear inside them. It's possible to lose half your money buying a country fund at the point where unluckier investors have already lost half theirs. But this is where calamity becomes opportunity. Countries don't go out of business. Sooner or later, they overcome their problems and their markets have another run.

If you can tolerate bottom fishing with a 600-foot line, then buying third world declines can be a winning strategy. Consider this: If horrendous timing caused you to buy Hong Kong at the top prior to the 1974 bear, losing 92 percent in the process, and you stuck with Hong Kong, you caught up to the Dow in 1987.

Markets don't always rebound in timely fashion. Japan didn't, which makes Japan a useful cautionary tale. From the U.S. vantage, the fall of Japan took everybody by surprise. In the late 1980s, any American who read the papers was convinced that the Japanese were taking over the world. Japan had bought Rockefeller Center, a major Hollywood studio, and the Pebble Beach Golf Course. Our consumers bought everything of theirs; their consumers bought nothing of ours. Their cars hogged our roads. We ate their raw fish. They made our VCRs. Our money crossed the Pacific and landed in Japanese banks. The yen rose; the dollar set.

Books were written about how the Japanese had lost the war but won the peace. In the summer of 1987, our Dow took a bow and their Nikkei stood up—two indexes; two countries headed in different directions. Ours was lazier, sloppier, less efficient; theirs was neater, more energetic, more cooperative. Our economists, pundits, and politicians asked: Why can't America be more like Japan?

The Nikkei continued on its merry rise from 25,000 yen to 39,000 yen. A small group of U.S. skeptics noted a Japanese bubble in the making, as Japan's stocks entered the realm of silly prices. Warning signs were everywhere—rising interest rates, a falling yen, widespread corruption that forced the Minister of Finance to resign—but they were widely ignored. Skeptics were hooted down by a larger group of enthusiasts, who claimed the Japanese had a different cultural relationship to investing, perhaps a gene that led them to buy stocks at 50, 60, or 100 times earnings without flinching. Weren't the Japanese devoted savers and investors, unlike the spendthrift Americans with their charge cards? Hadn't they purchased trillions of yen worth of the local version of mutual funds?

Wasn't it their patriotic duty to buy and hold stocks forever? Didn't government, banks, manufacturers, and the stock market work together, protecting investors from losses, eliminating the downside risk? Hadn't Japan proven its eternal bullishness by making it illegal and/or impossible to sell short? In sum, hadn't Japan, Inc., repealed the rules of markets and reached the permanent plateau of prosperity?

The answer was "Yes" on all counts, or so it seemed until 1990, when Saddam Hussein pricked Japan's bubble (being fully dependent on foreign oil, Japan was particularly vulnerable to any disruption along the pipeline). The "inferior" U.S. market picked itself up after a mild bear market; meanwhile, Japanese investors kicked the props from under Japanese stocks. The unsinkable Nikkei sank from 39,000 to 14,000 yen and the broader market went down deeper.

So the rules of the markets weren't repealed after all, and the permanent plateau of prosperity was flooded with red ink. The Japanese turned out to be long-term investors only to the point where they became losing investors. Then they bailed out en masse. They sold their mutual funds as readily as their individual stocks; in the much-touted Japanese mutual fund industry, nine-tenths of the assets disappeared through losses or redemptions. The government, banks, manufacturers, and stock exchange officials couldn't protect anyone from the losses, including themselves.

The Postal Savings System had announced, near the top, that it was putting employees' money into *Tokkin* (mutual funds) for the first time in Japanese history. Even one trillion yen in liquidity pouring into stocks couldn't buoy the prices against the tide of selling.

Ursa Nikkei knocked the country into deep recession. The world's richest country during the 1980s was being squeezed to death by corporate, household, and government debt. By 1997, Japan's economy was so thanatonic that 1 percent interest rates couldn't shock it back to life.

Pecuniary poohbahs who were surprised by the Japanese decline have been equally surprised by seven years without a comeback. Peter Lynch says that big companies take longer to turn around than small companies—could it be that big countries take longer as well? In the smaller emerging markets, the comebacks can be quicker.

Mexico is Exhibit A of how an entire market can go from can't-lose to can't-win and back to can't-lose again. In 1994, Mexico was touted as the darling of the smaller economies, the Latin American economic miracle, and living proof that cross-border capitalism works wonders. Cheerleaders in U.S. brokerage houses were predicting further advances in Mexican stocks after the upcoming election. Instead, Mexican stocks went south from mid-1994 through October 1995.

The Mexico Fund, one of several popular U.S.-based Mexican mutual funds, had its own mega correction, down from $39.50 to $10.75 in six months, the kind of result you'd expect from an obscure biotech company with no earnings.

Suddenly, you weren't reading about the "Mexican economic miracle" anymore. You were reading about a "submerging market" where talk was cheap and bribes expensive; a currency crisis where the peso went forth and multiplied; a corruption crisis; the Mexican narcocracy; murders in high places; civil unrest; high unemployment; insolvent banks, and no hope of improvement. The game was over. Mexico was terminal. You expected it to dry up and fall off the continental shelf.

Nevertheless, the $50 billion bailout package assembled by the United States was a strong signal that the financial overlords wouldn't allow Mexico to go out of business. While U.S. brokerage houses still advised caution, if not outright rejection of Mexican stocks, buyers of the Mexican fund doubled their money in 18 months.

Emerging bear market investing is like domestic bear market investing, only more so. You must commit funds when the bad news is out and the experts have nothing good to say about the place. It's getting such lousy press you wouldn't want to go there. It often helps to save the articles from six months earlier, when the same experts were giving the economic ministers rave reviews.

"Dogs of the Dow" investors have outperformed the averages for more than a decade by purchasing the Dow's underachievers at the end of each year, holding onto them through the next year, then repeating the process. What about Dogs of the Emerging Markets?

Here, you'd purchase country funds—or the indexes (called WEBS)—for the worst-performing markets in a given time frame, then hold on for the rebound. Several opportunities arose in Latin America in 1994–1996. Stocks in Argentina, for instance, fell 87 percent (in U.S. dollars), hitting bottom in March, 1995. A year later, they doubled in price; two years later, they'd almost tripled. The same story was repeated in Colombia; and in Brazil, after a 59 percent drop into early 1995, stocks rose to an incredible fivefold gain. (This data has been extracted from the database at ING Barings.)

Three years earlier, between 1989 and 1992, Korean, Indonesian, and Thai stocks went through bear markets that rivalled the 1997 sell-offs. The Indonesian Fund and the Korea Fund tripled off the bottom by mid-1994, yet this quick recovery from the last hopeless situation is omitted from the press coverage of the subsequent hopeless situation.

As this is written, the Asian bears (pandas, presumably) are having their way with stocks across the region. The panic spread to Europe, Latin America, and the United States, where the Dow shed 554 points in one session, an all-time Dow record. Stocks fell on the heels of falling currencies, in a replay of the Mexican crisis of 1994, when the Mexican peso couldn't keep up with the dollar. In the Asian version, the Thai baht, Malaysian ringgit, Indonesian rupiah, Korean won, and Hong Kong dollar couldn't keep up with the dollar.

The Asian bear market arrived, just as Mexico's had, when the cheerleaders in brokerage houses and the financial press were rhapsodizing the Asian economic miracle: high growth rate; PhDs on every block; tireless workers; devoted savers for the future; natural-born capitalists; swanky new hotels, high rises, and industrial parks; can't-lose stock markets. As happened in Japan a decade earlier, the Asian miracle became the Asian debacle overnight: growth rate sluggish to moribund; dispirited workers; funny money; phony earnings; lootocrats in government; con artists in boardrooms; empty hotels, unfinished high rises, abandoned industrial parks; can't-win stock markets.

Mexico quickly got its bailout package, so it was obvious that the United States wouldn't let its neighbor fail. No such unconditional guarantee was offered in Asia—at least not right away. A bailout loan for Thailand was advanced by the International Monetary Fund in August 1997, but Korea's bailout was still in doubt weeks after its market tripped over its fallen currency.

It's worth remembering anytime you speculate in stocks abroad, through mutual funds or otherwise, you're also speculating in currencies. That's why Asia 1997 was so unkind to U.S. investors—Asian stocks had a bear market, and so did the Malaysian ringgit, the Thai baht, the Korean won. The baht was off 70 percent versus the dollar, meaning U.S. investors would have lost that amount even if Thai stocks held their own, which of course they didn't.

The double jeopardy of currency loss and stock market loss is treacherous for bargain hunters. In early December 1997, the International Monetary Fund announced a Korean bailout, a perfect time, one might have supposed, to invest in the world's eleventh largest economy. But after a brief sucker's rally, Korean stocks fell another 50 percent, so you can be prudent, and wait for low prices and the news of a rescue, and still see your investment cut in half in two weeks.

It's anybody's guess where the Asian bottom is, but if tradition holds, someday this whole affair will be remembered as a great bear market buying opportunity.

THE GLOBAL HEDGE

IN THE SUMMER OF 1997, Jim Grant, editor of *Grant's Interest Rate Observer*, gadfly to the vested interests, and bearish on U.S. equities, began to promote certain Korean equities as alternatives to the overvalued domestic variety. Soon after he announced the discovery of the cheaper, and therefore safer, list of Korean stocks, Korea had its bear market. Investors who acted on Grant's advice to escape the U.S. bear ran smack into the paws of the Oriental variety.

Grant isn't alone in thinking that investing abroad is a possible hedge against a bear market at home. Many money managers and strategists, aghast at the high price of U.S. equities, have looked for safe havens in the stock exchanges of Latin America, Central Europe, Africa, and Asia.

Eric Fry is one such hedge seeker. He works for Holl International, a San Francisco firm. In early 1995, about the time a barrage of data convinced him that U.S. stocks were overripe, Fry searched the world for markets with a "low correlation with Wall Street." Along the way, he made a tongue-in-cheek study: Intel, a popular American high-tech issue and a beloved occupant of many domestic portfolios; and India, a less-popular investment absent from many domestic portfolios. It did appear in the portfolio of an Ohio investment club, which had mistakenly bought the India Fund when it meant to buy Intel.

DIFFERENCES, SIMILARITIES BETWEEN INDIA, INTEL

- India makes tea. Intel makes chips.
- Indians work in the Indus Valley. Intel operates out of Silicon Valley.
- India has Ashrams. Intel has D-Rams.
- India offers transcendent spiritual experience. Intel offers transcendent monetary experience.
- Intel is an expensive stock that doesn't trade on the Bombay Exchange. India is cheap, and doesn't trade on NASDAQ.

Joking aside, Fry saw no bargain in Intel or many other overrated U.S. companies, and many bargains in India, which he said had a "near perfect noncorrelation with the S&P 500." India was cheap in 1997. Stocks that had sold for thirty-five times earnings in 1992 had been knocked down to ten times earnings, half the price of the typical U.S. share. In other words, Fry could get twice as much India for the same amount of Dow Jones.

(In case you're interested, India can be purchased on the New York Stock Exchange, where three Indian country funds are listed: India Fund (IFN), India Growth (IGF), and Morgan Stanley India (IIF). Numerous regional and global funds carry Indian stocks in their portfolios as well. A few individual Indian stocks also trade on the NYSE.

That India was full of bargains in 1997 wasn't the only reason it fit Fry's conception of the perfect global hedge. India had "growing domestic liquidity," meaning easy credit was available from the central bank, and interest rates were in decline. "Don't fight the local Fed," says Fry, echoing Marty Zweig. He also noted India's independence from the foreign bankroll, in that much of its corporate activity is financed with local money. Thus, India isn't likely to witness the giant sucking sound of foreigners repatriating their investments.

Stephen Poloz, a bright light at BCA, a Canadian research firm, picks Japan and Italy as prime low-correlation candidates because their markets are "domestically driven." James Libera, editor of the *Closed-End Country Fund Report*, looks for countries where the currency isn't pegged to the U.S. dollar. This cuts out Hong Kong and most of Latin America.

Strategists at SBS Warburg have identified South Korea, Taiwan, South Africa, Thailand, and Japan as markets that could weather a U.S. selloff rather well. In picking these five, Warburg made three assumptions: (1) markets with heavy investment from U.S. investors will behave like the U.S. market in a crisis (this cut out Europe, Mexico, and much of South America); (2) markets that depend on dollar earnings will be adversely affected by a U.S. crisis (this cut out Hong Kong and Singapore); (3) markets where real estate is a dominant factor (again, Hong Kong and Singapore) would be undermined by rising U.S. interest rates.

In their own search for noncorrelation, the staff at Robert Fleming Securities in London (this via Jim Grant), rejected Hong Kong, Mexico, Poland, and Venezuela as "virtual satellites of Mother Wall Street" and found only five hedges to recommend: Botswana, Ghana, Mauritius, Slovakia, and India. It's doubtful you'll see Wall Street trying to crowd into the first four, and only India is big enough to accommodate high-volume institutional buying.

So, when the next U.S. bear rolls around, Fry's money may be hiding out in Bombay, Warburg's in Seoul and Johannesburg, Poloz's in Rome and Tokyo, and Fleming's in Bombay. Others hope that East European and Russian markets will march to their own balalaika, and expect Egypt and Turkey will go their own way no matter what.

India has had a stock market for 100 years; other potential candidates for U.S. noncorrelation are comparative newcomers on the financial scene. Most third world stock exchanges date from the 1980s and have grown up in a period when the U.S. market has been relatively flop-free. They weren't around for major U.S. declines in 1973–1974 or 1981. So there's little history to go on, except the Crash of 1987, the mild bear market of 1990, and a handful of minor declines, or "corrections."

Until the United States has the bear market so many have been expecting, there's no way to crash-test the foreign hedge theory. The recent Far East debacle proved one thing: India wasn't affected, therefore India noncorrelated with the Asian markets that Jim Grant assumed would noncorrelate with the United States. Whether two noncorrelations make a correlation is anybody's guess.

A review of corrections since 1964 reveals an interesting pattern. English-speaking markets—Canada, Australia, Britain, and the United States—move in lockstep. Japan and Italy generally go their own way. In the Crash of 1987, the losses in Canada, Germany, Switzerland, France, Italy, Britain, and Sweden equaled the losses on Wall Street. Australia lost even more; only Japan escaped with a modest decline. It was very profitable to exit U.S. stocks in the summer of 1987 and flee to Toyko, but the advantage was temporary. Any investor who hedged an investment in the United States by leaving money in Tokyo has been paying for that noncorrelation ever since.

A century ago, when London was the dominant stock exchange, British investors looking for noncorrelation thought they might find it in the emerging market of the United States. They didn't. With 40 percent of U.S. stocks and bonds owned by the British, there were frequent sympathetic swoons. "London Stocks Fall, U.S. Stocks Fall in Sympathy," was a common refrain after the latest bear market in London spread to the United States. Londoners would sell their U.S. holdings to raise the cash needed to support their fallen London holdings.

They did this in the Boer War bear of 1899–1902, and particularly after the scary decline known as Black Week.

For years, U.S. investors have been hearing that we live in a global economy in which the world's fortunes are linked as never before, but when Asia collapsed in late 1997, the tune changed, and experts said Asia's problems would have a negligible effect on U.S. corporate profitability. So which is it? Are we in a global economy or not? We'll find out.

PART FIVE

~

BEAR-PROOFING THE PORTFOLIO

The Bear Busters

Assuming you've decided to stay fully invested in stocks or stock mutual funds, it still may pay you to switch into types of stocks that have done well in different stages of bear markets. Bearish since 1995, the Leuthold investment group in Minneapolis has passed the time doing research on which sectors hold up best and worst. Here's the Leuthold lineup of nine "defensive sector selections" that performed well in eleven prior market declines:

1. *Soft drinks*. Soft drink companies either broke even or rose in price in four of the eleven bear markets. In five others, they lost much less money than the average stock. Only once, (1973–1974) did they lose more than the average stock.
2. *Pharmaceuticals*. Ethical drug companies rose in price in three of the eleven bears. In four others, they lost much less money than the average stock. Only twice (1962 and 1976–1978) did these companies lose more than the average stock.
3. *Food suppliers*. Food companies rose in price in three of the eleven bears. In four others, they lost much less money than the

average stock. In three additional bears, they lost somewhat less money than the average stock.

4. *Major oils.* Oil companies rose in price in one bear market (1983–1984). In five others, they lost much less than the average stock.

5. *Household products.* Companies that make small appliances and other household items rose in price, or nearly broke even, in four bear markets. In three others, they lost much less than the average stock.

6. *Telephones.* Telephone companies rose in price in three bear markets. In eight others, they lost less than the average stock. Telephones are eleven for eleven at beating the averages in these declines.

7. *Tobacco.* Tobacco companies rose in price in six bear markets; in a seventh, they lost only 1 percent. Their worst showing was in 1962, when they went down 43 percent. They matched the S&P 500 decline in the Crash of 1987.

8. *Electric utilities.* Electric companies rose in price, or nearly broke even, in five bears.

9. *Gold.* North American gold mining stocks rose in price in four bears. Two impressive advances occurred: 174 percent in 1973–1974 and 36 percent in 1976–1978. In three other bears, gold stocks lost much less than the average stock; in 1980–1982 and 1983–1984, they lost much more. "A stable or rising gold price is required to make gold an effective defensive group," says Leuthold.

Companies that profit from cigarettes, electric power, oil, food, drugs, soft drinks, telephones, and household goods share a key protective advantage in recessions or bear markets. People will continue to smoke, eat, drive cars, drink Coke, swallow medicine, run appliances, and make phone calls even when they're short on cash. They'll put off buying cars, houses, and major appliances, which is why automakers, homebuilders, and some retailers will suffer in recessions.

Being aware of this fact, investors won't unload recession-proof stocks as readily as they unload stocks in companies that are vulnerable to recessions. The prices of these defensive issues will hold up relatively well because shareholders expect the earnings will continue to grow.

Leuthold mentions two situations where his defensive sectors offer only modest protection or no protection in a Wall Street selloff. The first is when a crash brings rapid and indiscriminate selling. In the Crash of 1987, five of the nine groups mentioned above were down 20 percent or more, and only the telephones and the utilities managed to hold their losses to around 10 percent.

The second is when defensive stocks are overpriced going into a bear. Leuthold says that's the situation today, when premier defensive stocks such as Coca-Cola are selling for a posh 35 times earnings. With such a fancy pricetag attached, even a recession-proof company isn't likely to avoid a big markdown when Wall Street has a sale. The next time around, Leuthold doubts that drug, food, and household products manufacturers will offer much protection.

He favors utilities because their dividends remain relatively high. Their large debts and healthy appetite for investment capital make them less attractive when interest rates are rising, as in 1994. But in recessions, they're low-risk performers. Leuthold also thinks real estate investment trusts, insurance companies, and energy and natural gas companies will avoid major damage in the next bear.

Sam Stovall, editor of Standard & Poor's monthly newsletter and author of *Sector Investing*, did his own study of the fate of various industry groups in losing markets going back to 1946. Stovall, like Leuthold, concluded that no industry is exempt from decline, but some will decline less than others. This is his list of industries whose stocks held up better than the S&P 500 in eleven market declines since 1946:

Industry	Average Drop (%) in Each Decline	Number of Times Beat S&P 500
Containers (metal and glass)	−15%	11
Electric utilities	−11	10
Household products	−13	10
Tobacco	−11	9
Foods	−14	8

Stovall's outperformers are basically the same as Leuthold's, with one notable exception: containers! Companies that make cans and bottles have beaten bear markets 100 percent of the time. The reason? Edibles and drinkables, from borscht to beer, are sold in cans and bottles. As long as people keep eating and drinking, container companies will prosper in future recessions.

Electric utilities have beaten the averages ten out of eleven times in Stovall's study, the only exception being the 1973–1974 decline. Utilities posted a gain on two occasions: in 1976–1978, and in 1981, their best showing, when the S&P average was down 19 percent and utilities were up 23 percent.

In a second tier of bear-resistant industries, Stovall puts banks; drug, oil, and liquor companies; supermarkets; and gold mining—all of which have lost less than the S&P 500 in seven of eleven down markets. Gold turned in two amazing performances: 1973–1974 and 1976–1978, as mentioned on the preceding page. Both were periods of high inflation; otherwise, gold offers no advantage in bear markets. Twice, mining shares have lost money even as the price of gold was on the rise.

The worst performing industries, by Stovall's reckoning, are chemicals, financial companies, retailers, machine tools, building materials, homebuilders, trucks, machinery, airlines, and computers—in other words, any industry in which profits are vulnerable in a recession. Leuthold has his own list of industries to avoid:

Industry	Average Drop (%) in Each Decline	Number of Times Beat S&P 500 in Eleven Bears
Building materials	−26%	1
Machinery (diversified)	−28	2
Trucks & parts	−32	2
Oil equipment/services	−26	3
Textiles (apparel)	−31	3

THE SMALL STOCK ADVANTAGE/DISADVANTAGE

You don't want to own small stocks going into a bear. Whatever a typical big stock is about to lose, a typical small stock will lose more. For an extreme example, the Value Line Composite Index of 1,700 companies, most of them small, stood at $199.99 in 1968 and was on its knees at $46.50 six years later.

Researchers at Ibbotson Associates checked the damage from subsequent setbacks dating from 1978. On average, big stocks (the S&P 500) lost 18.1 percent while small stocks lost 23.9 percent in each decline—more evidence that small is unrewarding in down markets. Yet, when Ibbotson looked further, this discrepancy was found to apply to growth stocks and not to value stocks.

Growth stocks attract investors through their earnings. Value stocks are prized for their assets (land, factories, cash in the bank, franchises, merchandise, and so on). Value stocks tend to be cheaper than growth stocks in that they sell for lower prices relative to their earnings (a lower price–earnings ratio).

In its review of bear markets, Ibbotson found that small value stocks hold up rather well—losing only 4.8 percent, on average, in the setbacks mentioned above. This suggests a new strategy for coping with a bear: buy small value stocks or mutual funds that specialize in "small-cap value," and get the best of two worlds—protection on the downside and superior returns on the upside, when the market turns. For a list of low-risk small-cap value funds, see page 165.

Small stocks often outperform big stocks in the early stages of bull markets, as previously mentioned. There are periods when they underperform big stocks, as they did from 1983 through mid-1991. Although small stocks played catch up in 1992–1995, their poor relative showing in recent years is a troublesome factor in this can't-lose market.

How can you tell when small stocks are overvalued, or undervalued, relative to big stocks, so you know when it's likely to be more profitable to own one variety versus the other? Follow the New Horizons indicator (Exhibit 8). A familiar pinup on the corkboards of Wall Street, this chart tracks the price–earnings ratio of small stocks owned by the T. Rowe Price New Horizons fund, as compared to larger stocks in the S&P 500 Index.

Few small cap funds go back as far as New Horizons, which opened its doors in 1960. (It recently closed to new investors.)* Being unusually old for its class, New Horizons is closely monitored for its telltale ups and downs. Thanks to the savvy stock picks of John ("Jack") LaPorte, the fund has had a lot of ups. New Horizons was the largest institutional owner of Wal-Mart from the initial public offering through the 1970s.

When small stocks are in vogue, the New Horizons line rises above the 2 on the chart. At that point, investors are paying twice as much for small stocks as for big stocks, based on their earning power.

---

* The fund was closed in June 1997; so much new money was coming through the door the manager had more cash to invest than ideas for where to invest it. It was closed twice before, and severe bear markets followed in both cases. Is the closing of New Horizons another sign of a top?

Exhibit 8 T. Rowe Price New Horizons Fund (P/E Ratio of Fund's
Portfolio Securities Relative to the S&P 500 P/E Ratio)

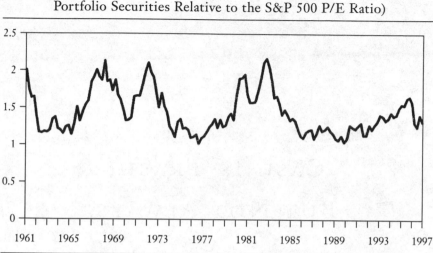

Source: T. Rowe Price Associates.

Three times in modern memory (1968, 1972, 1983) the line has risen above 2 on the chart. On all three occasions, it paid to get out of small stocks; on the first two occasions, it paid to get out of stocks altogether. Once these peaks of overvaluation are reached, small stocks may underperform large stocks for several years, as they did from 1983–1991. Nevertheless, the patient investor can avoid disappointment by investing in small stocks when the line is closer to 1 than to 2.

The chart is updated in quarterly reports sent out to shareholders, but since the funds isn't taking new investors, the easiest way to get the latest whereabouts of the line is to call T. Rowe Price at (800) 225-5132.

Cash Is Trash,
But Not Always

There's nothing wrong with cash. It gives you time to think.

Bob Prechter

IN A BEAR MARKET, a rube with money in the mattress can outperform momentum investors, value investors, small caps, large caps, growth funds, balanced funds, and even Dogs of the Dow. A savings account has a better rate of return than a brokerage account. A passbook is more lucrative than a share of Fidelity Magellan. A person who never met a broker and never heard of the S&P 500 can beat the S&P 500, Fidelity Magellan, and five thousand stock mutual funds. A 3 percent annual return always beats minus 20.

In this way, the bear market is a revolutionary act—the only time stockless and brokerless individuals can close the wealth gap between themselves and stockholders—not because the stockless are getting richer, but because the stockholders are getting poorer.

Exhibit 9 How Cash Fared in Down Years for Stocks

Year	Large Company Stocks	Cash (U.S. T-Bills)
1931	−43.34	+1.07
1937	−35.03	+.31
1941	−11.59	+.06
1946	−8.07	+.35
1957	−10.78	+3.14
1966	−10.06	+4.76
1969	−8.50	+6.58
1973	−14.8	+6.9
1974	−26.5	+8.1
1977	−7.4	+5.1
1981	−5	+14.71
1990	−3.2	+8.4

Total return with dividends, interest payments included.

You can avoid this impoverishment by removing your net worth from stocks and parking it safely in a passbook, a money market account,* or a three-month Treasury bill. (For simplicity's sake, these three options will be called "cash" throughout this discussion.) Jim Stack offers this extreme example: $10,000 riding on the Dow in February 1966 didn't catch up to $10,000 parked in cash, with interest compounding, until 1986! Stocks underperformed cash for two decades.

Exhibit 9 shows how cash fared in the various down markets.

As a general rule, it takes seven and a half years for a stockholder in a bear market to catch up to a cashholder, but cash does best in periods when interest rates are rising because it means that the yield on a

---

* The inventors of the money market, Bruce Bent and Harry Brown on the East Coast, and Jim Benham on the West Coast, deserve a statue in front of every bank. Not only did they give investors everywhere a new place to park money, but they also forced banks and savings and loans to compete with the money market by offering higher passbook rates. This put billions of dollars in customers' pockets that otherwise would have stayed in bankers' pockets.

money market account, a savings account, or a Treasury bill is also rising. Rising interest rates made the 1970s a cash Camelot.

In 1973, when Nixon resigned the White House and the bulls resigned from Wall Street, you made 6.9 percent on cash, a return that compared quite favorably to −14.8 percent in large stocks. A year later, if your cash was still riding on the money market, you made 8 percent, versus −26.5 percent in large stocks. After two years, the cashholding yokel turned $1,000 into $1,154, while the stockholding sharpie turned $1,000 into $627.

Cash beat stocks in 1977 and 1978 (but only slightly). In 1981, cash had its best showing of the century. Imagine making 14.71 percent for twelve months in the money market. People did, but that was the last hurrah for investing in money. Cash outperformed stocks in 1984 and in the bear market years of 1987 and 1990, but otherwise, stocks triumphed. The motto "Cash is trash" gained popularity, as investors forgot there was anything good about it. Markets are cyclical, and the money market will once again have its day and outperform Fidelity Magellan, taking Wall Street by surprise.

Although cash performs best when interest rates are rising and provides a safe haven whenever stocks are in a bear market even if interest rates are falling, it can't be relied on for long. Time is the stock picker's ally, but it's the enemy of wallet fodder. On the back of every U.S. bill, the words "In God We Trust" appear in large letters. Not "In Cash We Trust," because cash can't be trusted. The only sure thing about cash is: It will be worth less tomorrow than it is today.

More often than not, interest on cash can't keep up with inflation. If a lifetime of shopping hasn't convinced you of that fact, consult Exhibit 10. A percent here or there lost to inflation may not look like much, but, over the years, it matters. If you bought a $100 Treasury bill in 1925 (the money market hadn't been invented yet) and rolled it over in a succession of Treasury bills for seventy years, the $100 grew into $1,172. Subtract $813 for 70 years of erosion by inflation, and you

Exhibit 10   Inflation's Impact on the Dollar

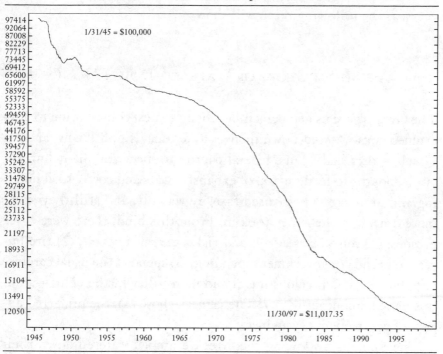

1/31/45 = $100,000

11/30/97 = $11,017.35

Source: Ned Davis Research.

got $359 to show for your efforts. The same $100 traveling in name-brand stocks over the same period grew into $79,187, after inflation was subtracted. Cash is no match for stocks in the average life span.

One school of economists sees inflation as foul weather, an unpleasant effect with multiple causes. Economists of the Milton Friedman school pin the blame on political regimes that cheapen the currency by producing too much of it, a reckless ploy to support their compulsive spending. Supporters of the tactic don't call it "cheapening the currency." They call it "expanding the nation's money supply."

No wonder George Soros has made billions betting against various Asian and European currencies—more profits than he ever made betting on stocks. Stocks have been erratically profitable for 300 years.

Governments have made currencies reliably unprofitable for 2,000 years, as the following recap will show.

THE SHORT STORY OF WATERED-DOWN MONEY

The Greeks gave us democracy, but their greatest contribution to government was watered-down money. Like today's politicians, ancient Greek leaders had a huge federal payroll to meet and many bureaucratic mouths to feed, on top of expensive wars and costly road building and drainage. They raised taxes repeatedly, and still they spent more drachmas than they took in. From this bind, there were three escapes: (1) raise taxes again, and risk a taxpayer revolt; (2) fire bureaucrats and cut government spending; (3) spend at the usual carefree clip, but put less precious metal and more filler in the coins—a numismatic hamburger helper. The Greeks chose (3), the preferred option of governments ever since.

The Romans, following the Greek example, watered down their coins to pay for their war against Carthage. Julius Caesar was a notorious coin-waterer, as was Emperor Augustus. Overeating and late-night partying may have contributed to the collapse of the Roman Empire, but financial historians cite weak money as a key factor. Consumers lost faith in pocket change, and merchants refused to accept coins as payment. Coins were so widely mistrusted that traders from Europe to Asia returned to the barter system. Barter was in vogue throughout the Middle Ages.

Paper money was issued by King James of Cataloria in 1250, and gained widespread popularity in Europe and America in the early 1700s. At first, people preferred the new paper to the old unreliable coins. But not for long, because governments and private banks used the printing press whenever they needed extra cash. The rebellious American colonies couldn't pay for their Revolution with taxes; they were in revolt against British taxes! They financed the war with a huge print run of "Continentals," sent to troops and suppliers as payment for their services. Tom Paine's pamphlet wasn't the most important printing job in the fight for independence—the Continental was.

Nothing of substance was backing this new currency, as the recipients soon discovered. The Continental lost half its value the first year, and when merchants refused to accept Continentals, the Revolutionary government made it a crime to reject the new money. Anybody who did could have his or her property confiscated.

Unwilling to risk confiscation, and equally unwilling to sell their foodstuffs, clothing, and other resources for worthless money, merchants finessed the problem by taking their goods off the shelves. This widespread hoarding of food and other necessities caused severe shortages and general starvation in Boston in 1779. Once again, people exchanged goods and services through barter.

The Continental Congress issued new paper to divert attention from the discredited old paper, a regular ploy of printing-press finance. Each of these newer Continentals was worth twenty of the originals, an admission that the old money had lost most of its buying power. The new money quickly lost most of *its* buying power as well. By issuing sham currency, the Revolutionary government had imposed what amounted to a 97.5 percent tax on the recipients.

On the economic front, with their restrictions on free trade, their overactive printing press, and their capricious new tax on distilled spirits, the Revolutionaries bore a striking resemblance to the odious Tories. This unpatriotic observation comes from turn-of-the-century curmudgeon William Graham Sumner, and was passed along by Harry Browne, author, Libertarian candidate for President in 1996, former gold bug, pop financial historian, and chronicler of government bungling.

By the late 1700s, paper money was discredited worldwide, and leading nations, including the United States, put themselves on a gold or silver standard. Banks could issue "notes" redeemable in gold. Every piece of folding money was backed by metal. You could walk into the

Bank of the United States, the original central bank, hand over a paper dollar, and receive a dollar's worth of gold in exchange.

This system created the first reliable cash in human memory. It also caused problems. Banks could only print as much paper as they had gold in the vault—a restriction most bankers and many politicians opposed. The Bank of the United States kept itself on the gold standard, but Congress refused to renew its charter. Its successor, the Second Bank of the United States, also succumbed to political attack, and its demise caused a national "panic" in 1819—the first time that word had entered the financial vocabulary, according to John Kenneth Galbraith.* The United States didn't get a third central bank until 1913, nearly 100 years later.

After the 1819 panic, the gold standard was relaxed, and hundreds of local and state banks appeared on the scene to take advantage. Each note and bill issued by this proliferation of banks was supposedly backed by a tangible asset, but, in reality, the banks printed far more cash than they could support with tangible assets. In the mid-1800s, the federal government forced state banks out of the money business by imposing a huge tax on their cash. Ever since, the U.S. Treasury has had a monopoly on the currency, challenged only by an occasional counterfeiter.

Governments worldwide, including the United States, stuck to the gold standard when convenient, and ignored it whenever an expensive war broke out. Typically, they ran the printing presses overtime to pay for a war, then reneged on their promise to exchange cash for gold. The U.S. Treasury created a huge supply of "greenbacks" to finance the Civil War, and terrible inflation resulted when a greenback proved as worthless as a Continental. The two World Wars and the Vietnam War were financed in similar fashion, and double-digit inflation followed all three.

---

* John Kenneth Galbraith, *A Short History of Financial Euphoria* (New York: Viking Press, 1993), p. 59.

On the one hand, the government creates inflation with a glut of money; on the other, it fights inflation by having the central bank raise short-term interest rates. This home remedy has produced several severe recessions.

In September 1944, politicians and bankers from the Allied nations met at Bretton Woods, a retreat in New Hampshire, to devise a new system of "fixed exchange rates" for world currencies. According to plan, each currency was assigned a price range within which it could trade, in relation to the U.S. dollar. If it strayed outside the range, central banks would take corrective action.

Harry Browne says the new system worked as follows. If the Swiss franc got too expensive vis-à-vis the dollar, the Swiss central bank would enter the market to sell francs and buy dollars. This balancing act would push the price of Swiss francs lower and, at the same time, boost the price of dollars. Likewise, if the dollar got too expensive relative to the franc, the U.S. central bank would enter the market to buy francs and sell dollars.

Under the Bretton Woods agreement, whenever a currency fell so far out of line that the corrective measures couldn't save it, the government in charge of that currency was urged to "devalue" it. For instance, if the Italian lira was devalued, it would take more lira to equal a dollar.

Devaluation is a painful and unpopular step, but a country with a weak currency had no choice. If Italy, for instance, refused to devalue, other countries would amass a huge pile of lira, approach the Italian central bank, and demand that Italy swap the pile for gold at the prevailing rate. Italy wouldn't be able to meet this demand without depleting its gold reserves, so devaluation was the lesser evil.

When Bretton Woods went into effect, the dollar was the world's strongest currency. Countries that signed the agreement were allowed to settle their debts with dollars as well as with gold and silver reserves. The dollar was considered "good as gold." In the late 1960s, however, the dollar began to lose its lustrous reputation—a consequence of expansion of the U.S. money supply to pay for President Lyndon Johnson's twin wars: Vietnam and Poverty.

As the dollar weakened, it lost credibility with international bankers. A number of countries appeared at the teller's window in the U.S. Treasury, seeking to exchange piles of dollars for gold. The U.S. gold reserves were soon diminished, and U.S. officials responded to this governmental demand the same way they had responded, on prior occasions, to private citizens' request at the same teller's window. They shut the window and suspended all paper-for-gold exchanges until further notice.

The rest of the world didn't appreciate this welching on a deal. Germany, which had joined the Bretton Woods fold after World War II withdrew temporarily in 1969; Canada dropped out in 1970; other countries relentlessly sold dollars in their possession, causing their currencies to strengthen and the dollar to sink far below its trading range. In December 1971, the United States did the unthinkable: it devalued the Almighty dollar.

The unmighty dollar continued to weaken until the Bretton Woods system was scrapped in 1973. Since then, the world's currencies have floated freely in the marketplace, rising and falling on the whims of bankers and speculators. The dollar has lost 71 cents worth of its buying power since 1973; other currencies have lost much more. Latin Americans endured triple- and quadruple-digit inflation manufactured by profligate poohbahs with high-speed printing presses. They switched into dollars or Swiss francs whenever possible, but, as their governments restricted such exchanges, they resorted to stealth and cunning to preserve their capital.

In the end, cash has a lousy shelf life, whether it's issued as bahts, sucres, remnimbi, lira, or dollars. When stocks are in a bear market, particularly of the inflationary variety, it pays to own cash, but don't make a habit of it.

Hiding in Bonds

In the old days, the confirmed bondholder was the savvy, sophisticated, level-headed bloke who realized how much money can be lost in stocks. These days, the confirmed bondholder is the slow-witted, anal-retentive fuddy-duddy who fails to realize how much money can be made in stocks. The life of the party is the stockpicker telling a story of how he retired on his Microsoft and his Hewlett-Packard. Crowds never gather around the bondpicker who brags about the Ford Motor Company 9½s of 2005, or how fifteen-year governments return an annual 6.1 percent.

Various brokerage houses have produced studies that show the chronic underachievement of bonds, dating back to the Spanish–American War. They all lead to the same conclusion: Bonds are for losers, and stocks are for future millionaires.

Bonds are the corporate or government IOUs given to lenders in return for various sums of money. Bonds pay a fixed rate of interest until "maturity," the date on which the original amount of the loan is repaid. Thus, most bonds provide a steady if unspectacular source of income, at a rate that varies with the trustworthiness of the issuer of the bond. The U.S. government offers less income on its bonds than, say, an X-rated movie company operating under an assumed name in the Bahamas.

People have become so convinced of the inferiority of bonds that if you asked yourself this question: Which had a bigger payoff from 1980 into the 1990s, bonds or stocks? your answer would surely be: Stocks. Actually, bonds and stocks were equally rewarding over that stretch; the souped-up zero-coupon bond (more on this later) outperformed the S&P 500 and the Dow.

For scholarly corroboration that there's something good about bonds, read Jeremy Siegel's *Stocks for the Long Run*, a book that has nice things to say about bonds in the long run. A professor at The Wharton School, Siegel studied the returns back to 1802, an effort that must have required an ample supply of No-Doz. While stocks may have outgained bonds over two centuries, Siegel shows how bonds outgain stocks in four years out of ten. Not only are bonds worth owning but, in certain periods, they're the only thing worth owning.

Bonds have one big advantage over stocks that pay paltry dividends or zero dividends, as in the case in today's who-cares-about-dividends environment. Bonds provide their owners a steady return through thick and thin—or, in the case of a bear market, through thin and thinner. This continuous yield gives bondholders something to bank on while the market value of the bonds is in decline. Better yet, they provide something to bank on while the market value of the bonds is in ascent.

Exhibit 11 shows how a typical government bond fared through nine periods when stocks were in arrears. As you can see, bonds provided a slight positive return in recent episodes, a terrific return in 1981–1982, and disappointing returns in three out of four bear markets dating from the 1970s. This brings up an important point: Bonds don't exist in a vacuum. Whether you own them outright or indirectly through mutual funds, you're advised to check the interest rate environment, and inflationary pressures, for favorable or unfavorable

Exhibit 11 Total Returns for Long-Term Government Bonds during Recent Down Markets (Inflation Adjusted)

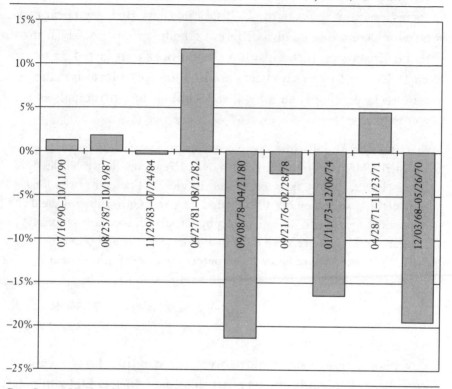

Data Source: Used with permission. © Ibbotson Associates, Inc. All rights reserved. [Certain portions of the work were derived from copyrighted works of Roger G. Ibbotson and Rex Sinquefield.]

surroundings. To buy the long-term variety, you must be somewhat confident of the economic prognosis.

A bond's reputation for safety comes from the fact that if all goes as planned and you hold the bond to maturity, you'll get your money back. Therefore, you lose nothing and earn interest along the way. This happy ending ignores inflation, which can sap the buying power of your original investment by the time you're reimbursed. (We're talking about U.S. government bonds here, which carry minimal risk of default. With other kinds of bonds, there's always a risk the issuer will neglect payment.)

With every drop in inflation and interest rates, a bond becomes more valuable. This was the case in the 1930s. With every rise, a bond becomes less valuable, as in the 1970s. Bonds have their own bear markets, which come and go on a different schedule than stock bear markets. For instance, in the insidious bond bear that lasted 35 years, from 1946–1981 (who says bears are in a hurry?) a loyal bondholder lost more face value than a loyal stockholder lost principal, as Jim Grant explains:

> Starting from the all-time low in government yields, 2.03 percent, set in April 1946, the (bond) market moved irregularly but relentlessly lower (lower, that is, in price; higher in yield). The end of the long bear market, in September 1981, found long-term governments yielding almost 15 percent. The price of a hypothetical, constant-maturity 2½ percent bond, purchased in 1946 at a price of 101 and blindly held until 1981, would have fallen by 83 percent, to 17 inflation-shrunken cents on the dollar.
>
> *The Trouble with Prosperity*, Times Books
> Random House, 1996

Few people besides bondholders were aware of this thirty-five-year misery, because bond bears never attract much notice. Did you realize that 1994 was the worst year for bonds in the twentieth century? That news is still news to a lot of investors.

Exhibit 12 shows four possible scenarios to consider: (1) stocks and bonds do well together; (2) stocks do well and bonds don't; (3) both are losers; (4) bonds do well and stocks don't. Which is worth owning at any particular time depends on inflation and on interest rates. Let's consider each scenario.

1. *Stocks and bonds do well together.* This happens when interest rates are falling and inflation is under control, a double benefit that investors have enjoyed from 1982 to 1997. Who but a Robinson Crusoe

Exhibit 12 Bond Prices (1945–Present)

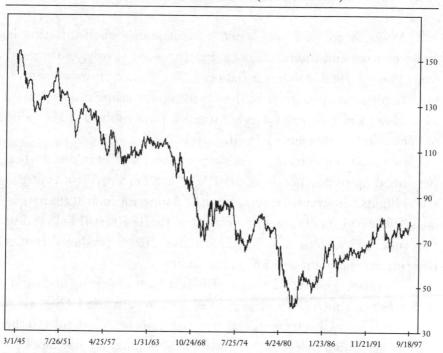

Source: Bob Prechter, Elliott Wave International, 20 Municipal Bond Index.

without a broker doesn't realize that stocks have enriched the rich and the not-so-rich during this period? Bonds have quietly done the same.

"Certificates of confiscation," bonds were called in the early 1980s, when they offered yields north of 15 percent. Some confiscation. Any investor who took Uncle Sam up on the offer and bought long-term governments in that period has collected 15 to 20 percent in annual interest payments ever since. This return compares favorably to the annual return from the most successful stock mutual funds of the era. Original owners of 1982 vintage thirty-year government bonds can look forward to fifteen more years of this posh harvest.

Although stocks and bonds have both continued to prosper in the 1990s, stocks have prospered more. That's because inflation has picked up a bit, and interest rates aren't falling as fast as they did in the 1980s.

2. *Stocks do well and bonds don't.* This happens when inflation is under control and interest rates are rising—but slowly, as they did from 1947 to 1968. Modest inflation didn't bother most companies. Higher corporate profits more than made up for rising interest rates, so stockholders prospered. Higher interest rates nibbled at the value of bonds, so bondholders suffered.

This wasn't the outcome conservative investors had in mind when they lined up to buy bonds in the 1950s—and avoided stocks as too risky! Bonds had won their reputation as a superior long-term investment twenty years earlier, and citizens of the 1950s still believed in that superiority. This was a costly mistake. Bonds produced results that might disappoint a slot machine addict.

3. *Both stocks and bonds are losers.* Interest rates are rising and inflation is out of control. The last such episode was in the 1970s, when bonds were lousy investments and stocks did worse. It's thanks to the income that bondholders in an inflationary bear market may fare better than stockholders.

Bonds throw off cash, which, in an inflationary bear market, can be reinvested at progressively higher interest rates.

4. *Bonds do well and stocks don't.* Interest rates are falling, and inflation turns to deflation—the only case where falling rates won't help stocks. The last time this happened was in the 1930s. With the economy in deep recession or depression, companies can't make money. Bonds are star performers because they generate cash payments when prices are in decline, making each monthly payment more valuable than the last.

If you decide stocks are too risky at present, how do you know when to buy long-term bonds, and when to take shelter in the money market? Marty Zweig, a nimble asset allocator, follows the ups and downs of the popular inflation gauge, the Commodity Research Bureau (CRB) index of prices, published in the financial pages. As long as the CRB index holds steady or declines from the current reading, bonds will give a better return than the money market or a three-month Treasury bill. When the CRB index rises a modest amount (9 percent or less, in a given year), bonds will beat the money market, but only slightly. When the CRB rises more than 9 percent, the money market will beat bonds.

Here are some final thoughts about bonds.

There's no law that says a "high" interest rate can't go higher. There's also no law that says a "low" interest rate can't go lower, although the lower it goes, the less chance you have of making money in the future. In Japan in 1997, you could buy a twenty-year bond paying 1.5 percent. For this investment to pay off, Japanese interest rates—along with the inflation rate—must hover near zero for two decades—a very debatable outcome.

If you're bullish on bonds, you can boost your profits with the zero-coupon variety, called "zeros" for short. Zeros are issued by the U.S. Government and carry the same high credit ratings as regular government bonds. The difference is in the way the payout is arranged.

When you buy a regular $10,000 bond, you pay $10,000 up front, collect interest along the way, and get your $10,000 back at the end. When you buy a $10,000 zero, you get an immediate credit for all the interest you'll be owed over the life of the bond. Let's say the zero will throw off $2,000 in interest payments over fifteen years. In that case, you'll pay $8,000 for the bond up front and $10,000 comes back at the end.

This plan helps the government save money now, because it has your $8,000 and doesn't owe you any interest for fifteen years. Meanwhile, you must pay taxes every year on the interest you haven't gotten yet. To avoid being taxed on this virtual interest, it's best to own zeros in tax-free accounts.

What makes zeros so profitable in a bull market for bonds? When you're paying only $8,000 for a $10,000 bond, you're using a form of

Exhibit 13   Total Returns of Bonds vs. Stocks (December 31, 1980 –December 31, 1997)

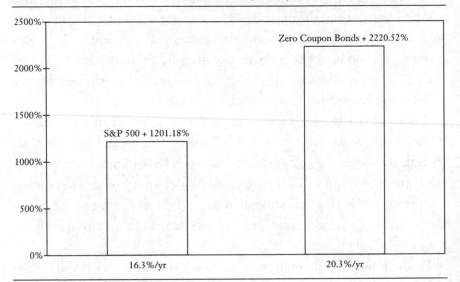

Source: Michael O'Higgins.

leverage. You get more bonds for the buck, and the market value of the zero will increase much faster than the market value of a standard bond. Exhibit 13 shows how zero coupon bonds have outperformed stocks by a wide margin since 1980. Naturally, this same leverage that produces such high returns will work against you when bond prices are falling. You don't want to own zeros in periods of high inflation.

In that case, you might consider the government's new inflation-indexed bonds, launched in 1997. Investors greeted this new product with a yawn, but the concept is intriguing. Inflation-indexed bonds pay a fixed rate of interest that is much lower than the interest on a standard bond. But on top of the fixed yield, you get an additional payment that's pegged to the inflation rate. This won't do you any good if inflation holds steady or falls, but whenever it rises, the bond yield rises with it. Inflation indexing removes the biggest fear of bondholders: That inflation will sap the buying power of the income they receive.

WILL GOLD
STOP A BEAR?

You have a choice between trusting the natural stability of gold or the honesty and intelligence of members of the government. And with all due respect to these gentlemen, I advise you, as long as the capitalist system lasts, vote for gold.

George Bernard Shaw

GOLD IS THE ICONOCLAST'S bankroll, the libertarian's retirement plan, the legal tender of the backwoods militia, but will it get you through the next bear market? The scorecard shown in Exhibit 14 tells the story.

It's obvious that gold isn't a sure cure for bear markets, although it has held up rather well on several occasions. Whether bought by the ounce (physical gold) or by the share (mining stocks), gold has gratified its owners in six of the eleven losing streaks for the S&P 500.

Homestake Mining Company (a proxy for the gold group) was a notable bright spot in the Great Depression. It offered no protection

Exhibit 14 Industry Performances during the Eleven Corrections
of 15% or More Since 1946

Correction Date	S&P 500	Physical Gold	Gold Mining Shares
May 46–May 47	−23	0	−28
June 48–June 49	−17	0	+3
July 57–Oct 57	−15	0	−18
Dec 61–June 62	−22	0	−3
Feb 66–Oct 66	−17	0	−10
Nov 68–May 70	−28	+4.11	−35
Jan 73–Oct 74	−41	+142.87	+144
Sept 76–Mar 78	−16	+60.72	+43
Nov 80–Aug 82	−19	−34.58	−60
Aug 87–Dec 87	−27	+7.90	−22
July 90–Oct 90	−15	+2.54	−8

Source: Sam Stovall at S&P 500.
Note: Gold price was "fixed" during the first few episodes, hence physical gold registered no gains and no losses.

in the selling panic of Black Monday, October 29, 1929, when it fell from $11 to $8 in short order. But when gold rallied through the wreckage of the bear market, so did Homestake. It hit an all-time high of $15 a share in 1932. By comparison, a share in a typical Dow component, General Motors, was marked down from $45 to $3.75 during the same period.

By gaining 30 percent while the Dow lost 89 percent, gold stocks posted a spectacular relative return. You didn't find a lot of gold investors sleeping in doorways and selling apples on the curb.

Toward the end of 1932, when the country was officially depressed, stocks of all stripes enjoyed a snappy recovery, carrying the Dow to a fourfold gain by 1937. Homestake Mining kept up with the crowd, advancing from $15 to $68, but here its similarity to the Dow ends. The Dow's fourfold gain was preceded by an eightfold loss; Homestake's fourfold gain came on top of a prior gain from

1929 to 1932. Overall, the owners of gold stocks came out four to six times ahead of the game, while owners of every other kind of stock were far from breaking even. A remarkable recovery from a bear attack doesn't mean investors are made whole. It depends on the damage.

Gold was expected to do well during periods of high inflation. For centuries, metal had been the best defense against the funny money routinely foisted on the world population by big-spending governments. That gold stocks could produce big profits in a period of deflation, when prices were falling, impressed a lot of people in the 1930s. Gold attracted a new fan club as the answer to any financial crisis, inflationary or deflationary.

This fan club overlooked the reason gold did well in the deflation of the 1930s. The price was fixed by government decree at precisely $20.67 an ounce. Thus, gold was sitting on a "floor" that saved it from the nasty tumble in other commodities: copper, wheat, real estate, lumber, theater tickets—you name it. Spared from the whims of the free market, the mining industry continued to reap profits while other industries reaped losses.

President Franklin Roosevelt raised the floor on gold from $20.67 to $35 an ounce in 1934, but this edict didn't help gold stocks in the decades ahead. In fact, investors who married their mining shares after the honeymoon of 1929–1937 were punished for their fidelity. By 1953, gold stocks were selling for half off their earlier high prices. Nevertheless, loyal investors in Homestake had doubled their money from 1929–1953, while loyal investors in Dow stocks were still in the red.

In 1933, President Roosevelt also signed legislation making it illegal for U.S. citizens to own gold. This metallic Prohibition was a shocker. You could own mining shares, but you couldn't keep gold bars, gold dust, or gold coins in the house (unless they were old enough to be valued as antiques). A well-stocked liquor cabinet was legal (this other Prohibition was abolished the same year gold was criminalized), but a nugget in the kitchen drawer could get you prison time.

The purpose of this strange law was to get gold out of the hands of the people and into the hands of the government, which needed every ounce to support the dollar, backed by gold in the international money system.

Although the words "redeemable in gold" disappeared from the dollar bill, cash was returned to a modified gold standard, even though for 40 years thereafter, it was a crime for the population at large to own the metal. In 1974, President Ford decriminalized it. For the first time since the New Deal, gold could be bought and sold by consenting adults at whatever price they consented to. It was subject to the same market forces as pork bellies or soybeans.

Gold got its freedom three years earlier, when President Nixon allowed the price to float freely in the commodity pits and elsewhere. This liberation came just in time for the bear market of 1973–1974, a period of pesky inflation and long lines at the gas pumps. The price of oil quadrupled, and the prices of other hard and soft assets tagged along. Stocks were in descent from a never-never land of valuation, where the so-called Nifty Fifty companies had sold for fifty to seventy times earnings. With inflation on the rise and stocks extravagantly priced, it was a perfect chance to buy gold stocks and sell the rest of the portfolio.

In the topsy-turvy trading of 1968–1974, mining shares rose with the overall market and fell with the overall market, but they didn't fall as far. At the bottom in 1974, when the Dow was down 40 percent, mining stocks were up and physical gold closed the year at $186.50 an ounce, up from $132.50, and far ahead of the 1973 low price of $66. From this new plateau, the gold price mounted an impressive drive. The 1970s, which began with the Dow at 1,000 and gold at $35, ended with the Dow at 800 and gold at $850.

The golden hoopla brought a surge in demand that pushed the price too far too fast. Since the top was reached in 1980, gold has disappointed its hoarders and its speculators. Communism fell, corporate profits rose, inflation was stymied, New England came back from recession, Texas came back, California came back, even Beirut came back—all part of a lingering nightmare for gold fans, because gold thrives on bad news.

On a few occasions, a slight upturn in the metals industry gave gold bugs (as gold bulls are called) false hopes, soon to be dashed by another positive development in world economics or politics that returned gold to its lowly rut. In the bear market of 1981, gold and gold stocks offered no protection. They were roughed up with the Dow, the bond market, and everything else. After 1981, gold, stocks, and bonds parted company. Paper assets had scraped the bottom of a long decline and were headed for renewed prosperity. Gold had retreated from a long advance and was headed back to inferiority. The 1980s were the 1970s in reverse.

Physical gold held up well enough in the Crash of 1987, taking only a tiny stumble from $480 to $450 an ounce, then rising to $500. Mining shares weren't as fortunate. Homestake dropped from $24 to $13 an ounce and ended the year at $17. Once investors were convinced that the world's central banks had averted a global depression by cutting interest rates, the rally in gold ended quickly, and the metal lost popularity. As stocks moved higher, gold sank as low as $250 an ounce before settling into a trading range of $300 to $400, its general range as this is written.

Since 1980, $10,000 invested in the Dow has returned $70,000 to the stockholder; $10,000 invested in gold has lost $5,000 to the oreholder. Does this mean the bear market in gold is almost over? Not according to Bob Prechter. Prechter was bearish on gold in 1980, and he's bearish today. His charts tell him gold could drop below $100 before this cycle runs its course. People who buy $300 gold as a hedge against an 8,000 Dow, says Prechter, will soon be sorry.

Gold may look cheap at $300, seventeen years after it fetched $850, but bear markets don't work on a schedule (some have lasted sixty years) and they don't have predictable bottoms. Compared to other commodities in the producer price index, physical gold at $300 is still more expensive than it was in the two centuries leading up to the 1970s, if you buy Prechter's data. (Much of his research on this subject comes from the American Institute for Economic Research, Great Barrington, MA.) To add to the risk, mining shares have been overvalued, as compared to physical gold.

If the inflation rate were on the rise, gold would also have a reason to rise, in spite of its being relatively expensive at the moment, says Prechter. But the inflation rate is falling, not rising, and many indicators point to deflation, gold's natural enemy. If the next bear market is deflationary, à la 1929–1932, gold will offer no protection, unless a reincarnated Franklin Roosevelt restores the floor under the price.

There are two sides to every gold coin, and the gold bulls (or bugs), rebut the Prechter analysis. They give at least four good reasons to buy gold today:

1. With the Dow up sevenfold since 1980 and gold down by half, the metal is exceedingly cheap compared to the average stock.
2. There's an endless supply of stocks and a limited supply of gold. The entire world inventory—coins, bars, necklaces, goblets, nuggets, fillings, and so on—could be smelted into a cube small enough to be displayed on the basketball court at Madison Square Garden. Mining companies are digging deeper and extracting less. According to nugget counters, $20 billion in new gold is coming onto the market every year. Bill Gates could afford to buy a year's supply.

The biggest deposit on earth isn't in a Russian, South African, or Australian mine. It's in the basement of the Federal Reserve Bank in New York, where many nations keep their gold bars—8,500 tons, worth $90 billion. The world's central banks own and control 40 percent of the world supply, stored in New York and elsewhere.

3. Demand is growing with the world population, and the recent decade has produced a billion new necks, two billion new arms, two billion ears, and 32 billion teeth, all waiting to be adorned with necklaces, bracelets, earrings, and gold fillings.

4. Governments on six continents are running record deficits and sinking deeper into debt. When all else fails (it always does), they'll rescue themselves with the printing press, making cash worth less and gold worth more. When all currencies lose their credibility, gold will benefit. The importance of gold as an antidote to politicians was emphatically made clear by Fed Chairman Greenspan in the 1960s, when, as a young economist, he was free to say such things:

The financial policy of the welfare state requires that there be no way for the owners of wealth to protect themselves. This is the shabby secret of the welfare statists' tirades against gold. Deficit spending is simply a scheme for the "hidden" confiscation of wealth. Gold stands in the way of this insidious process. It stands as a protector of property rights.*

The problem, at the moment, is that the very governments whose easy money policies make gold more valuable in the long run are selling, or threatening to sell, the gold in their vaults. Why are they doing this? For the same reason that a laid-off steelworker pawns his watch:

---

* Greenspan made this statement in an article entitled "Gold and Economic Freedom," published in *The Objectivist* magazine. It was later reprinted in a book, *Capitalism: The Unknown Ideal*, written by Ayn Rand.

they need quick cash. Every time the gold price begins to rise, another report of central bank selling drives it back down. In the spring of 1997, the Germans, Belgians, and Italians were reportedly selling. Even the Swiss, who love gold as much as chocolate, announced their intention to sell.

But don't give up on gold entirely. Even Prechter thinks gold has a bright future, but only after the latest bear market runs its course. "Then, if the Federal Reserve returns to the printing press to revive a dying economy," Prechter says, "a swift shift to gold will be essential."

What's the bottom line? It makes sense to invest in gold when gold is in a bull market, usually because inflation is in a bull market and the dollar is losing credibility. It doesn't make sense to invest in gold just because stocks are in a bear market.

THE DISAPPEARING DIVIDEND

OWNING STOCKS THAT PAY dividends is like owning rental property instead of raw land. In a slow market for real estate, land will just sit there, reminding you that you shouldn't have bought it. But rental property gives you income while you wait for that offer you can't refuse. In a slow market for stocks, a dividend is rent. It's the only reward you'll get, perhaps for several years, while you wait for stocks to appreciate.

When stocks are on a winning streak and investors are mesmerized by rising prices, it's easy to forget that dividends have accounted for a third of financial gains over the years. Benjamin Graham, the father of value investing, once said the primary purpose of a "business corporation is to pay dividends to its owners." This notion is all but forgotten today. Charles Carlson, editor of *Dow Theory Forecasts*, figures dividends accounted for half the gains between 1980 and 1995. Thus, it's a danger sign when stocks are so high priced that their dividend yields are negligible, as they were in 1997.

The income stream from dividends can keep a fearful investor from abandoning stocks near the bottom of a decline, when Wall Street is demoralized. A reliable dividend also acts as a brake whenever the stock price rolls downhill. For instance, if Philip Morris pays an annual dividend of $1.60, and the stocks sells for $40, the yield on the stock is 4 percent. If the stock price drops to $20, the yield jumps to 8 percent.

With its steady cash flow in a recession-proof industry (people smoke cigarettes no matter what), Philip Morris will have no trouble paying its dividend. Investors know this. Investors who hadn't thought about buying the stock before now find the 8 percent yield irresistible, and the new buyers will bid up the price. In today's market, a powerful company that pays you 8 percent a year to own it isn't likely to stay down for long.

One way to prepare for a bear without cashing out of stocks entirely is to pack your portfolio with dividend-paying companies, or to invest in mutual funds of the "growth and income" variety, which follow the same strategy. In that way, you'll avoid smaller, iffier companies that don't pay dividends because they'd rather spend every available dollar on their own fast growth. You'll end up owning larger, stodgier companies that survived hard times in the past and can be counted on to do so again.

The stodgy group includes utilities, banks, drug companies, and oil companies. It also includes industrial heavyweights that have fallen out of favor, such as the "Dogs of the Dow," the five worst performers among the thirty Dow Industrials in any given year. The Dow dogs pay high dividends because their stocks are down; hence, their yields are up. They make a habit of outperforming the other Dow stocks the year after they're put in the doghouse. It also turns out they've outperformed the rest of the Dow in five out of six stock market declines shown in Exhibit 15 provided by Michael O'Higgins. The irrepressible O'Higgins, a money manager out of Albany, New York, and now Miami, Florida, masterminded the Dogs of the Dow technique of investing in last year's losers.

Exhibit 15   Dogs of the Dow in Down Years

Year Ended	DJIA	5 Stock Strategy
31-Dec-69	−11.60%	−10.09%
31-Dec-73	−13.12	+19.64
31-Dec-74	−23.14	−3.80
31-Dec-77	−12.70	+4.50
31-Dec-81	−3.40	0.00
31-Dec-90	−0.58	−15.20

Source: Michael O'Higgins.

Since recessions and bear markets often go hand in hand, a portfolio of dividend-paying stocks must be carefully chosen. Bear-proofing on the basis of yield alone can be dangerous. Because a dividend isn't an obligation (compared to an interest payment on a bond, for example), a company is free to reduce or suspend payment at will, and usually does so when it lacks cash.

Such suspensions are common in hard economic times. Even in prosperous times, a high dividend may be a sign that a company is already in trouble. Investors may be dumping the stock because they expect the dividend to be cut. This causes the stock price to fall and the yield to rise, but the yield means nothing if the company stops paying it.

More important than the dividend per se is the company's ability to make future payments. The "payout ratio" tells you whether a company can afford to keep paying at the current rate. If a company earns $1 a share this year and plans to pay $1 a share in dividends, it has no margin for error. A slight drop in earnings puts the dividend in jeopardy. On the other hand, if it earns $3 a share and pays $1 in dividends, it has a comfortable margin for error. A 3–1 payout ratio is considered quite safe; 2–1 is reasonably safe; and 1–1 is very risky.

Any stockbroker with access to in-house research can give you the rundown on payout ratios for a variety of companies. For a more comprehensive source of information on dividends, consult Moody's, the bond rating agency and all-around statistical service.

The staff at Moody's keeps tabs on a group of "dividend achievers"—companies that have raised their payouts at least ten years in a row. At last count, 345 such achievers were listed in Moody's handbook on the subject, published annually for $24.95 (800-342-5647).

Moody's handbook is an excellent place to start bear-proofing a portfolio. If it appears on Moody's list, a company must have increased its dividend through good markets and bad.

With more than 4,200 stock-oriented mutual funds in existence today, Moody's shows remarkable restraint in resisting the temptation to start a Dividend Achievers' Fund. However, there's an ample selection of funds that specialize in dividend-paying stocks, and are likely to hold up well in bear markets. Examples that are rated low-risk by Morningstar appear in the "growth and income" category on page 189.

What can the dividend yield on a popular stock index, such as the Dow or the S&P 500, tell us about where stocks are headed? At the top of a bull market, the yield on these key indexes will be much lower than it was at the bottom of the market. Therefore, the lower the yield, the closer you get to a bear.

There are only two ways a company can pass its wealth on to its shareholders: (1) paying dividends or (2) doing something to boost the stock price, also called "creating a capital gain." When dividends are high, stock prices are low, which means investors are pessimistic about future capital gains. When dividends are low, stock prices are high, so investors are optimistic about capital gains. Since investors are most optimistic at a market top, and most pessimistic at a market bottom, dividend yield is also a useful contrary indicator.

Because dividends compete with bonds and other income-producing investments, they become more or less attractive as interest rates rise or fall. Looking at the *real* dividend yield for stocks, going back to 1900—that is, subtracting for inflation—we get the interesting picture shown in Exhibit 16. Notice when dividends are *really* high, as opposed to apparently high.

A high "real" yield on the Dow or the S&P 500 has always been a sign of a great buying opportunity in stocks. This certainly was the case in 1918, when the real yield on the Dow was a generous 9 percent, or in 1931, when the real yield was an astounding 14 percent. In 1931, the market was paying 14 percent with zero inflation to own the best American companies. Who could pass up such a deal?

Many people couldn't, which is why America had a great bull market (1932–1937) in the middle of the Great Depression. Should a similar opportunity repeat itself, don't pass it up. It hasn't happened in six decades, and only twice in that stretch (in 1973 and 1982) has the real yield on the Dow reached 6 percent. Both entry points were extremely profitable for investors in stocks.

A high real yield is a buy signal, but no convincing case can be made for a low real yield as a sell signal. A once-popular formula, "Sell stocks when the yield on the Dow falls below 3.5 percent," failed its

Exhibit 16   Real Dividend Yield on Dow

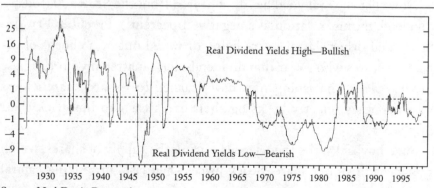

Source: Ned Davis Research.

practitioners twice: in the late 1950s, when stocks quadrupled after dividends fell below that benchmark, and again in the 1990s.

It's true that you avoided the October 1987 Crash by fleeing the stock market when the yield on the Dow dropped into negative territory in mid-1987. But unless you returned to the market in timely fashion (the dividend yield didn't give a clear signal to do so), you missed ten years when the Dow quadrupled.

More recently, if you abandoned stocks when the Dow's real yield went negative in 1988, you missed 5,000 points of Dow appreciation.

In 1997, the Dow's yield was stuck in negative territory, while the yield on the transportation index hit an all-time low. Bob Prechter, who provided this tidbit, sees these skimpy returns as profoundly bearish and notes that a year's worth of dividends can't cover the cost of the average commission to buy and sell the average stock in the S&P 500—and that's before inflation is subtracted.

Prechter marvels at investors who choose stocks paying 1.6 percent over government bonds paying 6 percent or Treasury bills paying 4.5 percent, risk-free. Eric Fry, an astute money manager for Holl International in San Francisco, shares Prechter's amazement. Fry sees stocks at current prices as collectibles, like old lava lamps, plastic battleships, or souvenir ashtrays where the market price has nothing to do with underlying shlockholder value.

Now that the real yield has disappeared from the S&P 500 (today's dividend, minus inflation, is a negative 1 percent!), Prechter, Fry, Jim Stack, and other alarmists are being drowned out by a chorus of expert witnesses who swear that dividends don't matter anymore. These experts claim that companies have learned to reward shareholders in other ways, mostly by using their extra cash to buy back their own stock.

Such buybacks, the theory goes, shrink the supply of shares, which raises earnings per share. Stock prices then rise, producing capital gains and paper profits that more than make up for the lack of dividends. Shareholders are so happy they forget about dividends.

Skeptics of this theory have found a savvy ally in Larry Tisch, billionaire investor in CBS and Loew's properties, among other holdings. In 1997, Tisch surprised the audience at Jim Grant's annual bearfest with evidence that stock buybacks are a ruse and a sham. He focused on Microsoft to show how this works.

According to Tisch, while Microsoft was buying back millions of shares in the open market, it was adding the same number of shares by awarding them to corporate insiders as stock options. Thus, the potential benefit of the well-publicized buyback was negated by the poorly publicized bestowing of stock options at headquarters. The campaign to "enhance shareholder value" is really a tricky maneuver to enhance insider value.

When a company gives its insiders more in options and less in salary (a popular maneuver these days), it boosts the stock price, indirectly. By reducing salaries, the company also reduces expenses, which adds to earnings. Higher earnings convince investors to pay higher prices for the stock. The problem arises when the recipients of options decide to convert their options into actual shares. This puts more shares into circulation, which lowers earnings per share and makes the stock less attractive. When enough bigwigs sell their shares to reap their rewards, the stock price will fall, subverting the aforementioned buyback. Investors will wish the company had sent them a dividend instead of spending the money on internal maneuvering that did them no good.

Jim Stack waits for the next bear market to restore dividends to the importance they deserve. For the S&P 500 to return to its average yield, he says, stock prices would have to drop 50 percent from today's lofty levels.

JUMPING ON THE
NEXT BULL

THE BEAR MARKET IS OVER and stocks are coming back. But which stocks? What got you through the bear with minimum loss can't be expected to give you maximum gain in the next bull. "Defensive issues"—utilities, soft drinks, grocery stores, and so on—that held their ground during bad times have lagged behind in every recovery since 1966. Utilities have been particularly unproductive in the early stages. Steels, automakers, home builders, lumber mills, and other "cyclicals"* have led the advance.

As consumers regain confidence, they head for the auto showrooms, appliance stores, and new subdivisions. Rising sales of big-ticket items (cars, houses, refrigerators) bring business to the smelters, fabricators, and ore pits up the line. Truckers, railroads, and airlines prosper as the orders trickle up. Advertising agencies produce more ads, newspapers

---

* A "cyclical" is a company that does well when the economy is strong, and not so well when the economy is weak.

sell more space, TV stations sell more time. These industries (advertising, broadcasting, and trucking) have been star performers after all nine recessions since World War II.

The best time to buy cyclicals is before the experts have convinced themselves the recovery is for real. As in other bear market maneuvers, it takes courage to invest in steel mills or homebuilders when the economic EKG is flat and pessimists abound. Two years after the recession of 1990, economists still were doubting the recovery. But with large institutions buying cyclicals early to get ahead of the crowd, you must do the same to get a decent price.

"As a new bull market begins," notes Marty Zweig, "the economy has six months or more left on the downside. Worse results for corporate earnings usually lie ahead." Wait for hard evidence of a recovery to trickle down from the economists to the newspapers, and you're likely to miss the best gains. A rising stock market has "predicted" 100 percent of the economic recoveries since World War II—not the other way around.

If you're thinking about buying specific companies (as opposed to mutual funds), the big winners from the previous bull market aren't likely to win big in the new bull. The charms of "Stocks That Would Have Made You a Fortune Already" aren't easily forgotten, but try to forget them if you can. "Avoid yesterday's darlings" is a Wall Street motto that deserves to be sewn on a pillow.

Copper companies were yesterday's darlings in the early 1900s, before steel companies stole the role. Oil companies were resplendent until the bear of 1919 and were duds thereafter. RCA was a big winner until 1929, but was mediocre in the 1932 rally and beyond. The stars of the 1930s—Philip Morris, Western Auto, and Coca-Cola—were has-beens in the 1940s and 1950s. Go-go stocks of the 1960s never recovered their pizzazz after the subsequent bear.

There's a psychological reason a yesterday's darling has a hard time recovering from a bear market loss. It attracted a large following in the preceding bull market; buyers paid progressively sillier prices to own it. On the way down, those owners become progressively more disgusted. They promise themselves they'll unload that lovable loser as soon as it reaches the break-even point on the way up. Thus, when stocks are on the move, all the ex-darlings must swim against a strong tide of selling from owners who are getting out at the same price they paid when they bought in. Break-even selling can retard a stock's progress for years, even if the company itself is thriving.

The ex-darling syndrome explains why smaller and less well-known stocks often outgain the better established names at the start of the latest bull run. Small companies are newcomers to the market; they are too young and too obscure to have disappointed a crowd of investors in a previous bear market. With no history of disappointment to hold them back, they can travel upstream unimpeded, as publisher William O'Neil describes:

> The greatest opportunities of the next three or four years [following a bear market] will be popping out one after another all over the place. These new leaders are setting up new bases from which they'll rise five or ten times. . . . As soon as the market turns, they'll start jumping out right and left. This is absolutely the worst time for anybody to get scared. . . .
>
> Many will be issues that recently got their start as public companies. Look for ones where the price is down, along with all the other stock prices, but the earnings are up . . . maybe 50–100 percent over the past two years. They have new products that are selling quite well, yet most people haven't heard of these companies. These are your new leaders.

O'Neil says these new leaders move up quickly because big institutions who've done their homework invest in future success stories posthaste. As soon as they're convinced the bear market is over, institutions step in and buy millions of shares. For example, in 1990, Cisco Systems rose nine points the week stocks escaped Saddam Hussein's bear hug. From that point, Cisco advanced 100 fold in seven years.

If past performance counts for anything, you'll enhance your profits by switching into small stocks or small stock mutual funds coming out of the next bear market. Also called "small caps" or "secondaries," small stocks have outrun big stocks in the early stages of every new bull market since 1932. Far-sighted bargain hunters are buying these young, fast-growing companies when they're cheap, hoping they've jumped onto the next Microsoft or Wal-Mart.

The harder stocks fall in the prior decline, the better the small caps do on the rebound. In 1973–1974, they went on a tear, more than doubling off the bottom in seven years. (The Dow lost 10% in the same time period.) A young Fidelity fund manager named Lynch went on a tear of his own, filling his portfolio with small stocks other fund managers had snubbed. They were buying yesterday's household names; Lynch was buying tomorrow's.

True to form, small caps outgained big caps coming out of the Saddam Hussein bear of 1990. The Russell 2,000 Index (another proxy for small stocks) sprinted far ahead of the S&P 500 in 1991–1992. Small stocks held their advantage into the mid-1990s. By then, big stocks were cutting into the lead.

The small-cap advantage often lasts several years, or until small caps become overpriced compared to big caps, and the bargain hunters who bought on the cheap are selling and taking their profits. Sensing the good times are about to end, cautious investors are pinning their money on seasoned companies with a record of solid earnings and a proven ability to withstand economic abuse. Soon, the small stocks will stop rising and the big stocks will continue to slog ahead, into the arms of the next bear.

PART SIX

~

My Mutual
Funds Will
Save Me and
Other Fallacies

MUTUAL MISERY

ARE YOU CONVINCED THAT mutual funds will protect against bears? Your fellow investors seem to think they will. "Stocks may be risky to own at today's high prices," goes the standard refrain, "but in a stock fund you can't lose much. Fund managers are too smart to let a decline get out of hand. At least mine is. He's been brilliant. He's tripled my money in seven years."

Everybody's brilliant fund manager has tripled everybody's money in the latest U.S. bull, leading to the widespread conviction that fund managers can't go wrong. Meanwhile, stock funds have proliferated, creating thousands of opportunities for brilliancy. Stock funds outnumber common stocks that trade on the New York Stock Exchange (4,200 funds, 2,907 stocks!) Stock funds have multiplied faster than stocks—further evidence that institutions are in control and won't let a bear market happen.

After all, won't the baby boomers continue to pour money into stock funds as they prepare for retirement? Isn't the huge fund industry that deploys this money a new factor in the market, giving it ballast and keeping prices afloat? Aren't the professional investors employed in that industry less likely to panic than skittish amateurs who once caused bear markets by capricious selling that drove prices off cliffs? How can the market fail, when mutual funds ARE the market?

Jim Stack, our skeptic out West, has completed a "mutual fund reality check" that puts a kink in this line of reasoning. What he has already told his subscribers he's willing to repeat here for free: Stock funds won't stop the next bear market because they failed to stop the two biggies in this century.

Stack discovered "déjà vu all over again" in two prior periods when mutual funds were wildly popular: the 1920s and the 1960s. The earlier of these manias was little noted nor long remembered, but Stack's research uncovered persuasive evidence that it occurred. One reliable source reports that 450 investment trusts, as funds were called back then, had attracted $3 billion in public money in the 1920s.

Apparently, these trusts "caught on like wildfire" in 1922 and continued to spread. To meet the demand, new trusts sprung up so fast that, by 1928, the *Saturday Evening Post* observed: "It is hardly possible to find enough experienced operators." A historian of the period added his two cents: so many trusts were launched so quickly that, by 1929, the "promoters were having some difficulty finding distinctive names for their organizations."

What endeared the masses to the trusts will sound familiar to any modern fundholder. People thought that professional managers could fend off the bears. Stocks they might not have bought for themselves—too risky—they were willing to own collectively in a fund. "These trusts act as great cushions against the market's shocks," marveled a financial writer in *The Outlook & Independent* magazine (September 18, 1929). "Such influence, such terrific resources in constant reserve have given the market an internal buoyance it never possessed in the old days."

This claim sounded rather hollow by the end of 1929, and hollower still in 1932, when it was obvious that investment trusts had provided zero internal buoyancy during the Great Decline, and more likely

helped accelerate the sinking. The trusts themselves, also lacking buoyancy, sank with the market, and the majority never resurfaced. Their
remains were scattered among clients, as a memento of their losses.

Once these pioneering mutual funds had proven they couldn't prevent a decline any better than they could protect their clients' assets
in the midst of one, the fund industry fell out of favor and stayed that
way for thirty years. In 1940, only an oddball would buy a stock mutual fund, and fewer than 300,000 oddballs had done so. It wasn't until
the 1960s—by then, the investment trust fiasco was erased from the
public memory—that funds were reintroduced as an exciting new concept that took the fuss, bother, and danger out of owning stocks.

By the early 1960s, three million Americans had bought shares; by
1969, the number reached 10 million, or one in four adults. Funds
were peddled door to door like vacuum cleaners or encyclopedias; the
peddlers were schoolteachers, shoe salesmen, engineers working after
hours. The moonlighting sales brigade helped the industry capture
nearly $60 million in assets, and the number of funds more than dou-
bled, from 150 in 1965 to 350 in 1970.

"Almost as fast as Americans have been buying funds, other Americans have been starting them up," observed Solomon Freedman at the
SEC. The agency didn't have a count on the exact number. "We're too
busy to poll all our five branches to find out how many there are," he
told a reporter at *Dun's Review* (July, 1969).

The flamboyant Gerry Tsai left Fidelity in 1966 to make a solo
launch of the Manhattan Fund. Expecting to raise $25 million, Tsai at-
tracted ten times that amount. Manhattan was tagged a "go-go fund"
in honor of Tsai's strategy of buying high-tech companies with abun-
dant promise and a lack of current earnings. In 1967, his fund recorded
a 39 percent gain, besting all competitors in its class.

"Nothing mysterious about investing," Tsai told *Newsweek*. "Look,
I am really very conservative. There is no such thing as go-gos. It's a
lot of hooey."

Fred Mates of the Mates Investment Fund out-go-goed Tsai with a 153 percent gain in 1968, and his mailslot was clogged with new money, just as Tsai's was. William O'Neil, who went on to launch *Investor's Daily*, had his own hotshot fund in the go-go era. The clever O'Neil was farsighted enough to see the future in computers. He installed a computer system—a novelty at the time—to track earnings growth, price volume, and relative strength of 2,000 different stocks. "The computers do 80 percent of the work for us in stock selection," O'Neil told *Forbes* Magazine in December 1968. "They're going to put a man on the moon with computers. The stock market isn't that complicated." O'Neil's computers seemed to be working—fundholders made a 100 percent profit in 1968 alone.

~

About the time O'Neil installed his database, mutual funds and related institutions held a third of all shares listed on the New York Stock Exchange and accounted for a third of the buying and selling. This bothered almost nobody except a minority of worrywarts at the SEC, who saw danger in the fact that "markets for many securities can be significantly influenced by the decisions of a single fund manager."

The danger wasn't that Tsai, Mates, O'Neil, and others would keep on buying, but that they might someday decide to start selling. A couple of megafunds unloading their biggest holdings—would that be enough to scuttle the market? If average investors thought so, their fears were put to rest by expert commentators.

"The funds are still well fortified with cash reserves," *Forbes* reassured its readers on September 15, 1968. "They've been taking in new cash from the public at an average of over $200 million a month so far this year. They could, accordingly, continue buying more stock than they sell for many months and at a rate high enough to keep the overall price movement rising or at least out of serious trouble."

"It is, of course, the theory that any sharp drop in the market will be cushioned because the mutual funds in particular, attracted by all the bargain-priced stocks, will immediately start buying and thus shore up the entire market," echoed *Dun's Review* in September 1968.

These cheery pronouncements came to a sad end in the bear market of 1969–1970. Mutual funds, obviously, couldn't shore up the entire market, or even a chunk of it. In a clear example of Pogo's advice, "We have met the enemy and they is us," investors who adopted funds as the safest form of enrichment subverted the process by fleeing their funds to the safety of cash. To finance these redemptions, managers were forced—often against their better judgment—to put their favorite stocks on the auction block at giveaway prices. A brilliant fund jockey couldn't protect clients who stayed on from losses created by clients who sold out. What did it matter that you were a long-term holder, when your mutual fund became a short-term seller at a disadvantageous moment?

The go was soon gone from the go-go funds. Their concerted selling drove prices lower. While O'Neil can't confirm this—"that's a long time ago," he says—records show his fund lost 54 percent in the 1969–1970 bear alone. Tsai's was down 57 percent, Mates's 77 percent. As fundholders grieved for their portfolios, *Forbes* answered its own rhetorical question:

"What happened to the proud boast that mutual funds would help stem any bear market? That, being levelheaded, long-range investors they would step in and buy when others were selling in a panic?

"These funds had to sell stock into a declining market to raise cash. They worsened the decline rather than stemming it."

Stocks hit bottom in May 1970. Managers like Tsai and Mates were sitting on a pile of cash they'd squirreled away—either because they expected prices to fall even lower, or because they wanted to cover the next round of redemptions they thought might come their way. A frustrated Mates asked the SEC to let him suspend redemptions altogether—in effect, forcing his clients to stick with the fund. The SEC turned him down. With the threat of withdrawals hanging over them, funds couldn't take advantage of the bargains that were everywhere.

Amateur stockpickers with homemade portfolios had more flexibility than professional fund managers. Amateurs weren't forced to sell at depressed prices to raise cash. Nor were they forced to sit on their cash and miss a buying opportunity. They could participate in the bargain phase of the summer rally that began in 1970. Many funds had to pass up the chance.

Funds didn't buy stocks in earnest until they were convinced the redemptions had ceased, and by then, the rally was half over. They continued to buy, at progressively higher prices, until they ran into a second vicious bear, in 1973–1974, that came on the heels of the first. This was a bleak phase for the fund industry. Its clients had lost money and faith, and its funds had lost their credibility, just as investment trusts did in the 1930s.

O'Neil sold his operation, merging it with Lincoln National Life; Mates's was disbanded; other big-name funds from the 1960s were gone by 1974. Fund assets nationwide dropped by a third. *Business Week* lamented, "In contrast to the seemingly unlimited prospects of five years ago, there is today the conviction that the fund industry must change dramatically if it is to survive at all."

"Talk with these people at any length," said *Forbes* in 1974, referring to the mob of dissatisfied customers coast to coast, "and you quickly understand why they are more sour on mutual funds than on stocks. They always knew stocks were a gamble. But they thought of mutual funds as an investment. The point is that mutual funds were for safety. Or so they thought."

Forbes quoted a widow from an unnamed small city near Portland, Oregon. "No, never again," exclaimed the widow. "When I bought my mutual funds I paid three times what they're worth today. It would take me twenty years to break even."

For eight straight years, from 1974 to 1982, more money flowed out of stock funds than flowed in. Even Peter Lynch's high-performance Fidelity Magellan had trouble attracting customers. The owners of funds with less stellar records (which means most of them) waited for their monthly statements to show they'd reached the break-even point, then sold their holdings. Steady withdrawals put a drag on the Dow and other indexes, which gained no ground for the balance of the decade.

When stock prices took off in 1982, stock funds were still out of favor. The newly created money market funds captured the public's fancy and the biggest share of its investment dollars. Why risk losses with unreliable equity managers when you could make a sensible rate of interest from a low-risk money market? Most people chose the latter, when prevailing opinion pushed them into this new form of cash. The less popular choice—stocks—proved to be the winner.

By 1987, the Dow had nearly tripled off the 1982 bottom. Then stocks crashed. The crash had the unlikely result of bringing stock funds back into favor. People who had soured on the fund concept years earlier and had taken investing into their own hands were traumatized by the crash and sought professional help. Money was moved out of the homemade portfolios and back into managed care, and stock funds entered their third heyday—the 1990s.

President Dwight Eisenhower once said: "Things are more like they are now than they ever were before." So are stock funds in the 1990s. There are more of them—4,200 at latest count, divided into at least thirty categories. Funds once took the confusion out of picking stocks; now there are funds of funds to take the confusion out of picking funds. Momentum funds are a lot like go-go funds. Gerry Tsai is played by Garrett Van Wagoner; Fred Mates by Louis Navellier; William O'Neil by William O'Neil. In 1992, the publisher of *Investor's Daily* started the new USA Mutual Fund, which closely resembled his 1960s version. He sold the fund in 1997.

The SEC worrywarts from the 1960s would be chewing their nails over the size of the fund industry today. More than $2 trillion worth of stocks are held in U.S. stock mutual funds at present count. Fidelity Magellan is now worth $55 billion by itself. The size of the industry, and of its most popular funds, brings comfort to people who think these funds are too big to fail. Jim Stack thinks they're too big not to fail. "When they start selling," he wonders, "who are they going to sell to?"

He concedes they won't have to sell unless fundholders decide to take their money out, but past performance suggests a mass withdrawal is far from implausible. Today, it's easier to take money out than it was when you had to send a letter to quit a fund. Today, you can quit with a phone call. In the old days, you might have hesitated to leave a fund and forfeit the entrance fee. Today, with those fees eliminated or reduced, there's no reason to hesitate. Also, the cash held in funds is at the lowest level in 20 years.

William O'Neil insists that funds are for holding, not for selling, and overall, he's right. But as in individual stocks, buy at the wrong time and you may face a long wait before you see any profit. Sometimes, funds never come back.

Evidence of the downside in a popular fund was buried in a Q&A page of *Kiplinger's Personal Finance* magazine in August 1993. It's worth exhuming. A reader asked the following: "I invested $500 in the no-load Investment Indicators Fund in 1971. The president of the fund was Charles Schwab. Are my shares worth anything?"

Answer: "They're not worth much. You now own 39 shares of the American Heritage Fund, which you can redeem for a total of about $55...."

It turned out Schwab (the famous Schwab) sold his fund to another fund, just as O'Neil did. That other fund went on a losing streak, until it was merged into the American Heritage Fund in 1993. At that point, according to Kiplinger's, the reader's original $500 was whittled down to $6.72.

Stock funds won't start a bear market, but if one happens, don't expect a brilliant manager to save you. The manager won't, and neither will Uncle Sam, even though a lot of people are misguided on this point. In a Lou Harris poll in 1996, more than 20 percent of the respondents insisted their stock funds are guaranteed against loss by the U.S. government. Good luck collecting on that.

BEAR-FRIENDLY FUNDS

UNDER THE CIRCUMSTANCES described in the preceding chapter, you can hardly expect a standard stock fund to offer much protection in a bear market. That doesn't mean you're out of luck if you own one, but you have three choices when you feel a bear coming on:

1. You can exit your stock funds, switch into bonds or cash, then reenter the funds at lower prices later. To profit from this switch, you need to sell high and buy lower, which requires smart or lucky timing.

2. You can keep the funds you've got, refuse to sell into the decline, and hold on for the comeback. The best performers in the comeback (emerging growth funds, for instance) are likely to fall the farthest in the setback, so owning them through the worst will require a lot of conviction about their lasting qualities.

3. You can buy bear protection by moving out of the most vulnerable types of funds (growth funds, for instance) and into the defensive camp. Funds that limit their losses in a bear tend to make a dull impression in a bull, so it's unlikely you'll find them on any list of winners from, say, 1990 to 1997. They tend

to be overlooked at the very point they're worth noticing; near a market top, when they could save a lot of people a lot of money.

Defensive funds can be categorized in various ways. This chapter describes some likely candidates: (1) Funds Run by Fogies Who've Seen the Worst, (2) Balanced Funds, (3) Dividend-Oriented Funds, (4) Asset Allocation Funds, (5) Growth and Income Funds, (6) Value Funds, (7) Utilities, (8) Funds That Sell Short, and (9) Hedge Funds.

All but the fogie funds (the author's invention) and the hedge funds (which aren't counted as mutual funds, since not everyone can buy them) are listed by category in the mutual fund guide published by Morningstar, the *Consumer Reports* of the industry. This excellent resource is updated twice a month and is available in local libraries. It gives all the important details about thousands of individual funds: what they own, who the managers are, the profits, the losses, how they rate against the competition. If you wouldn't buy a television or a toaster oven without consulting *Consumer Reports*, why buy a fund without consulting Morningstar?

The Morningstar staff assigns each fund a risk rating, based on past performance. Do you know the risk rating of funds you already own? If not, you might want to look it up (Exhibit 17). It's easy enough to understand. A fund with a "1" rating takes average risk in the fund arena; more than "1" indicates more risk; less than "1," less risk.

Using the risk score, you can get double protection against bear-market losses by investing in low-risk funds in low-risk categories. By the way, you can't always tell a fund's strategy by the category that Morningstar assigns to it. For instance, a fund that invests in out-of-favor companies that pay dividends might show up in the value category, even though it could just as easily be included in the equity-income category. These distinctions are somewhat arbitrary, and also inexact.

Whatever the category, funds listed in the pages that follow all received the lowest risk ratings in the Morningstar database as of this

Exhibit 17 Morningstar Low Risk Funds

Fund Name	Risk 3 Yr.	Phone Number
Utilities		
UAM SAMI Preferred Stock Income	0.11	800-638-7983
Putnam Utility Growth & Inc A	0.37	800-225-1581
Putnam Utility Growth & Inc B	0.39	800-225-1581
MFS Utilities A	0.43	800-637-2929
Hancock Utilities A	0.44	800-225-5291
Contrarian Funds		
ONE Fund Global Contrarian	0.39	800-578-8078
FBP Contrarian Balanced	0.55	800-543-0407
FBP Contrarian Equity	0.63	800-543-0407
Kemper Contrarian A	0.85	800-621-1048
Fidelity Contrafund	0.87	800-544-8888
Robertson Stephens Contrarian	1.12	800-766-3863
Asset Allocation		
Gabelli ABC	0.08	800-422-3554
Maxus Income	0.22	800-446-2987
Merrill Lynch Asset Income A	0.23	800-637-3863
Merrill Lynch Asset Income D	0.23	800-637-3863
Merrill Lynch Asset Income B	0.24	800-637-3863
Small Cap Value		
Royce Total Return	0.20	800-221-4268
Evergreen Small Cap Eq Inc Y	0.33	800-343-2898
FBL Managed	0.39	800-247-4170
Delafield	0.41	800-221-3079
Wilshire Target Small Value Inv	0.49	888-200-6796
Mid Cap Value		
American Century Equity Income Inv	0.40	800-345-2021
Pegasus Intrinsic Value A	0.40	800-688-3350
Pegasus Intrinsic Value I	0.40	800-688-3350
Zweig Appreciation A	0.50	800-444-2706
Wright Selected Blue Chip Equity	0.51	800-888-9471

Exhibit 17 (Continued)

Fund Name	Risk 3 Yr.	Phone Number
Large Cap Value		
Vontobel U.S. Value	0.35	800-527-9500
Monitor Income-Equity Trust	0.44	800-253-0412
Smith Barney Premium Total Return A	0.44	800-451-2010
Primary Income	0.45	800-443-6544
Smith Barney Premium Total Return B	0.45	800-451-2010
Equity Income		
Capital Income Builder	0.35	800-421-4120
American Century Equity Inc Inv	0.40	800-345-2021
Heartland Value Plus	0.43	800-432-7856
Monitor Income-Equity Trust	0.44	800-253-0412
Smith Barney Premium Total Return A	0.44	800-451-2010
Balanced Funds		
UAM FPA Crescent Institutional	0.24	800-638-7983
Rea-Graham Balanced	0.25	800-433-1998
Norwest Advant Strategic Income I	0.29	800-338-1348
Goldman Sachs Balanced A	0.34	800-526-7384
Evergreen American Retirement Y	0.35	800-343-2898
Funds That Sell Short		
Caldwell & Orkin Market Opportunity	0.33	800-237-7073
Calvert Strategic Growth A	2.35	800-368-2748
Comstock Partners Strategy O	0.72	800-373-9387
Crabbe Huson Special Prim	1.15	800-541-9732
Dreyfus Premier Value A	0.97	800-554-4611
Growth & Income		
Gateway Index Plus	0.29	800-354-6339
T. Rowe Price Capital Appreciation	0.31	800-638-5660
Vontobel U.S. Value	0.35	800-527-9500
T. Rowe Price Dividend Growth	0.39	800-638-5660
Endowments	0.48	415-421-9360

Source: Morningstar.

writing. Names and descriptions of "outstanding examples"—funds that not only are low-risk and offer strong bear repellent, but also have other favorable attributes—are provided in the text below. A few extraordinary performers, such as Michael Price's Mutual Shares, are omitted here because they are closed to new investors.

You'll notice several funds with the same name followed by an A, B, or C. These letters refer to the different loads and fees that fundholders are required to pay; otherwise, you're getting the same portfolio and the same manager.

FUNDS RUN BY FOGIES WHO'VE SEEN THE WORST

Who better to guide your money through a melee than an experienced bear handler? Finding one is a challenge. The longer a bull market lasts, the fewer veterans from the previous bear are left to handle the next bear. The list of active fund managers involved in the routs of 1969–1971 and 1973–1974 grows shorter by the year. Fewer than 500 of today's stock fund were doing business in 1973, and only 36 have retained the same manager.

A couple of fogies are worth mentioning. One is Marty Zweig. Zweig developed a lifelong respect for bears in the early 1970s and has protected his clients' assets from claw marks ever since. His most popular mutual fund, Zweig Strategy Fund, held up well in the bear market of 1990. Other funds in the Zweig universe are designed to outperform in market declines, as Zweig moves into cash to reduce exposure. Zweig Total Return and the Zweig Fund trade on the New York Stock Exchange. Others that can be bought directly from the Zweig organization include Zweig Managed Assets (global stocks and bonds), and Zweig Growth and Income. Telephone (800) 272-2700.

Another is Shelby Davis. The manager of New York Venture and Selected American Shares recently passed the reins to his son, Chris, but Shelby still looks over Chris' shoulder as chief investment officer. Like Zweig, the elder Davis learned about bear markets the hard way, with big losses in the early 1970s. Since that time, the Davises have packed the portfolio with value stocks that sell at low prices compared to their growth rates. This ought to help temper the downside. Telephone (800) 279-0279.

BALANCED FUNDS

A balanced fund owns stocks, bonds, and cash (Treasury bills) in fixed percentages. The manager may change the percentages every so often, but generally, he keeps the same mix.

Outstanding Examples

UAM FPA Crescent. It's not your average balanced fund that combines stodgy stocks and high-grade bonds. Here, manager Steven Romick combines small companies trading at discounts to private market value with lower grade bonds that offer high yields and where credit quality is on the mend. Romick's knack for stock and bond picking has given him a terrific risk score and many happy returns.

~

Carillon Capital. Carillon doesn't make Morningstar's top ten in the risk category, but its score isn't far behind the winners, and Morningstar has called it "the least volatile domestic hybrid fund by nearly every measure." Carillon has produced annual returns of 11 percent since 1990 in spite of a hefty cash position.

"George Clucas is one of the most risk-averse managers in (this group)," says Morningstar. For Clucas, an ideal mix is a two-thirds stocks, a third bonds, and the rest cash, but in recent years, he's been light on the stock part because he thinks they're overvalued.

A small loss in 1990 is Carillon's only loss in this decade. At today's price, it yields 3.8 percent on top of whatever capital gains it can gather. You can reach Carillon at (800) 999-1840.

DIVIDEND-ORIENTED FUNDS (EQUITY INCOME)

For details on the advantages of dividends in a bear market, see page 163. Funds listed in Morningstar's equity income category invest at least 65 percent of their assets in companies that pay dividends.

Outstanding Examples

Heartland Value Plus. This unusual fund buys small stocks selling at discount prices, making it a value play. It's also a dividend play because about 20 percent of the small stocks in this portfolio pay dividends, a rarity in the small-cap arena. The manager boosts yield and adds ballast with corporate bonds. Where else can you find a small cap fund that's fortified with dividends?

~

American Century Equity Income. "A haven for risk-averse investors," says Morningstar. "Although the fund is too young to have been tested in a bear market, its performance in the market's recent rough patches has been encouraging." It lost half as much money as the Dow in a recent 10 percent correction.

American Century is well fortified with utility stocks. The managers are on the lookout for companies that offer higher-than-average yields and lower-than-average price-earnings ratios.

ASSET ALLOCATION FUNDS, ALSO CALLED FLEXIBLE FUNDS

Like balanced funds, these funds own a mix of stocks, bonds, and cash—but the mix can change and often does. In some funds, computers do the allocating; others rely on humans.

Michael Lipper's organization, which tracks fund performance a la Morningstar, has identified flexible funds that held up best in three prominent bear markets: 1981–1982, the crash of 1987, and 1990. A few actually made money. One exceptional fund, IAA Trust, shows up on all three lists. Names and phone numbers appear below.

Exhibit 17 on pages 188–189 is Morningstar's list of low risk flexible funds.

Exhibit 18 Flexible Portfolio (Asset Allocation) Funds

1981–1982 Bear Market

Fund Name	04/30/81– 07/31/82 Total Return	Rank	Phone Number
IAA Trust Asset Allocation	10.98	1	800-245-2100
Merrill Capital	−6.59	2	609-282-2800
Franklin Asset Allocation	−9.17	3	800-342-5236
Stein Roe Balanced	−11.82	4	800-338-2550
Phoenix Strat Allocation	−13.11	5	800-243-4361
General Securities	−13.74	6	800-577-9217

1987 Crash

Fund Name	08/27/87– 10/22/87 Total Return	Rank	Phone Number
Rightime:Blue Chip Fund	0.72	1	800-242-1421
Stagecoach Asset Allocation	0.38	2	800-222-8200
IAA Trust Asset Allocation	−3.79	4	800-245-2100
Strong Asset Allocation	−8.58	5	800-368-1030

1990 Bear Market

Fund Name	07/19/90– 10/11/90 Total Return	Rank	Phone Number
IAA Trust Asset Allocation	0.89	1	800-245-2100
FBL Series	0.80	2	800-247-4170
SCM Portfolio Fund	0.20	3	770-834-5839
Strong Asset Allocation	−1.56	4	800-368-1030
Stagecoach Asset Allocation	−2.58	5	800-222-8200

Source: Lipper Analytical Services, Inc.

Outstanding Examples

Merrill Lynch Asset Income. Started 1994. Keeps roughly 60 percent of assets in bonds, the rest divided between stocks and the money market. Owns some foreign stocks, but most of portfolio is U.S. based. As this book went to press, the fund had an annual yield of 4.3 percent.

~

The Value Line Asset Allocation Fund. It's not in Morningstar's top ten, but the management team has taken a low-risk posture. Since 1993, this fund has kept up with the S&P 500 even while it was weighed down with a large supply of bonds and cash. Managers allocate conservatively: 55 percent or so in stocks, 35 percent bonds, the rest cash. Stock portion is invested in fast-growing small companies with strong earnings and price momentum; bonds and cash reduce the risk of investing in such companies. Lately, portfolio is somewhat bullish with 65 percent of assets in stocks. Telephone: (800) 243-2729.

GROWTH AND INCOME FUNDS

Similar to equity-income funds, except these invest in high-performance growth companies that pay dividends. The dividend component may help moderate the losses in a bear market. In 1973–1974, when pure growth funds lost 46.4 percent on average, the stodgier growth and income funds lost 29.9 percent.

Outstanding Examples

T. Rowe Price Capital Appreciation. Most funds in this category are at least 60 percent invested in stocks, this one keeps more conservative 50 percent stake. The rest of the money is invested in bonds and cash. According to Morningstar, manager Richard Howard's "value orientation" protects clients in down markets, while his relatively low fixed-income exposure prevents the portfolio from becoming too interest-rate sensitive.

~

T. Rowe Price Dividend Growth. Manager William Stromberg recently dumped pricer holdings in favor of mid-cap value names. In a typical move, he sold General Electric shares and bought Trimas, because Trimas offered better earnings growth at half the price. Until recently, this fund kept up with the gains from the S&P 500 at much lower risk.

VALUE FUNDS

Value funds own stocks in companies that carry low price-earnings ratios and that sell at relatively low prices based on the companies' book value. In other words, cheap stocks as compared, say, to stocks in fast-growth companies that carry high price-earnings ratios.

Morningstar divides the value camp into three divisions: funds that buy stocks in large-companies(large cap), mid-sized companies (mid-cap), and small companies (small cap). As mentioned earlier, small cap value funds have held up well in bear markets in the past. It's no surprise, then, that Heartland Value Plus is a low-risk performer in the equity income category. It's also a value fund, and could just as well be included here.

Outstanding Examples

Royce Total Return. Charles Royce runs several low-risk funds, and considers this one the safest. Since it opened for business in 1993, Total Return has suffered one quarterly loss. The portfolio is populated with small-cap stocks that pay dividends, the bear-proofing formula that's worked in the past. A small company that pays a dividend is already in decent financial shape, or else it couldn't afford the largess. By picking stocks of this type, Royce avoids more dubious prospects.

Total Return has a large cash stake at present, because the fund recently merged with another Royce product. This cash stake adds to the bear protection.

~

Vonotobel U.S. Value. This is a large-cap version of Royce's fund. The manager, Ed Walczak, follows a disciplined routine and sells stocks when they reach target prices, so he won't be caught holding overpriced merchandise in a sell off. He keeps a cash stake of 20 percent or more; recently, he's upped the cash to 35 percent. He's a buyer of strong franchises at cheap prices, which led him to the prosperous financial sector in the mid-1990s.

~

American Century Equity Income. Managers pick companies with yields in the top third of the equity universe and price-earnings multiples in the bottom third. They use convertible bonds to add stability. Morningstar notes: "Although this fund is too young to have been tested in a bear market, its performance in the market's recent rough patches has been encouraging."

UTILITIES

These funds invest in electric, gas, and telephone companies. Most utilities pay a more generous dividend than the average company does, which helps prop up their stocks in bear markets.

Outstanding Example

MFS Utilities A. Its five-year returns top the Morningstar charts, and its risk scores are the lowest in the category. Fund manager

Maura Shaughnessy uses bonds to keep the yield in line with other utility funds; invests in utilities in emerging markets and small-cap natural gas producers to add pizzazz.

CONTRARIAN FUNDS

Eleven mutual funds with the word "contrarian" in their name, plus one "contrafund" show up on the Morningstar screen. They hold about $2 billion in assets combined. Just because they call themselves contrarian doesn't mean their portfolios have anything contrary in common.

Five of these eleven contrarian funds look and act like the typical "value" fund, according to Morningstar. They may be contrarian to the extent value stocks are less popular than growth stocks, and value stocks hold up relatively well in bear markets. (Morningstar says these funds performed in line with the value group in two recent corrections.) But it doesn't mean they're contrarian the way Robertson Stephens Contrarian is contrarian.

That eccentric vehicle is parked in San Francisco and managed by globe-trotting stockpicker Paul Stephens. Although Stephens doesn't describe himself as a bear, a lifesized replica of one sits in his office. He feeds his bearishness with a large short position—mostly technology stocks—that involves about 25 percent of the fund's assets. The balance is invested in natural resource companies, gold mining in particular.

After producing excellent gains in 1995–1996, Stephens' fund was thwarted with double-digit losses in 1997 when gold had a bear market and Silicon Valley didn't, exactly the reverse of what the fund was designed to handle. Nevertheless, if you believe what comes out of a mine will prove more valuable than what comes out of the minds of nerds in Silicon Valley, Stephen's fund is a convenient way to take advantage.

Outstanding Example

One Fund Global. Manager Jean-Marie Eveillard rarely strays from the long side; this fund also falls in the value category. Eveillard packs the portfolio with commodity-related companies, and bypasses the standard manufacturing companies. Stocks comprise 70 percent of holdings, divided 50/50 between foreign and domestic. The balance is deployed in cash and bonds.

FUNDS THAT SELL SHORT

Only a tiny percentage of mutual funds takes a "short position" and bets against stocks. Thus, it's a rare fund that will turn debacle into profit, or sell short on a less ambitious scale where the proceeds can offset losses in the rest of the portfolio. This lack of short selling is part cultural. Most managers are eternally bullish, as their career advancement depends on outbulling their peers.

Short-selling is a volatile business, which explains why the risk scores are all over the map.

Outstanding Examples

Caldwell & Orkin Market Opportunity. A computer model helps the manager divide the portfolio among domestic and foreign stocks and high-quality corporate debt. Manager also takes short positions and has positioned fund to weather a bear market. Had an outstanding year in 1996.

Four short-selling funds with higher risk scores have unusual features that are worth mentioning:

- *Crabbe Huson Special—Primary Shares.* Played short side of technology stocks in 1995 and 1996, which hurt results. Recently buying health care stocks at depressed prices. Manager a contrarian investor with an admirable 10-year record.

- *The Prudent Bear Fund.* This one doesn't make the first-tier of funds covered by Morningstar, and its $60 million in assets puts it in the pipsqueak category, but it's the only mutual fund where shorting individual stocks is the primary purpose. For every $100 invested in the portfolio, $65 ends up on the short side, $10 on the long side, $5 or so in stock options, and the rest in cash.

    Prudent Bear was the number one performer among 3,703 funds tracked by Morningstar during the October 1997 selloff. On the day the Dow was down 554 points, Prudent Bear was up 10.9 percent. It lost money in 1996 and again in 1997, but less than one might have expected, given the gains in the market.

    In bearish circumstances, Prudent Bear will be a sure winner. "People who try to protect their assets by keeping 40 percent of the portfolio in bonds or cash," manager David Tice argues, "might do better to keep 80 percent in stocks and 20 percent in a fund that sells short. That way, they have more money at work on the upside when stocks are rising, and a more effective hedge on the downside when they are falling."

    A $2,000 minimum investment gets you into the fund. For more details, call 1-888-PRUBEAR.

- *Rydex Ursa.* With a name like that, how could it be bullish? Based in Bethesda, Maryland, Rydex Ursa has one purpose in life: it plays the short side of the S&P 500 index "futures" to the maximum extent possible. It ends each day 100 percent short. On a bad day, week, or year for stocks, Rydex Ursa has a good day, week or year.

    Ursa was launched in 1994 and ran into a bear market of its own: three down years in a row. The result would have been worse except the Treasury bills Ursa holds as collateral brought in some much-needed income. You wouldn't be happy investing in Ursa unless you were convinced the bears were about to gain the advantage, but in that case, your money would be riding on them. Telephone: (800) 820-0888.

- *Lindner Bulwark.* A not-so-distant cousin of Robertson Stephens Contrarian, described above. Run by a managerial troika, Bulwark invests in "microcaps" (very small companies), several of which are involved in mining. On the short side, it buys put options and bets against a variety of likely stories. Lately, its biggest investment (45 percent) is cash. "Only doomsday prophets would find this portfolio useful," says Morningstar. On any inflationary doomsday, it will shine. Telephone: (314) 727-5305.

HEDGE FUNDS

Hedge funds can make bets in any direction by going long or short, or a little of each. They aren't limited to stocks. They can own or disown currencies, commodities, domestic debt, foreign debt, or anything that trades on any exchange worldwide. No opportunity eludes them, and no market is too big.

Hedge funds aren't mutual funds, because they aren't publicly traded. They're limited partnerships, which exempts them from certain SEC restrictions and regulations that apply to mutual funds. For instance, they can go 100 percent short if the managers are so inclined.

Hedge funds often require daunting initial investments ($1 million or more; often, as much as $5 million). To date, only a fat cat could afford to join one. However, recent changes in regulation allow hedge funds to expand their customer base, which may cause some of them to relax the entrance requirements. That would make them accessible to leaner cats.

The hedge fund population now stands at 4,700, according to the Van advisory service in Nashville. It's no secret why the funds are popular with the proprietors. The proprietors take home 20 percent of the profits, an incentive that far surpasses the 1 to 2 percent management fee collected annually by proprietors of mutual funds.

That's how hedge funds made George Soros a billionaire. He raises giant sums, makes giant profits, and he and his staff get 20 percent of the take. During 1995, in a typical example, Soros's funds made $4 billion from hedging, outgaining Merrill Lynch and its 40,000 employees worldwide. In the first half of 1997, Soros's $3.6 billion Quota Fund was up 50 percent; his $8.5 billion Quantum Fund was up 14 percent.

Are Quantum fundholders jealous of Quota fundholders? Jealous or not, Soros's take of the two funds' profits was $598 million—for six months. Imagine if Fidelity Magellan was a hedge fund. Magellan generated approximately $10 billion in capital gains through December 1997. A 20 percent take-home on those profits would put $2 billion in Fidelity's pockets.

Such stories cause mutual fund managers to wonder: "Why don't I start one of those?" Many have, including former Magellan manager Jeff Vinik. Some managers are bi-fundal and run mutuals as well as hedge funds. Marty Zweig, for instance, has several mutual funds (open to small and large investors but primarily appealing to the former) and three hedge funds. This is common practice on Wall Street today.

From the client's point of view, hedge funds are attractive because they can prosper in good markets and bad. Recently, they've proved they can prosper in the good ones, but the question remains: What chance do they have to prosper in the bad? The vast majority of hedge funds have played the long side on U.S. stocks in recent years—fully invested and then some—because they borrow money to augment their positions. In other words, the hedge funds aren't hedged.

Harry Strunk, a Palm Beach investment adviser who connects wealthy clients to short sellers and hedgers who are hedged, has a hard time finding the latter. "I ask if they have any short positions," says Strunk. "Most don't."

The record of hedge funds in recent market declines proves they aren't hedged. 1994 was a down year for stocks and for most hedge funds, which lost money in spite of their ability to protect the portfolio with futures, options, and short sales. July 1996 was a down month for stocks, and two-thirds of the hedge funds tracked by an outfit called Managed Account Reports reported losses.

Lois Peltz, a spokesperson for that organization, told *Barron's:* "It turns out a good number of long-only managers were calling themselves hedge funds to get the great incentive fees. A lot of them got caught unhedged."

According to Barton Biggs at Morgan Stanley, who recently checked himself into the bears' camp, hedge fund performance in the Ursa Major of 1973–1974 was far from enriching. Biggs stumbled across a list of hedge funds in an article from an old (May 1971) *Fortune* magazine. Hedge funds were in vogue; yet, at bear's end, most of the names from the 1971 article were defunct.

The best thing you can say about hedge funds that survived Ursa Major is: They did no worse than the normal aggressive mutual fund—that is, they lost a lot of money. None of the survivors from that period has a hedge fund today. Michael Steinhardt stayed in business the longest, but he closed his shop in 1995.

Biggs tells the story of a successful hedge fund manager who bought a new house in Greenwich, Connecticut, while stocks were rising and new money was pouring into the office. When stocks retreated, this manager did the same: He shut himself in his new bedroom. His wife begged him to come out, and his office pals advised him that his behavior was upsetting the limited partners. Still he refused to budge. Eventually, his pals closed the fund, and his wife sold the house out from under him and moved to Wyoming, never to be heard from again.

"Are things different now?" Biggs wonders. "Will hedge funds as a class make money in the next bear market? I don't know, but I doubt it. So far the results don't seem very encouraging."

Short-selling purists like Bill Fleckenstein, in Seattle, argue that unhedged hedge funds will have a hard time preserving capital in a violent decline. "People are deluding themselves," says Fleckenstein, "if they think their hedge fund manager can turn around and go short during a market drop, especially a quick one. They're also deluding themselves if they think they can exit the market by calling 1-800-GETMEOUT. When the great gong goes off, you're either going to be there [short] or you ain't getting there, because you've got to be positioned ahead of time."

If you're in a hedge fund or you're thinking about investing in one, find out: (1) how the fund has fared in drops in the market to date; (2) whether the manager has ever taken a short or hedged position, and if not, why not; and (3) what steps the manager plans to take in the next calamity.

PART SEVEN

~

WINNING
FROM LOSING

THE SHORT SALE
MADE SIMPLE

SHORT SELLING GOES BACK thousands of years to the ancient grain markets, but only recently have the financial whizbangs been provided with a vast array of short selling opportunities. Today, you can short entire stock markets, or any number of individual stocks or stock indexes.

Most investors will be happy enough to limit their losses in a bear market, but more aggressive types will try to profit from calamity. How do you win when others are losing? You sell short. You borrow somebody else's stock and sell it at today's high prices, then replace what you borrowed with stock you buy at tomorrow's lower prices. You're selling high and buying low.

Discussions of short selling often begin with a quote from Daniel Drew that sounds like a Burma Shave commercial from the 1950s: "He who sells what isn't his'n, must give it back or go to prison." It's hard to explain the popularity of this ditty. It gives the wrong impression and makes the practitioners out to be criminals, even though the poet was a chronic short seller himself.

Although it's legal in most countries, short selling is vastly confusing to most investors, and 350 years of lengthy explanations in dozens of languages have added little clarification. No doubt more people would be interested in selling short to make a profit in bear markets if they understood the mechanics.

Imagine this situation. Your husband (or wife, squeeze, friend, relative, or neighbor) invites you into the garage to see the new $799 Toro riding mower he purchased at the local garden store. You suspect he overpaid for this machine; he overpays for everything. Your suspicion is confirmed when you check the paper and find an ad for the identical Toro offered at Home Depot for $599.

You think about mentioning this $200 difference, but there's no point in bruising your husband's ego. Instead, you hatch a plan to "short" the lawnmower and recover the $200 he overpaid. As soon as he leaves the house for work, you roll the machine into the family pickup truck and return it to the garden store for a full $799 refund. This is leg one of a typical short sale: receiving money for merchandise that belongs to somebody else.

Refund in hand, you drive to Home Depot and buy the identical Toro for $599. You load it onto the truck, transport it back to the house, remove the tags, and park it in the same spot in the garage where your husband left the original. This exchange hasn't cost your husband anything, but you're $200 richer for it. Whether you share the proceeds or treat yourself to two rounds of golf or a day at the spa, you've made an easy profit.

Take this scenario one step further. Imagine that your husband tells you he bought 1,000 shares of Toro stock, which trades on the New York Stock Exchange, for $10 per share. Checking a financial Website on the Internet, you discover that fifteen out of fifteen analysts who follow the company think Toro is overpriced at $10. You think about sharing this news with your husband, but there's no point to your bruising his ego. So you call your broker (assuming you're a two-broker couple) and instruct her to short 1,000 shares.

This requires no effort on your part, and hardly any on the part of your broker. She borrows the 1,000 shares from another customer—it could be from your husband, but he'll never know it, just as he never knew you pulled a switcheroo on his lawnmower. His brokerage statement will continue to show 1,000 shares of Toro resting comfortably in his account, with no mention that the shares are involved in a short sale. Every day on Wall Street, millions of shares are lent to short sellers without the owners' being aware of it.

Your broker takes the borrowed shares and sells them at the current price—let's say it's still $10 apiece. The proceeds from this sale (1,000 shares times $10 equals $10,000) are credited to your account. You sit on this cash and wait for the stock price to drop. Let's assume the market obliges. Six months later, Toro stock is trading for $5 a share. You decide to take advantage of this markdown and close out your short position.

You call your broker and instruct her to buy 1,000 shares at $5 apiece (this costs you $5,000) to replace the 1,000 shares you borrowed six months earlier and sold for $10 apiece. This leaves you with a $5,000 profit, minus commissions and carrying charges.

On paper, your husband has lost $5,000 on his Toro investment, but you've made up for it with your timely short sale.

Short sellers come in all varieties. Some specialize in small stocks; others, in larger ones; some use leverage, others don't; "theme players" bet against hot industries; "value players" bet against overpriced issues; "terminal shorts" bet against fraudulent management and flawed products that will put companies out of business.

If short selling had a warning label, it would read:

SHORT SELLING IS REWARDING ON OCCASION. IT CAN BE HABIT-FORMING AND POTENTIALLY RUINOUS TO WEALTH.

In 200 years of American investing, not a single short seller stands in the winner's circle to rub wallets with Astor, Vanderbilt, Rockefeller,

Carnegie, Buffett, or Gates. Two of the major players from the 1920s—Bernard Baruch and Joseph P. (Joe) Kennedy—died rich, but only because Baruch gave up shorting for politics, and Kennedy for rum running and politics.

Other major players (there weren't many) came to a sad end when their talent for losing great sums proved greater than their talent for making them. The list includes: Jacob Little, a short-selling bon vivant from the 1830s who had little to show for it twenty years later; Daniel Drew, a sneaky short seller who nearly brought down the mighty Cornelius Vanderbilt but died insolvent and unnoticed in 1879; Jesse Livermore, a high-volume short seller whom banker J. P. Morgan saw as a threat to put America out of business. Livermore shorted himself with a bullet to the head in the men's room of the Sherry-Netherland Hotel in New York in 1940. He left an estate worth less than $10,000 and a note to his wife: "My life has been a failure."*

The most celebrated short sellers of the recent era, Jim Chanos and the Feshbach brothers (see "Bears' Hall of Fame"), made a profitable run until their luck ran out and their clients did the same. The Feshbachs lost their billion-dollar bankroll and their corporate jet ("Air Bear") and gave up shorting except for their own account, which isn't what it used to be. Chanos lost a chunk of his half-billion-dollar bankroll, but managed to stay active in the shorting business, a triumph in itself. Lately he's attracted new clients.

There are three main reasons why selling short has foiled top practitioners:

1. Stock prices rise in the long run, a big problem when you're betting against them.
2. A stock you're sure will go down goes up instead. It happens all the time. You come across a company where the CEO is indicted, the accounting firm has defected, and a big bank loan

---

* Tom Shachtman, *The Day America Crashed* (New York: G. P. Putnam's Sons, 1979).

is in default. Then the company reports "disappointing results" (translation: huge losses). You short the stock at $20 ex-
pecting it to hit zero, and it doubles to $40. What gives?
Optimistic investors are looking on the bright side and buying the stock.

3. You get scared out of your best ideas. With every uptick in the
stock, your losses mount. That puts you in the same stew as a
poker player in a high-stakes game. You're sitting on three kings
while a guy across the table bets the limit. It takes an ample supply of courage and chips to see the bet. The short seller often
runs out of both, and folds a winning hand.

The 1990s have taught professionals like Chanos and the Feshbachs
an expensive lesson they're willing to share for free. Year in and year
out, short selling is a tricky business. Still, there are various ways to
use the technique in a bear market, to protect your portfolio by balancing losses with gains. This gives you a bear market insurance policy. Here are the pluses and minuses of each protection method.

Shorting the Individual Stock

To provide useful information on how to short individual stocks is beyond the scope of this book. A little knowledge can be a costly thing, especially in short selling. The amateur who seeks advice puts himself in
the same position as the bloke in the auto showroom who inquires about
the price of the Rolls Royce: "If you have to ask, you can't afford it."

Shorting a Stock Index, Such as the S&P 500

Instead of betting against a specific company, you're betting against
an entire index; if the index is the S&P 500, your money is riding on
the decline of 500 different stocks. This puts you in the "futures

market," which requires a hefty cash outlay and can produce profits or losses far beyond the actual amount invested. This author learned this the hard way in 1996, when he "shorted" a single S&P futures contract and the S&P didn't cooperate. After the first week, he found himself $20,000 poorer. His wife insisted on closing out the position, or he would have lost five times that amount in two months. He was glad she put her foot down.

A tamer alternative to shorting a stock index "future" is shorting the S&P Depository Receipts (symbol: SPY) that trade on the American Stock Exchange. SPY is the entire S&P 500 rolled into one stock: bulls can buy it, bears can short it. Shorting SPY has two main advantages over shorting S&P futures: (1) it's cheaper and (2) if you're wrong, your mistake isn't compounded by 15–1 leverage.

BUYING A "PUT OPTION" ON A STOCK INDEX SUCH AS THE S&P 500

Again, you're betting against an entire index—if it's the S&P 500, you're opposing 500 companies at once. However, the put option has an important safety feature: you can lose only the amount you invest. It also has a disadvantage: the expiration date. The typical put option is valid for only a few weeks. Once it expires, to renew the wager you must buy another put. Continuous buying of puts while you wait for stocks to go down is an expensive proposition.

One way to avoid this problem is to buy long-term puts—called LEAPS—that don't expire for a year, although you may end up paying a big premium for the privilege.

HIRING A PROFESSIONAL

You can avoid all the aforementioned complications by hiring a professional short selling manager, giving him or her some money, and hoping for the worst. There's no point in doing this unless you have a sizable portfolio to protect. Most "short only" managers operate hedge funds that require a $1 million to $5 million minimum investment. Some operate smaller partnerships on the side ($250,000 minimum), but again, you'd have to have several million invested on the long side before you'd want to spend $250,000 on an insurance policy.

Harry Strunk, of Palm Beach, Florida (561-659-9599), can tell you whom to hire. After inheriting an ample lump sum from his family's publishing business, Strunk stumbled into a new career: helping other wealthy families invest their lump sums. He set up shop in a PaineWebber office in Palm Beach, where wealthy families are as prevalent as golf carts.

"When people have already made a fortune," Strunk says, "their main interest is in protecting it. They've done a lot of thinking and strategizing about how to prepare for bear markets."

One of his earliest clients, an investor from Omaha (not the investor you're thinking of), asked Strunk to compile a list of successful short sellers. Finding names was hard enough; getting them to agree to an interview was even harder. Money managers on the long side rarely miss a chance to trumpet their services to potential clients, but short sellers refused to take Strunk's calls. "It's a very secretive bunch," he says. "Which is no wonder, considering how the system is stacked against them."

Strunk started tracking short-selling managers in 1985. Of the original twenty-six practitioners he identified, only sixteen are investing on the short side today. The others went out of business or turned themselves into hedge funds.

One out of ten wealthy families in Strunk's Rolodex used short sellers as portfolio insurance, but half of those have given up the short side after several years of nagging losses.

WHERE ARE THE SHORT SELLERS' YACHTS?

Selling short, it's not unAmerican.
Marty Zweig

We had no short seller as a speaker, because none has a pair of shoes to wear today.
Jim Grant, at his annual conference, April 1997

PROFESSIONAL SHORT SELLERS don't start out betting against their Little League teams, rooting for earthquakes and plane crashes, or doubting the tooth fairy at an early age. They don't fly the British flag on the Fourth of July, wear black at weddings and white at funerals, or douse apple pie with tabasco sauce.

Most have routine childhoods, attend college, graduate from business school, and arrive on Wall Street expecting to live a normal life as analysts or fund managers. Then, for some unknown reason, they get bored with touting stocks they hope will go up. They stumble onto a company that's deep in hock and a poor bet to succeed, and they write a sell recommendation. This gets them excited. The next thing you know, they're selling the stock short. When the price drops, they make a quick profit. Now, they're hooked.

Ignoring the strong and healthy companies they might recommend to clients, they search for more losers with fatal flaws. The stream of negative reports coming from their offices puts them in a bad aura with their bosses, who are catching flak from companies that dislike being downgraded and put on a sell list.

The bosses encourage, cajole, and command staff pessimists to think positive, play the game, and write buy recommendations like everybody else. But budding short sellers can't help themselves. They continue to accentuate the negative until they're forced out of the firm that hired them and start their own "boutique," where they can hector the hokum and sell short at will.

Known short sellers suffer the same reputation as the detested bat. They're reviled as odious pests, smudges on the walls of Wall Street, pecuniary vampires who suck profit out of healthy stocks until those stocks are too weak to stand up in the market. Their friends are vastly outnumbered by their foes, who'd gladly bludgeon them with nine irons, pepper-spray their martinis, or put their monitors out if they could get away with it. No wonder typical short sellers keep a low profile and avoid the camera, the microphone, and the notebook.

They're accused of selling their country short as well as their stocks, even though admitted short seller Joe Kennedy fathered a president; and Bernard Baruch, another notorious practitioner, was sidekick to President Roosevelt. Baruch and Kennedy were Democrats, as short sellers tend to be; the rest of Wall Street is staunchly GOP. If Wall Street had ever become staunchly Democratic, these Wrong Way Corrigans no doubt would have converted to the GOP. Under either banner, they don't have much use for big government. Bill McGarr, a.k.a. McBear, a noted short seller and libertarian, explains:

"There's a big difference between the two parties. The Republicans want to take away all your freedom. The Democrats want to take away all your money."

Short sellers are an oppressed minority whom nobody seems to care about. Because they may profit from the misfortunes of others, they are accused of causing the misfortunes and end up in the same category as arsonists who sell fire insurance. Short sellers were blamed for the Crash of 1929, though detailed studies later proved them innocent. They faced Senatorial inquisition, and the president at the time (Hoover) was convinced a bearish conspiracy had sunk the market. Cooler heads observed that the amount of stock sold short in 1929—one-eighth of one percent of all shares outstanding—could hardly sink a rowboat.

When an individual stock has its own bear market, short sellers take the blame. The company calls a press conference and accuses the "short interest" of putting out false rumors to scare investors into dumping the stock. In some cases, these accusations have validity, but, as a rule, short sellers are no more guilty of hyping a stock down than management is of hyping a stock up. Turning bears into scapegoats is a company's way of diverting attention from its internal problems, the real cause of the stock's poor performance.

"It's ludicrous—the business establishment wants protection against short sellers," sniffs Harry Strunk, a conduit between short sellers and wealthy investors. "Especially when there are 1,000 mutual funds on the long side for every fund that's primarily short; 100 buy recommendations on Wall Street for every sell recommendation; and all the prominent short sellers have been put out of business in the latest bull market. If anything, the short sellers need protection from the bulls."

Other oppressed groups find a friend in government, but government is the short sellers' sworn enemy. On numerous occasions, the practice has been banned in England, France, Japan, the United

States, and other countries with stock exchanges, usually at the end of a massive selloff when the damage already is done. Malaysia is the latest example: the currency collapsed, short sellers were fingered as culprits, and the leader there put the kibosh on them. He made short-selling a crime, although if tradition holds, eventually he'll learn that short sellers serve a useful function and the practice will be decriminalized.

Even where short selling is permitted (as it is in most countries today), it's restricted. On the long side of the market, it's a free country. You can buy a stock anytime, at whatever price consenting adults consent to. But you can't short a stock anytime. You must wait for an "uptick," when the price is on the rise. The uptick rule deprives pessimists of their best chance to make a profit—when prices go into free fall, as they did in the Crash of 1987. Unless you were short going into that decline, you couldn't take advantage. There weren't any upticks.

Short sellers put up with this constraint because they lack the power to have it removed. But imagine how bulls would react if the SEC ruled you could only buy stocks on a downtick. Wall Street would go on strike. Ticker-tape-burning ceremonies would be held outside SEC headquarters, and a Million-Investor March would clog the streets.

Bullish analysts can flog a stock and keep their jobs even if they're wrong and the company falters. Bearish analysts can pan a stock and take flak from their superiors if they're right and the company falters. Too many negative reports, even prescient ones, can spoil a career. "I find that negative research on a company is usually superior to positive research," says Marty Zweig. Yet bullish reports outnumber bearish reports by a wide margin.

Bullish fund managers meet over lunch or swap stock picks on the phone and during coffee breaks at conferences, but nobody accuses them of conspiring to drive stock prices up. Get two short sellers in an elevator and it's an automatic conspiracy to drive prices down.

When it comes to the IRS share of any profit, bulls are taxed plenty, but bears get taxed more. Hold a stock on the long side for more than a year, and you get a break on the capital gains tax when you sell it. Hold a short position for a year, 100 years, or 1,000 years, and you pay the maximum short-term rate.

Until recently, you could defer capital gains through a maneuver called "shorting against the box." The details would take at least six paragraphs to explain, but there's no point wasting time on this, because the government has nixed shorting against the box, adding to the long list of short selling no-nos.

Meanwhile, under the "short-short rule," a mutual fund couldn't earn more than 30 percent of its annual income from stocks held less than three months. Any fund that made a quick buck from its limited ability to sell short into a crash would flunk the "short-short" test and face a phenomenal tax bill: 35 percent of all income and capital gains for the entire year. (Elaine Garzarelli's fund was hit with this tax in the late 1980s.) The short-short restriction was lifted in 1997, making it a bit easier for funds to play defense with this tool.

In sum, short sellers get short shrift, in spite of the useful public service they perform: putting a lid on prices in an exuberant market, and putting a floor under prices in a downtrodden one. In the former instance, a short seller who publicizes the defects of an overrated company can scare off would-be investors, thereby depressing the price, which helps buyers get better value for their money.

In the latter instance, the short sellers come to the rescue via the "buoyant effect," as described by Phil Carret: "Near the bottom of a market, when pessimism has triumphed and nobody wants to buy stocks, the only buyers are short sellers covering their positions. Without them, the people who want to unload stocks would have nobody to sell to."

The famous rally in stocks at the end of 1929 may well have resulted from short sellers' covering their positions. This rally gave other investors a chance to escape at a favorable price, a fact that eluded the vigilantes of the day. They accused Sell 'Em Ben Smith and other bearish investors of causing the crash, ignoring the silly bulls who overpaid for the merchandise.

If short selling were more widespread and various obstacles were removed, we might see more happy faces during bear markets. There'd be more new buyers for the mansions put up for sale at Newport and Palm Beach; new customers for yachts, limousines, minks, and caviar; new faces on the luxury liners and in the posh restaurants now short of clientele. That a gang of enriched bears could revive the economy and spare it from recession or depression is doubtful, but surely they could give a boost to the upscale retailers and other purveyors of high-priced goods and services. That is, if their bodyguards could protect them from the lynch mob.

PART EIGHT

~

BEAR'S GAZETTE

HALL OF FAME

JIM GRANT

PROMINENT BEAR WHO constantly reminds his followers: A Dow that goes up must come down. Writes, edits, publishes notorious newsletter: *Grant's Interest Rate Observer*. Intellectual refuge for gold bugs, short sellers, hedgers, bondholders—people who refused to hitch their bankrolls to stocks during the irrational exuberance.

Conference room contains rolltop desk, manual typewriter, fireplace with wastebasket deployed in spot where fire would normally be lit. Room also contains plastic blow-up: copy of Munch's *Portrait of a Scream*, wearing a surgical mask. To stifle screams on up days in stocks? At a previous address, Grant kept a lifesize stuffed teddy bear on display.

A slim 6'5", Grant bears no resemblance to stuffed teddy. Intense, bemused—all at once. Has gawky lope of Ichabod Crane; more closely resembles Savanarola, Florentine monk who poohpooed Medici bull market of 1400s. On Savanarola's orders, wealthy Florentines threw prized possessions onto original bonfire of the vanities. Savanarola tried to save his flock from God's wrath; Grant tries to save his from decline in S&P 500.

Even in bull market, Grant makes occasional prescient call. Was right about collapse of junk bonds and Drexel Burnham Lambert. Right about real estate disasters in Texas, New England, and California. Right about misadventures of Donald Trump and Reichmann brothers. Right about Citicorp and banking sector choking on their own bad loans. Wrong to mortgage his house and bet against bank stocks in 1989–1990, just in time for Fed to lower interest rates and bail out bankers. "The liquidity I'd built for myself vanished," Grant said of that unrewarding episode.

While ranks of bearish newsletters have thinned considerably, Grant's has prospered. Survives on provocative opinion, sassy prose. Entertains loyal base of paid-up subscribers with steady stream of witty commentary on dull subjects (subprime lending rates, for instance).

Recently expanded with *Asia Observer*, *Municipal Bond Observer* on top of original newsletter. Has proven literate bear can turn bull market into cash cow.

BERNARD BARUCH

Along with "Rockefeller," "Morgan," "Carnegie," "Vanderbilt," "Astor," "Buffett," and "Gates," name "Baruch" synonymous with "rich person." Only millionaire of consequence who sold short and stayed rich. Hooted down by press, politicians. Wrote pamphlet, *Short Sales and Manipulation of Securities*, to convince public he wasn't a Benedict Arnold or Satan's moneybags. Said short sellers performed a useful public service: "keeping people from buying securities at extraordinary high prices." Convinced almost nobody.

Shorted Radio Corporation of America before Crash of 1929, gained reputation as genius who profited from Crash. In fact, Baruch lost money in Crash, like everybody else. Showed forecasting ineptitude in cheery telegram sent to Winston Churchill, in November 1929: "Financial storm definitely passed."

Turned from stocks to politics. Prominent adviser to Democrats Roosevelt and Truman. Irked Wall Street Republicans.

JOE KENNEDY

Father to a President (assassinated), a would-be President (assassinated), and another would-be President (never nominated). Got his start on Wall Street, playing tricks on Yellow Cab. Hired to defend that company from short sellers, ended up shorting the stock himself. Used proceeds to acquire large portfolio on the long side. Thought market was doomed when shoeshine man gave him a stock tip. Sold portfolio pre-Crash; shoeshine man saved him millions. Rumored to have made extra $15 million on the short side of the rout. Biographer disputes story.

ALBERT WIGGIN

President of Chase Bank, known as most "loved banker on Wall Street." Pulled fast one, shorting Chase stock, betting against own firm, in September 1929. Let bet ride into December for $4 million profit. Financed bet with Chase bank loan; similar to baseball manager betting against team with loan from boss. Retired with large Chase pension plus hefty bonus for meritorious service. Ploy undiscovered.

"MARTY MARTINO"

Martino not real name. Alias used here to protect perpetrator from jealous admirers. If you make money in bear market, don't tell the neighbors. In 1987, pulled off most profitable short trade in Wall Street history.

A rising briefcase in his thirties, Martino occupied mid-level perch in Morgan Stanley's equity derivatives department. This included "portfolio insurance," popular practice of protecting against downside with stock index futures. Martino noticed "commonality" between 1987 and 1929: stocks overvalued, "massive draining of liquidity," bonds going down, "technical pattern that mirrored 1929."

Stocks kept going up because "everybody said the Japanese would take them off our hands, at even higher prices."

Unlike bullish colleagues, saw dim future for stock index futures. Doubted "portfolio insurance" would work as advertised. Thought the opposite: portfolio insurance would lead to crash. Searched for way to turn calamity to advantage.

Found inexpensive "put options," selling for six cents apiece. Puts are a wager stocks will go down. Martino's were "out of money" puts—they only paid off if stocks went way down. Got clearance from Morgan Stanley to buy put options for himself, for his mother, for few interested clients, for Morgan Stanley itself. Went to trading desk to complete transaction, heard trader laugh at this "stupid investment." For ten days, Martino added to stupid position, thousands and thousands of six-cent puts.

As stocks toppled, six-cent puts were worth 30 cents. Martino and clients made five times investment in short order. Some clients took profits, Martino hung on. Later in October, puts were worth $1, $5, $10, and more clients took profits. Martino hung on, by now vastly enriched. Also held on for his mother's retirement account.

Martino and mother stubbornly held onto thousands of puts going into Black Monday. Dow dropped 500 points, 22 percent in time it takes to see triple feature. Nearly $1 trillion of investor wealth disappeared; Martino's wealth, mother's wealth expanded by undisclosed millions thanks to puts. Exact amount Martino refuses to reveal; even under an alias protection. Here's a hint of how much he made: thousands of six-cent puts were worth $53 apiece when he sold them.

That Monday night, many investors stayed awake counting losses. Martino stayed awake counting gains, worrying whether parties who owed him millions had ability to pay. (In options trading, one person's profit is another person's loss.) Financial system survived, losers paid, Martino quit job for Idaho ski resort. Lives happily ever with children, first wife. "I loved Wall Street and Morgan Stanley," he says. "But my father died when I was young, and I wanted to watch my kids grow up." Thanks to put options, Martino has.

$53 return on six-cent investment in one month is same as $848 return on $1 investment, or 10,176 percent compounded annually. Contemplating this result from Idaho, Martino wonders: "Why me?" He's happy but not complacent. "You're only as good," he says, "as your next trade."

ROBERT PRECHTER

Steadfast bear since late 1980s. Built forecasting system on theory of ingenious crank, R. N. Elliott. Elliott reduced wars, plagues, conquests, migrations, other significant human events to series of waves. Prechter took Elliott's waves, applied them to bonds, commodities, stocks. Made numerous correct calls.

In 1980, called halt to 13-year bull market in gold. Gold bulls called Prechter crazy. They were wrong. In 1982, at Dow 900, Prechter foretold rise to Dow 3,900. Brokers, analysts, strategists, investors large and small called him crazy. No way Dow would hit 3,900 in their children's lifetimes, let alone in theirs, they said. Dow topped 3,900 in 1995.

"If our ongoing analysis is correct," Prechter wrote, "the current environment is providing a once-in-a-lifetime money-making opportunity." It did.

In mid-1987, Prechter picked Dow 2,700 as a temporary top. Market obliged, crashed in October. Economy ignored fatal diagnosis, rallied, took stocks with it. Prechter out of sync and out of favor since. From 1987 to 1997, he missed a triple, but he caught the triple from 1982 to 1987. Most investors missed that.

People who couldn't imagine Dow rising to 3,900, as Prechter predicted in 1982, now think Dow 8,000 is sensible level and can't imagine it falling far below 3,900, where Prechter says it's headed. Bullish when public was exceedingly bearish; now bearish when public is exceedingly bearish. Colleagues from Garzarelli to Granville have thrown in the growl.

Ten years with no sign of undertow hasn't shaken Prechter's faith in Elliott's waves, even if others see them as hogwash. "Today, stocks are popular because they WERE good investments," says Prechter, "not because they ARE good investments. A bear market will correct the misimpression."

EDSON GOULD

Student of stock charts, Dixieland music, crowd psychology. Worked in research department at Moody's. Launched market-timing newsletter in early 1960s. Predicted Dow would rise 400 points in 1962. It did. Predicted eight years of trouble for stocks, starting in 1966. Stocks had trouble. Called for 100-point rise in Dow in 1972. Dow rose from 900 to 1,040. Three days later, at Dow 1,070, predicted major bear market. Dow dropped in half.

Based market calls on investor sentiment. Relied on "Senti-Meter"—price of stocks divided by their dividends—to pick tops and bottoms. Devised "three steps and a stumble" theory—that stocks fall after Federal Reserve raises rates three times. Three steps and a stumble gained widespread popularity; later, Gould himself admitted it hadn't worked too well.

In 1979, with Dow at 850 and investors gloomy, predicted Dow would hit 3,000 in ten years. Ten years and eight months later, Dow peaked at 2,999.75. Gould wasn't around to see it. Died in 1983, at age 81.

JOE GRANVILLE

Longest-running bear on record: 1982–1996; 14 years and 168 *Granville Reports* newsletters, with hardly a bullish forecast among them. Saw trouble just around the corner—as Dow rose tenfold through two Reagans, one Bush, and a Clinton and a half. Still has subscribers. Convinced by market action on July 16, 1996, the bull was no fluke. Issued belated buy signal.

Mother an heiress; grandfather a well-known physicist. Economics major at Duke. Studied waves and cycles. In World War II, served in South Pacific, manning decoding machine, playing poker and piano. Came home, tried acting. Hosted radio show in Kansas City. Wrote two books about postage stamps, plus *How to Win at Bingo*. Enlisted as stockbroker, failed test. Hired by E.F. Hutton to write newsletter.

Chart reader, technical analyst. Said stock prices move in "syncopations" like music. Wrote book on subject, early 1960s. Disliked brokerage business, called brokers "stupid." Wore wild sportcoats and slick hair-dos. Left Hutton 1964 to start his own newsletter. In early 1970s, separated from first wife, lived in office. Too broke to fix car, pay printer.

After several erroneous forecasts, got in sync with market in mid-1970s. Made accurate predictions on gambling stocks; attracted subscribers. Joined lecture circuit, appeared on stage in blinking bow ties, togas, electrified sunglasses, Elvis costumes, chicken feathers. Dropped pants to read stock quotes printed on underwear. Brought monkey to podium. Dressed like Moses, delivered Ten Commandments of Investing, invited audience to "touch me and be wealthy." Dressed like Ayatollah; arrived at lecture halls on dogsled, in rickshaw. Had plank installed inches below the surface of swimming pool; walked on water.

August 1979, predicted earthquake. On radio show and in newsletter, called every move in stocks from 1979–1981. Gathered more subscribers. Became double-digit millionaire (his own estimate).

Issued buy signal April 21, 1980. Dow obliged with fifth biggest one-day gain in history. At year end, issued sell signal: "Market top has been reached." Caused waves of selling in Europe; U.S. Dow closed down on unprecedented heavy volume. "One Forecaster Spurs Hysteria," said the *Washington Post*. "A mindless wave of selling that destroyed billions of dollars in stock value from a forecaster who drops his pants in public to get attention," said *Business Week*. Granville's mug seen on front page of the *New York Times*.

"Many have said I have four times the power of the Federal Reserve," Granville told *Newsweek*. "I have solved the 100-year enigma, calling every market top and bottom." Predicted he'd win Nobel Prize. Nobel Committee didn't cooperate.

Said major quake would hit Los Angeles 5:31 A.M., April 10. City didn't feel a thing. Eight thousand people jammed entrance to latest Granville lecture. Appeared in *People* magazine photospread making weird face. Said he was a nut, a "nut who makes you rich." After United Airlines flight left the gate without him, Granville threatened to "drop the stock ten points." VIP golf cart arrived to escort him to another flight.

Played Carnegie Hall, June 1981. Clowned on Steinway. Took show on road to Europe that September, told London radio audience markets would fall. London fell, New York fell, Tokyo had biggest one-day drop ever. Stocks hit bottom in summer of 1982.

Emerged from coffin filled with tickertape; too drunk to give lecture. Stocks advanced, Granville more bearish than ever. Suckers' rally, he said. Predicted another Great Crash. Studied 1928–1929 editions of *Wall Street Journal*. Compared himself to Roger Babson, economist who cried *Bear!* back then. Appeared on Lou Rukeyser's TV show, called Rukeyser "Crab Louis" for making light of his predictions. Predicted another earthquake. Nothing quaked.

Stocks continued to rise. Rise will be brief, Granville said. Remained bearish through most of 1980s. Subscribers defected. Turned bullish in time for 1987 Crash. Temporarily back in sync, 1987–1989. In that period, newsletter reviewer Mark Hulbert named Granville top newsletter for profitable advice.

In 1990s, turned bearish again. Said new bear market had begun, 1992. Said Dow would drop to 1,500 or lower by year end, 1994. Predicted crash in "about three months," May 1995. Predicted "headlong swan dive," February 1996. Said market would witness "legendary disaster," October 1996.

Mark Hulbert named Granville least profitable newsletter for twelve-year span, "dead last" with 93 percent loss from recommendations. Granville disputed Hulbert's math.

July 16, 1996, turned bullish. Granville charts show low-priced stocks will "go berserk on the upside." Tells *Kansas City Star*, "There's so much momentum nothing can stop it." Has heart attack. Stops smoking. Stops drinking hard stuff.

Shares Kansas City apartment with third wife, Karen, and Lucky the parrot. Tries to teach Lucky to say "buy" and "sell." Hounded by IRS for back taxes. Sees Dow 10,000 by end of 1997.

(Sources for this section: *Barron's*; *The Kansas City Star*; Don Katz in *Worth* magazine.)

ELAINE GARZARELLI

Most famous she bear on Wall Street. Little competition in that department; she bears even rarer than he bears. Keeps distance from reporters, sometimes shows up on CNN. Seems to follow Joan Didion's advice: "Talking to a reporter can only get you in trouble."

Turned bearish in summer of 1987. Said so on CNN week before October Crash. Ran mutual fund at Shearson-Lehman based on "sector analysis." Mostly in cash when market collapsed.

Born in Springfield, Pennsylvania; graduate of Drexel University, MBA in economics. Allocation system based on fourteen key factors. Hot ticket after 1987. Money poured into fund as fund flopped: in 1988, down 13 percent with market up 16.6 percent. Garzarelli turned bearish before Saddam Hussein decline, 1990. Posed for No-Nonsense pantyhose, 1993. Turned bullish. Lost job at Lehman, 1994, after Lehman separated from Shearson. Started Garzarelli Capital, *Garzarelli Outlook* newsletter.

Turned bearish, July 1996, in promotional mailing. "Sell NOW," flyer warned, in red ink. "Get OUT of all U.S. stocks and mutual funds." Media critic called Garzarelli mailout "one of the most alarming pieces of junk mail in history."

Garzarelli saw following negatives: yield on stocks at all-time low, rising credit card losses, disappointing corporate earnings, corporate cash flow drying up, public too bullish with 63 percent of net worth in stocks, highest ever. Mentioned she has called "every market crash for the last twenty years with zero false alarms."

Appeared on CNN July 23, 1996, to reiterate sell signal. Prepare for 15 to 25 percent drop, Garzarelli said. Dow dropped 44 points, Garzarelli named culprit. Stocks rallied next day, Garzarelli issued buy signal two weeks later. Turned bearish again, almost immediately.

Wall Street Journal reports feud between Garzarelli and Phillips Publishing, July 1997. Phillips handled her newsletter. Public flap over who's responsible for controversial flyer, tacky sweepstakes promotion. Mistimed bearish call cost 30,000 subscribers, according to Phillips.

JOHN KENNETH GALBRAITH

Harvard economist, ivory tower bear, author of *The Great Crash (1929)*, *The Affluent Society* (Galbraith didn't like it), *The New Industrial State* (didn't trust it), *Short History of Financial Euphoria*. Warned of crash in early 1987. Occupies Warburg Chair at Harvard, named for Paul Warburg, a founder of Federal Reserve System. Warburg warned of crash in early 1929. (Is Galbraith Warburg's medium?)

Galbraith put warning in writing; *New York Times* rejected piece as "too alarming" for all the news that's fit to print; his news didn't fit. Submitted same piece to *Atlantic* magazine; *Atlantic* published it. Angry reader complained: "Galbraith doesn't like to see people making money." Six months later, market crashed.

New York Times relented, interviewed Galbraith too late for anybody's benefit. Galbraith swamped with letters, phone calls, mostly complimentary. Journalists, commentators from Tokyo to Texas lined up for interviews. The world found out Galbraith thought the market would crash, but by then, it already had.

JIM CHANOS

King of the short sellers; occupies office on middle floor of Citicorp Center, New York. (For explanation of this activity, see page 207.) Rents space from big client, the Ziff family, formerly in publishing. No stuffed or ceramic bears, no pictures of bears. Nothing to suggest Chanos isn't normal bullish fund manager, except he dresses casually. His suit isn't pinstriped.

Office contains standard props of high finance: prospectuses stacked on desk, computer that blinks gains and losses, photos of family ski vacations, "deal toys" to commemorate successful trades. (Chanos's deal toys commemorate stocks that failed.) He points to

Ugly Duckling logo on baseball cap perched atop computer monitor: "This company, Ugly Duckling, was in the used car business, had bad accounting, and the guy who ran it was a convicted felon, which didn't stop people from buying the stock." (Chanos marvels at the investor obliviousness that lifts issues of this caliber.) "Eventually, it went down and my clients made money on it. One of my better plays of late."

Chanos trained as analyst. Fresh out of Yale, began career with small investment house, early 1980s. Analyzed Baldwin-United, finance company highly recommended by seasoned colleagues. Went against crowd, advised clients to sell Baldwin short. Stock price promptly doubled; Chanos rebuked. As clients' losses mounted, Chanos stuck to bearish opinion; vindicated after Baldwin exposed as fraud, stock approached zero.

Investment house balked at Chanos's offer to manage short-selling fund; quit firm and started his own, Kynikos (Greek for "cynic"). Extracted money from few deep pockets, 1985. Installed computer, searched for next Baldwin using Warren Buffett style of analysis in reverse. Scanned financial reports for lost causes—companies in serious hock, with big debts, phony earnings, lousy products, felonious CEOs. Favorite targets: real estate boondoggles, banks on the ropes, leveraged buyouts gone bust.

Made money on shorts, even while stock market rose. Large institutions (pension funds, investment houses), perennial bulls at heart, took notice. Saw Chanos as perfect insurance policy. He'd booked 40 percent annual profits on short side in bull market; no telling how well he'd do in bear.

Institutions upped ante in 1990, sent $500 million Chanos's way. Most celebrated short seller in what looked like short sellers' paradise: Gulf War, recession in progress, banks flirting with insolvency. Paradise became hell for Chanos and for short sellers in general. They'd bet against a shaky bank, fraud, company in distress; these stocks would go up. In 1980s, companies in distress went bankrupt. In 1990s, easy credit kept them alive.

"You'd find a black cloud over a company," says Chanos. "And nobody cared. As long as the stock was rising, fund managers were buying more. They couldn't afford not to. Momentary underperformance could cost them their jobs."

Chanos's clients lost money; Chanos lost clients. His bankroll had a bear market, down from $500 million to $300 million. Adding insult to losses, "Short Busters" club formed by bulls. Purpose: to foil the likes of Chanos by buying stocks he'd already sold short. Result: prices rose, adding to Chanos's losses, forcing him to abandon his favorite investments in so-called "short squeeze."

In 1997, full-time short sellers could be counted on two hands—a decade before, there had been several dozen. Survivors lost 90 percent of capital sent their way. "Whereas the smart circles of the 1980s thought short selling was a clever idea, the same circles in 1997 think it's the province of fools," says Chanos. "Nobody wants to admit publicly he does it. We're so discredited, if we offered to give people $2 back for every $1 in their pocket, they wouldn't take us up on it."

Chanos is still in operation, a remarkable feat under the circumstances. He's king of short sellers, because who else is there? Has to make up a lot of losses before he gets cut in on profits. "The losses have been so substantial," Chanos says, "I'd have to be up 500 percent before I earn my fee."

FESHBACH BROTHERS

Notable short sellers, like Chanos. Tossup who started first "short only" fund: Chanos on East Coast, or Feshbachs on West Coast. Chanos came out of Yale; Feshbachs, out of surfing (Kurt), tennis

(Matt), and less than a year at Utah State (Joe). Three California kids with no patience for suits, ties, or popular opinion.

Learned basics of securities analysis from father, oil company deal-maker. Early in 1980s, risked a few thousand dollars on first short sale. Made progressively larger bets against Charles Keating, ZZZZ Best, other corporate frauds. Attracted clients, then crowd of clients, as Feshbach's fund compounded at an astounding 40 percent per year, 1985–1990. Outgained Warren Buffett, Peter Lynch.

Headquarters in Palo Alto, California: front door scratched, dented like a service entrance. Inside, fax machine to right, two plastic chairs in middle, bookcase to left. Feshbachs' group portrait sits on book-case: three male Graces, one turned sideways to show logo on back of jacket: a Merrill Lynch bull with red slash through it, indicating "Just Say No To Bulls."

Joe's inner office: couch to left; pillow done in needlepoint, "The Only Cash Flow is Negative Cash Flow"; Ron Hubbard Scientology poster on wall; crystal and china bears on shelf; desk to right. Joe sits at desk. Brother Kurt stands behind, surfer-length hair, wire-rimmed glasses, staring at Quotron like home-plate umpire. Joe tells story of how Feshbachs rode high, with $1 billion in assets, before luck changed and assets vanished: half through losses, half carted out by dispirited clients.

"The press wrote Wells Fargo did us in," says Joe, referring to the bank stock that rose from $50 per share to $200 per share, with the Feshbachs on the wrong (short) side of it. "We got out of Wells be-fore it killed us. The bull market was the problem. Everything went up; we went down. Stocks on NASDAQ gained 50 percent in 1991, we lost 50 percent. We could easily have lost more than we did."

"About that Buffett story," he volunteers, talking about a "Fuck Buffett" T-shirt the Feshbachs allegedly sent clients when they were short Wells and Buffett was buying it. "We never produced such a T-shirt. Never would have. I sent Buffett a letter to that effect. Got back a nice reply."

1990s cruel to Feshbachs: prior success created a glut of short sellers, too many people chasing too few good ideas. Billion-dollar fund too big to take advantage of short selling opportunity. In 1993, with losses mounting and clients defecting, Feshbachs made a startling decision. They switched from short to long.

"It wasn't a market call," says Joe, "the way a lot of people think. It was a response to how the nature of short selling had changed."

Either way, other short sellers were stunned; remaining clients abandoned fund. Who wanted to invest in Feshbachs as bulls? "Clients told us, 'When you prove you can do it on the long side, call us back,'" Joe recalls. "Those were the polite ones."

Today, the Feshbachs are back to playing with their money, on the long and the short side. Kurt taking a few short positions, once again with some success. "Mercury Finance, I nailed it," says Kurt, flashing a smile. "Remember Unioil?" Joe adds, nostalgically. "An oil and gas company with no oil and gas! We nailed that one, too."

GERALD LOEB

Stockbroker, financial advice columnist, 1930s. Wrote best seller, *The Battle for Investment Survival.* Sold most of personal portfolio before 1929 Crash. Avoided big losses, but 1929 experience made him a skittish trader for life.

Like Buffett, Lynch, and Beardstown Ladies, Loeb believed stocks are people's best chance to increase wealth in long run. However, didn't believe in owning stocks all the time. Advised buying in moderation, keeping large cash reserve on hand. Sold stocks automatically whenever price fell 10 percent; added to position as price rose, sold a tenth of portfolio at end of each year.

Developed strategy in period when stocks took two steps back as often as they took three steps forward. Market too fickle, he thought, to provide security to investor who analyzed companies on merits and bought accordingly. Said it was "safer to buy and sell a stock a dozen times starting at $40 and ending at $100 than to buy and pay $40." Capital, he said, was "best deployed like a rabbit darting here and there for cover."

When conditions unfavorable, Loeb sat on cash and waited. Avoided bonds altogether; realized that when interest rates rise, a bond can lose money as fast as a stock. "Those who imagine they are interested only in 'income' are knowingly or unknowingly not alive to the facts. They run the risk that at some future date their capital will have shrunk in excess of total income received in the interim."

"Of course, what everyone knows isn't worth knowing," Loeb wrote, meaning that whenever the investing public falls in love with any strategy, it will cost those investors money. Few people know about Loeb, so maybe he's worth considering.

CHARLES ALLMON

Called "contrarian chicken." Once worked for United Fruit in Honduras, later turned from bananas to stocks. Publishes newsletter: *Growth Stock Outlook*. For many years, managed mutual fund, Charles Allmon Trust. Sold fund in 1995. Allmon Trust only publicly traded fund to post a gain on Black Monday, 1987, the day the Dow lost 22 percent.

Bearish through late 1980s into 1990s: biggest position in fund and in newsletter model portfolio was cash. In spite of this drag on performance, Allmon's stock picks were smart enough to earn clients 18.9 percent compounded since 1974. Major stock indexes earned less than 10 percent.

Recently, Allmon's model portfolio held 90 percent in cash—more cash than he had held before Crash of 1987.

COULD 1929—THAT IS, 1932—
HAPPEN AGAIN?

THE YEAR 1929 IS famous as the Titanic of financial disasters. Yet this Titanic didn't sink. The Dow was up for the first nine months that year, fell 39 percent in October–November, then staged a rally and rose in December. If you held stocks from the beginning of 1929 to the end, you made money.

The real Titanic year was 1931, when the Dow lost 53 percent—the bulk of which disappeared in a single month, Black September. Nobody talks about the Crash of '31, though it ranks first on the list of obnoxious periods for U.S. stockholders. Nobody talks about Black September. Everybody talks about the Crash of '29, which comes to mind whenever the bear word is spoken.

The typical modern account of the Crash of '29 tries to convince investors that another '29 will never happen, thus helping them to sleep better at night. As mentioned above, the original '29 didn't happen—at least not in '29. It happened two years later. This confusion over the date is just one of several misconceptions about the entire ordeal (1929–1932) which, for simplicity's sake, will hereafter be referred to as the Great Decline.

After six decades of revision and amplification, the likely story of the Great Decline goes like this. In 1929, banks lacked deposit insurance, the monetary system was in the straitjacket of the gold standard, and the stock market was untrustworthy and easily rigged, with no SEC to police it.

Wall Street was a casino where high rollers hoodwinked the lower rollers, who got in on the action by buying shares at 10 percent down and borrowing the rest from a brokerage house. (This kind of loan is known as "margin"; the lower rollers were called "margin millionaires.")

The economy in 1929 was primitive: the government was only a small part of it. The Federal Reserve System was immature, having just turned 16. Its bankers lacked experience in how to handle an emergency. At the key moment when the Fed should have lowered interest rates to prevent economic arrest, the Fed raised rates and strangled the patient. Thanks to the Fed's bungling, the Great Decline became the Great Depression.

The margin millionaires soon became the margin penniless, forced into liquidation and then into bankruptcy because their losses far exceeded their net worth. Some ended up on the street selling pencils. Others ended up on the street after jumping from high windows, in a mass reenactment of plunging assets. This tragedy encouraged architects to design high buildings with windows that don't open, a common feature today.

The average person wasn't affected by the Great Decline per se, because the public wasn't in the market, even though shoeshine boys and elevator operators on Wall Street gave hot tips to tycoons. Without the ballast of long-term investors holding onto their shares, stocks lacked stability. Thus, the Great Decline resulted from an archaic situation. It won't be repeated and can't be repeated, because the modern financial system won't allow it.

Not on today's Wall Street, with a quarter of the U.S. adult population owning stocks and providing ample ballast for the market; with mutual fund professionals controlling the bulk of the assets; with a well-trained Federal Reserve delivering exactly what the doctor (Greenspan, that is) ordered; with insured bank deposits, a watchful SEC, a global marketplace, and computers that tell every detail about every company; with economists and forecasters on the lookout for any and all problems; another Great Decline is out of the question.

So what's the real story? A lot of data went uncollected in the 1920s, so nobody really knows how many Americans owned shares. But there's evidence the public was involved in the market in a bigger way than has been advertised. How could it not be, with Edgar Lawrence Smith's *Common Stocks as Long-Term Investments* a national best-seller? How could it not be, in the mutual fund mania (funds were called "investment trusts" then) that erupted?

As to whether the Great Decline took people by surprise, warning flags were flying all over the place in the summer of 1929. Paul Warburg, a founder of the Federal Reserve, warned of irrational exuberance, as Alan Greenspan did sixty-eight years later. Roger Babson had issued his famous call: Get out of stocks. Charles E. Merrill, the Merrill Lynch Merrill, advised his own customers to get out of stocks. (Apparently, Merrill endured twenty-eight sessions with a psychiatrist after colleagues questioned his sanity.) Dean Witter, *the* Dean Witter, sent an interoffice lament in April 1929: people were buying stocks without regard to "value, earning power and dividends, present and prospective. They were buying stocks only because they hoped stocks would go higher."

"I can remember distinctly that I could find no justification for values which existed in 1928," Witter later recalled, "and in many cases recommended sale or advised against purchase. I was decidedly wrong, as prices went much higher in 1929. I was only wrong however in that I failed to pick the very top of the market."

The part about the Fed causing the Great Decline by raising rates when it should have lowered them is only half true. The Fed did raise rates in 1929, to counteract several years of easy money, which resulted in the exuberant market that was sobered up in the Crash. But after the Crash, in 1930, the Fed lowered rates (six times, no less) just as the modern Fed would (and did) after the Crash of 1987. The Fed bankers of the day weren't as clueless in emergencies as they've been made to seem.

The Crash caused no noticeable increase in the suicide rate in lower Manhattan. [For details, consult William Klingaman, *1929, The Year of the Great Crash* (Harper & Row, 1989).] Jumps from high windows were rare, and usually not Crash-related. A radio executive exited an upper floor of the Hotel Shelton on Lexington Avenue, leaving a note that said "We are broke," but that was on October 3, two weeks before the financial plunge. A crowd gathered the morning after Black Monday to watch what appeared to be a despondent investor perched on a girder. It turned out to be a hardhat having his lunch. Winston Churchill was staring out the window of Manhattan's Savoy Plaza Hotel when a falling body passed through his line of sight; but again, there was no evidence this jumper was an investor.

Nationwide, a few bereft shareholders took their own lives, but gravity was not the weapon of choice in any of these fatalities: two bankers from New York and Philadelphia (pistol); the wife of a Long Island stockbroker (same)—her husband's clients wished she'd shot him, instead; a Rochester utilities executive (head in the oven); an individual investor from Milwaukee (same) who left a note that said: "My body should go to science . . . my sympathy to my creditors."

A Rhode Island man died in his broker's office (heart attack, ticker-tape fright), but this wasn't a suicide. Harry Crosby, the son of a partner at J. P. Morgan, was found dead in the arms of a Mrs. Bigelow, who apparently had joined him in a fatal opium orgy. Police concluded this exit had nothing to do with stocks.

Ivar Kreuger, a.k.a. the "Swedish match king," the Bill Gates of the matchbook industry, shot himself in Paris in March 1932. Kreuger was depressed over the lowly condition of his company's stock, owned by so many Americans that *Time* magazine had made him its coverboy a few weeks before the Crash. News of his death caused a minipanic on the floor of the New York Stock Exchange in 1932, but by then stocks had nearly reached bottom.

How the tall tale of ruined investors dropping en masse from tall buildings got started is a mystery. Perhaps it came from the night-clubs where comedians had turned the Crash into fresh material. Will Rogers said:

"The situation has been reached in New York hotels where the clerk asks incoming guests, 'You wanna room for sleeping or for jump-ing?' And you have to stand in line to get a window to jump out of."

Rogers was in a laughing mood because he followed the advice of tycoon Bernard Baruch and exited the market near the top. Baruch himself was still in the market, a fact that wasn't discovered until the 1980s. The discoverer was Jim Grant (see page 223), who, in ad-dition to his regular bearish commentary, took time out to write Baruch's biography.

There are as many similarities as differences between 1929 and 1997. The 1920s had low inflation and perky corporate profits, the same as the 1990s. We have the best-selling Beardstown Ladies, they had the best-selling Edgar Lawrence Smith. Mutual funds were wildly popular in 1929, the same as in 1997. Both periods were showcases for American ingenuity: in the 1920s, Henry Ford and related entre-preneurs put cars on the highways; in the 1990s, Bill Gates and related entrepreneurs put data on the information superhighway. Car com-panies were the stars of the New York Stock Exchange; computer com-panies are the stars of NASDAQ.

There was a mutual fund mania then, and there is another one now. Fundholders in the 1920s believed they had safety in numbers and trusted that their excellent managers could protect them from a Great Decline—same as fundholders today. Stocks sold for silly prices in 1929 (more than twenty times earnings) and for sillier prices in 1997.

In some ways, the United States was in better shape in the 1920s. It had the fastest growing economy in the world, no trade deficit, no federal deficit, low taxes, and low levels of personal, corporate, and national debt. Today, we have slow growth and a big trade deficit. We're the world's biggest debtor. Taxes are high. Many families pay more in taxes than they spend on food, clothing, and shelter. Instead of ten factory workers for one government worker, as in the 1920s, we now have more government workers than factory workers.

Market cheerleaders continue to reassure us that there will never be another Great Decline, because the world that produced it no longer exists. If that's the case, why does this description from Frederick Lewis Allen's reminiscence of the 1920s, *Only Yesterday*, sound so familiar?

> Time and again the economists and forecasters had cried wolf, wolf, wolf, and the wolf had made only the most fleeting of visits. Time and again, the [Federal] Reserve Board had expressed fear of inflation, and inflation had failed to bring hard times. Business in danger? Why nonsense! Factories were running at full blast and the statistical indices registered first-class industrial health.
>
> Was there a threat of overproduction? Nonsense again! Were not business concerns committed to hand-to-mouth buying, were not commodity prices holding to reasonable levels? Where were the overloaded shelves of goods, the heavy inventories, which business analysts universally accepted as storm signals? And look at the character of the stocks which were now leading the advance! At a moment when many of the high-flyers of earlier months were losing ground, the really sensational advances were being made by the shares of such solid and conservatively managed companies as United States Steel, General Electric, and American Telephone—which were precisely those which the most cautious investors would select with an eye to the long future. . . . What the bull operators had long been saying must be true, after all. This was a new era. Prosperity was coming into full and perfect flower.

Survivors from the Crash of '29 Speak Out—All Are Bearish Today

THREE EYEWITNESSES OF the Crash of 1929, all of whom had money riding on the outcome, are still at work in the stock trade: Phil Carret, Phil Fisher, and Roy Neuberger. Carret was 100 in 1997; the other two are in their 90s. As of this writing, all three can be found in their offices, hitched to their desks alongside colleagues who could be their great-grandchildren. What the last surviving Confederate widows were to the Civil War, this hoary trio is to Wall Street.

Combined, they have 200 years of experience in owning stocks in bull and bear markets. Are they telling us something by turning bearish for only the second or third time in this century? Here are their investment life stories, in truncated narrative.

PHIL CARRET

Carret turned 60 before angioplasty was invented; 70 before aerobics classes, cable TV, and personal computers came on the scene; 85 before Microsoft became a public company. He knows the score of the first Harvard–Yale game in 1913 (36–0, Harvard) because he was there, as a Harvard student. He has more hair on his eyebrows than on his head, giving him the appearance of a well-fed bald eagle. He dresses in the investment adviser style (suit, tie, and wingtips), and, at age 100, puts in a normal workweek at his firm's ninth-floor office in midtown Manhattan.

Inside his cubicle, Carret has surrounded himself with pictures of wolves, eclipses, and Warren Buffett, plus two antilawyer slogans—the famous Shakespeare quote about killing the lawyers, and a blurb in Italian that roughly translates to: "A mouse in the mouth of a cat has a better chance of survival than a client in a lawyer's clutches."

Carret's friendship with Norman Vincent Peale, author of *The Power of Positive Thinking*, makes him an unlikely bear. He once volunteered to write a companion piece called *The Destructive Power of Negative Thinking*, but Peale wanted no part of it. "Even though I was agreeing with him," Carret says, "just the word 'negative' was enough to turn Peale off." For having survived every bear market since 1893, Carret deserves mention here. His involvement with total eclipses (he has witnessed nineteen in person) tells us the man has some fascination for the dark side.

In 1927, Carret came to New York and joined forces with Blyth, Witter & Company, until Blyth and Witter got a divorce. He stuck with Blyth as an in-house economist, and soon found himself managing an early version of a mutual fund—the American, British & Continental Investment Company. Because several big-name foreign banks were connected to this fund, investors bid up the price to $40 a share when Carret figured it was worth $1 a share, at best. After the Crash of '29, it was worth less than $1 at best.

Of all the panics and crashes he has survived, Carret has the clearest memory of the '29 episode, which he says was far less traumatic than people think. The only jumping out of windows he can recall was a swan dive at 120 Broadway, but that happened in 1931. "The '29 Crash was more exciting than frightening," he says. "Most experts saw it as necessary tonic that sobered up the market and took the froth out of it."

Two weeks after the froth was gone, Carret attended a meeting of the Harvard Economic Society and heard the nation's top business forecasters, including Leonard Ayres of Cleveland Trust, insist that the hangover would be short-lived. Most economists were still bullish, as they had been in the summer before the crash when, as Carret remembers, "almost no American, from Wall Street executives to steel workers in Gary, Indiana, saw any clouds on the horizon. America was rich and increasingly prosperous. The country was growing. Its people were energetic. There seemed no reason why prosperity shouldn't continue, if not forever, at least for a long time."

By 1932, a quarter of the workforce was out of a job, including Carret. He and two friends started their own mutual fund, the Pioneer Fund, mostly out of desperation; Wall Street wasn't hiring, and it was a waste of time to apply for a position.

For 50 years thereafter, the Pioneer Fund enriched its shareholders to the tune of 13 percent compounded per annum, in spite of its losses from the early 1930s. After Pioneer was merged into a bigger fund, Carret left the fund business. He and a small staff, including one of his sons and a daughter-in-law, now manage $225 million worth of private portfolios.

In his career at Pioneer, Carret almost always sided with the bulls, although he "lightened up" on stocks during a few of the big declines. He was giving a speech to the Rotary Club in Rome, Italy, the day the Dow shed 500 points in 1987. "They all wanted to know what was going on," he recalls. "I didn't know myself. I still don't know," he says of that perplexing episode.

Carret confides he'd never been more pessimistic about stocks than he was at Dow 7,000 in 1997, and from that level he foresaw a 1,000- to 2,000-point drop. "I'm not doing anything about it in my own portfolio," he says. "If stocks go down, they go down. I'm 100 years old and due to conk out any minute. If I conk out at the bottom of a bear market, it would save a lot of estate taxes."

PHIL FISHER

Phil Fisher's office in San Mateo, California, involves two rooms, two desks, three chairs, a couple of file cabinets, Fisher, and a secretary. On his desk are four pencils (one is a nub) and five sheets of paper. No computer, no tickertape, no Bloomberg, no Quotron.

Weather permitting, Fisher walks to work a half mile or so past a "lovely garden." Otherwise, his wife drops him off.

At 90, he's still an active money manager with several big clients. Fisher visits every company in his portfolio at least twice a year. This forces him to limit his holdings to a few stocks—"five and a half positions" is the latest tally, the "half" being a tentative purchase of a small number of shares. "I'd prefer to own 6 to 9 companies," he admits, "but I don't want to lower my standards to get the other three."

As to which stocks he owns, Fisher refuses to comment. "My clients pay me to pick stocks, so it wouldn't be fair to give them out for free," he explains. Most money managers can't wait to broadcast their top holdings, but not Fisher.

A fax machine is the only hint this might be 1997 and not 1929, when Fisher entered the investment business and made a canny forecast: Get out of stocks, a huge bear market is on its way. Instead of heeding his own advice, he bought a couple of stocks that looked cheap, on the theory that not everything would go down when the market dropped. He was wrong and he lost money. Though that experience might have convinced him to lighten up in bear markets, for six decades thereafter, he stayed fully invested through all the ups and downs.

Only twice since 1929 has Fisher sensed another Great Decline was imminent: (1) in 1987, when he'd just turned 80, he issued a bear market alert in a column in *Forbes* Magazine (although he remained fully invested through the decline); and (2) in 1997. "Don't take my word for it," he says of his recent bearish forecast. "But I have a feeling the path we're on today is somewhere between 1927 and 1929.

"Enough people are scared so maybe we haven't reached the top, but when I hear the talk about how this is a new era, a permanent plateau of prosperity, and other such baloney, I get upset. It's the same stuff I heard from the other Fisher [Irving] just before the 1929 Crash."

Now, for the first time in his long career, Fisher is playing cautious, keeping some of his portfolio in cash and advising his clients to do the same. "They resisted my advice at first," he says, "because I taught them it's foolish to time the market. But I've convinced them at this point, they'd be better off with a little more cash."

ROY NEUBERGER

"There's been a big ruckus around here," says Roy Neuberger's secretary, leading the way to Neuberger's office. "Half the firm didn't want him to do this interview." Bears are a touchy subject at Neuberger & Berman. Most of their clients are on the long side of $45 billion worth of mutual funds.

Neuberger just turned 94, but age hasn't dulled his wit or his memory of the Crash of 1929. That was the year he left Paris and life among the artists and writers, for Wall Street and life among the brokers and traders. He bought his first stocks in March, about the same time Phil Fisher was buying his. He also sold a stock short—Radio Corporation of America, the famous RCA. A "bull pool" was buying

RCA shares to push the price up and attract suckers, who in turn would push the price even higher so the pool operators could exit with a large profit. The hustlers in this particular hustle included Walter Chrysler of Chrysler and Charles Schwab of U.S. Steel, the grandfather of Charles Schwab the discount broker.

"RCA reached a high of $574 before it split five for one, and nothing seemed to justify the extravagant price," Neuberger recalls. "I asked older investors to explain it, and got no intelligent answers. People said, 'We are entering the radio age.' "

Neuberger had a hunch the stock would collapse once the hustlers took their profits, and it did. Eventually, RCA hit $2. Meanwhile, the young short seller was making his own profit on the drop.

Meanwhile, Neuberger (age 25) was employed in the back office of a brokerage house, recording transactions. He remembers Black Thursday, October 24, as a hectic affair. Ditto Friday and Saturday, when the exchange was open two hours. So many shares changed hands in those three trading sessions, Neuberger was up late three nights in a row catching up with the paperwork. "Since the brokerage houses were so far behind posting the trades," he recalls, "people didn't realize how much their stocks had fallen until the next day."

Monday, October 28, brought more of the same, and Neuberger was on the job past midnight. He took a taxi home for a two-hour nap, returned to work, and recorded trades until dawn. He doesn't recall much gloom around the office. "Five months later, the Dow had recovered half its losses. Financial and political leaders proclaimed the panic an aberration and predicted prosperity was just around the corner. They were mistaken, of course."

Neuberger broke even on the Crash and its aftermath; the gains from his short position equaled the losses from his long positions. "Maybe my little account was the first hedge fund on record," he jokes. Soon, this Francophile cum speculator was managing other people's money. He preserved their capital with a few well-timed short sales as stocks hit their Niagara in 1932. He got married June 29 that year, the day the Dow Industrials registered an all-time low: 41.22.

In 1939, Neuberger started his own firm. From that point forward, he's been bullish "95 percent of the time," with an occasional bet on the short side. "I hedged my portfolio in late 1972–1973," he recalls, "when stocks in the so-called Nifty Fifty companies were selling at fifty times earnings, a very unnifty price. I hedged in 1987, after a ridiculous runup in prices. Today, I'm only managing money for myself and my family, but stocks have had another ridiculous runup, so I'm hedging one more time. At this moment, I'm short index futures, short Microsoft, short Coke, the world's favorite drink."

Neuberger swivels his chair around to face the computer screen. He's tracking the prices of Coca-Cola (KO) and Microsoft (MSFT), which at the moment are down on the day. (The Dow has dropped 160 points during the interview.) "I also wanted to short Intel," he says, "but I'm not allowed to short anything we own in the firm's mutual funds."

He pulls up the Coke chart, which shows the stock trading at forty-two times earnings for the past twelve months. "With sales growing at just 3 percent in 1996, I can't figure out why people will pay forty-two times earnings," he says. "That's why I'm short 2.5 million shares. But so far, I've been a dumbbell about this. I should have realized the world is addicted to Coke."

We head out for lunch at a shish kebab restaurant forty floors down and across the street. Neuberger, having donned a porkpie hat and topcoat, and now holding a cane, crosses in sprightly fashion. "Bring me a diet Coke, even though I'm short the stock," he says to the waiter. During the salad course, he compares Coca-Cola to Johnson & Johnson and finds the latter a far better investment, because of its diversified product line. By the time the entree arrives, he's calling for an SEC investigation of companies that buy back their own shares at high prices, which squeezes the short sellers. "Coca-Cola has been doing that aggressively," he says. "It's all across American industry. They buy their shares instead of building new plants or equipment, and they use borrowed money to do it. They pay too much."

"Do you realize," he says, as the waiter drops the check on the table, "Coke's book value is less than $3 a share? But who wants value these days? In this crazy market, the best stock to own is an overpriced stock. It attracts more buyers, who make it even more overpriced."

The Pessimists'
History of the World

Onward and upward. I've never uttered those words.

Jim Grant

While it may be true that U.S. stocks in the twentieth century have provided an annual return of approximately 9 percent, a more common characteristic of economic development throughout history is the recurrent massive destruction of wealth.

Marc Faber

MARC FABER, A PONY-TAILED gadabout, lives in Hong Kong, where his Eurasian wife runs a Thai restaurant. Faber, meanwhile, passes the time writing the *Gloom, Boom & Doom Report* (emphasis on Doom). He also manages money by plunking it down where others fear to plunk, such as Venezuelan bonds when rioters are in the streets of Caracas and the President's bags are packed for Miami. A latter-day financial Gibbon, Faber also follows the declines and falls of a long list of formerly prosperous societies:

- Memphis, Akkad, Lagash, Ur, Thebes, Babylon, Avaris, Nineveh—all gone from glory, most gone from the map.
- Babylon, the gem of Mesopotamia, but today, archeologists can't find it.
- Jericho leveled by Joshua.
- Mayans AWOL.
- Greek, Roman, Byzantine, and Holy Roman empires downsized.
- Incans and Aztecs trumped by Spaniards; Spaniards by Latin liberators; Napoleon by the British; the British by the Yanks; Tsars by the commissars; the commissars by capitalists.

Taking the truly long-term view, as Faber is inclined to do, the prudent investor has to be bearish and nimble. Faber notes a "continuous shift in the centers of prosperity, because of . . . war, decay, hyperinflation, depression, changing trade routes, internal strife, plagues, expropriation, etc. Furthermore, when disaster strikes and wealth vanishes, it's always in an atmosphere of great confidence and invincibility."

In the spirit of full disclosure, and as an antidote to the prevailing "myoptimism" and a cautionary tale for complacent stockpickers, here's a Faberian run through the red ink of yore.

In the trade that handed over Manhattan to the Dutch settlers for $24 worth of beads, the Indians avoided three centuries of fires, broken water mains, brownouts, work stoppages, padded payrolls, missed trash pickups, double parking, burglaries, assaults, murders, rapes, and higher taxes.

At the Jamestown colony, John Rolfe almost lost his head and investors lost their shirts. Few if any colonizing ventures in America were profitable to venture capitalists who supplied the bankroll. Backers of the Pilgrims were never fully repaid; ditto for the backers of Rhode Island and Massachusetts Bay. The New World (like much of the Old World) was built on false hopes and bad debts.

The French lost their life savings in a boondoggle contrived by John Law, a Scottish carpetbagger, in the early 1700s. Already on the lam for killing a critic in a duel, Law took up residence in Paris where his scheme for getting France out of debt caught the fancy of the king's babysitter, a.k.a. regent, who ran the country at that point.

Law got the regent's OK to start a Royal Bank. The bank issued "notes" to be sold to the public; the proceeds were to be used to pay down the government's extensive debts. These notes were salable only because the Royal Bank promised to exchange them, on demand, for gold nuggets equal to the face value of the paper. The nuggets would come from vast deposits in the French-controlled territories in Mississippi. The visionaries behind this ambitious mining venture financed it by selling shares of stock in the newly formed Mississippi Company to the French public, in 1718.

Mississippi shares were so popular that the offering caused huge carriage jams in the streets that doubled as a stock exchange al fresco. Respectable ladies offered their bodies to any broker who would sell them a piece of the action. In their desire to acquire, buyers forgot to ask whether gold had ever been found in Mississippi. Alas, it hadn't.

Once this sad truth began to be suspected, the Mississippi stock price dropped 99 percent in thirteen months, a major downgrade that led to the collapse of the Royal Bank and the French banking system at large. Having no gold to exchange for paper, Law's bank promptly reneged on its promise and said its notes were no longer convertible. In 1720, a run on the bank's main branch left fifteen depositors crushed to death in a single bloody afternoon. Before the survivors could take their anger out on Law, he skipped town and moved to Venice, where he found religion.

Across the channel in England, a Mississippi-style opportunity, the South Sea Company, was offered to British investors, who embraced it as enthusiastically as the French had. South Sea organizers promised to pay off the large British government debt with profits from trading with the colonies. This required ships, warehouses, employees, and assorted gear, all financed by selling South Sea shares.

Again, the demand was strong. Before South Sea had turned a farthing of profit, the share price rose from 2 British pounds to 1,000, for what Peter Lynch would call a "500 bagger."

The 500 bagger was soon deflated in the South Sea bear market of 1720, and investors were left with hot air and a whopping 84 percent loss. Other stocks traded on the London exchange fared as badly or worse. When the total losses are added to the partial losses, the average stock in London was down 98 percent in less than two years.

The exchange itself was shut down for a half-century thereafter, and the government made it a crime to be a stockbroker. England fell into six decades of depression; industrial production was basically stalled. The hard times brought on by the South Sea fiasco left the English chronically short of money, which is why the leadership decided to shake down the American colonies for spare revenue. The Americans responded by starting a revolution. Meanwhile, an investor who bought London equities near the top in 1720 didn't break even until 1784.

America Was Conceived in Debt and Born in Reorganization
Headline in *Barron's*, February 7, 1994

In order to unburden themselves of the British deficits, for which they were heavily taxed, the colonists ran up a big deficit of their own. With no power to tax anybody, the Continental Congress paid its bills by borrowing money and running the printing press. The latter was the source of 80 percent of wartime revenues. The victors got the spoils, including raging inflation and a federal debt equal to four-tenths of the gross national product.

Alexander Hamilton proposed to consolidate the nation's arrears and settle with the creditors on an easy payment schedule, the kind today's creditors seek by dialing 1-800-FREEDOM (or JUSTICE). He realized debts couldn't be paid without a source of income, so he lobbied for a tax on imports. Congress passed Hamilton's Tariff Act in 1789, and it became law on July 4. This decreed a tax on "distilled spirits," which led to an uprising known as the Whiskey Rebellion. This was a Boston Tea Party with hooch, making it far more rowdy. The American lawmakers and not the British were the villains of this uprising—one reason the Whiskey Rebellion isn't reenacted in school pageants.

The West was won by the robber barons who ran the railroads. In spite of getting a third of the country's real estate free from the government, the railroads couldn't make ends meet. Railroads were the serial defaulters on Wall Street, ruining bondholders and stockholders alike. More than half the investment in the U.S. emerging market came from European (mostly British) pocketbooks. A sizable chunk was lost to bankruptcies, defaults, and bear markets. What made America great in the 1800s made Europeans go broke, just as what made Asia great in the late 1900s is making Americans go broke.

Every twenty years or so, banks failed en masse, with no deposit insurance to protect the customers. The emerging American economy lurched from collapse to collapse. A collapse in 1819 brought the word "panic" into the financial vocabulary. Another collapse came in 1837 when Mississippi, Louisiana, Maryland, Pennsylvania, Indiana, and Michigan repudiated their debts like ancestral banana republics. Bondholders, again mostly from the other side of the Atlantic, were never fully repaid, although the states made halfhearted attempts at partial restitution. Instead of the unpaid creditors getting mad at America, Americans got mad at the creditors. Why, people demanded to know, should foreigners make a bad situation worse by demanding repayment?

Another collapse in 1857 may have helped cause the Civil War, according to some economic historians. The war itself was financed with the printing press, as usual. In April 1862, federal authorities issued notes that proved as worthless as Continentals. A national spending spree followed as the public tried to get rid of the cash as quickly as possible. Prices of food, clothes, and other items soared in the inflationary spiral that grew from the Treasury Department. Authorities reneged on a prior promise to convert paper money into gold.

Inflation turned to deflation and then to the depression of 1873. President Ulysses S. Grant was pressured by colleagues to print more money to revive the economy, but resisted. Grant (along with Grover Cleveland) has been a hero of the "hard money" crowd ever since.

There was a business collapse in 1893 and a bear market to go with it. America's trading partners lost confidence in the dollar and exchanged their greenbacks for gold. Ocean liners were weighed down with gold bars traveling from U.S. bank vaults to their new homes in European bank vaults. The silver mining industry collapsed when "bimetallism"—a plan to back the dollar with silver as well as with gold—was nixed by President Cleveland. Aspen, Colorado, was abandoned; more railroads went bankrupt.

The U.S. economy fell into depression in 1907, slumped in 1911, and again in 1917–1919. The newly established Federal Reserve pumped money into the banks to revive the economy; inflation was revived as well. In 1921, the Fed reversed course and drained money from the banks; inflation was checked but the economy faltered. Later that year, the Fed reversed course a third time and liquefied the banks. The money pump continued to run for eight years, to 1928, sending stocks to record highs, and causing another run on the national gold supply.

In 1929, the Fed turned off the pump and opened the drain, and the stock market crashed. In 1930–1931, it closed the drain and started pumping to lift the economy out of recession. This rescue failed.

In the 1920s, the total debt in the United States hit a record high of 190 percent of the gross domestic product, exceeded only by the 220 percent reached in 1997. Either way, the nation's debts and unfunded obligations have reached the point you could sell off the entire national net worth—real estate and stocks—in a giant flea market and the proceeds wouldn't cover the debts. Bob Prechter says the 1920s and 1990s are the only two decades when U.S. liabilities exceeded the assets.

Prechter adds other reasons we are worse off than our ancestors: In the 1920s, the federal budget was in the black and the government ran a surplus. Today, we are running in deep red. Then you had high private sector debt and low public sector debt. Today, both are at the highest levels in peacetime history. If the stock market crashes, Prechter wonders, what will be left to pay off these debts?

Michael Metz, chief market strategist at Oppenheimer and Co., has surveyed the nation's pocketbook, and notes the following progression: In the 1970s, the typical family learned to make ends meet by sending the wife into the workforce and gaining an extra paycheck. Two incomes proved insufficient to cover expenses, and in the 1980s, that same typical family used credit cards as a third source of income. The family bought now and hoped to pay later. When interest charges on the unpaid credit card balances got too big to handle, the typical family took out a home equity loan, refinancing their debts at a lower rate but sucking most of the equity out of their house. This left the typical family living near the edge of insolvency, or over the edge, as a million Americans a year now file for bankruptcy.

Metz says the typical family has no choice but to reduce consumption, buy less, cut back, the effect of which will be lower interest rates and a slower economy. High debt levels in this country and in others eliminate the "spending option" that can save an economy from a severe downturn. Metz sees disinflation, sluggish real estate sales, and a bull market in bonds that will help stocks until "you start to see a falloff in profits."

Meanwhile, U.S. foreign debt hit a record $900 billion in 1996, up 25 percent from the prior year; the national savings rate was puny, in spite of 45 million households owning mutual funds; in the ballyhooed government budget deal for which both parties took ample credit, nothing was done to curtail future shortfalls in Social Security, Medicare, and Medicaid. Unless something changes, those senior sweepstakes will produce liabilities the next generation can't afford.

Today's economists and market strategists offer a constant reassurance: the world has changed for the better. Does this mean New York, London, Paris, Hong Kong, Peking, Tokyo in the twenty-first century can't go the way of Nineveh, Ur, or the Mayans? Marc Faber doubts it.

Bearish Odds and Ends

Bears' Favorite Day of the Week

IT USED TO BE MONDAY. Between 1953 and 1991, the Dow gained 2,341 points overall, but lost 1,897 points on Mondays during that winning stretch. On the NASDAQ market, stocks also put in their worst showing on Mondays. What accounted for this? On weekends, people had time to fret about inflation, recession, world problems, and so on and Monday was their first chance to sell on bad news.

However, Yale Hirsch, editor of the *Stock Trader's Almanac* and the source of this data, reports a surprising twist: Since 1990, Mondays have been bullish. Stock prices have risen more on the first day of trading than on any of the other four. Does this mean people are so optimistic about stocks that a weekend's reflection on the world's problems no longer fazes them?

Bears' Least Favorite Days of the Week

Wednesday and Friday. On Wednesdays, stocks have registered their biggest gains overall. But the most spectacular advances have occurred on Fridays, partly because investors are optimistic going into a weekend.

BEARS' FAVORITE MONTHS

September is the only month that shows a loss over 47 years from 1950–1997. February, May, and June show negligible gains; August and October are mediocre.

> October is one of the peculiarly dangerous months to speculate in stocks. The others are July, January, September, April, November, May, March, June, December, August, and February.
>
> Mark Twain

BEARS' FAVORITE QUOTES

> If bankers are busy, something is wrong.
>
> Walter Bagehot, journalist, Nineteenth century

> The country can regard the present with satisfaction and anticipate the future with optimism.
>
> Calvin Coolidge, message to Congress, December 4, 1928.
>
> Harry Browne

BEARS' LEAST FAVORITE QUOTES

> Remember, my son, that any man who is a bear on the future of this country will go broke.
>
> J. P. Morgan

> The only thing we have to fear is fear itself.
>
> Franklin D. Roosevelt, 1933

As has been proven numerous times on Wall Street, the only thing investors have to fear is their lack of fear, which causes them to pay excessive prices for overvalued merchandise.

SHUTDOWNS AT THE NEW YORK
STOCK EXCHANGE

1873. The NYSE was padlocked in the aftermath of the "Jay Cooke panic," when the collapse of that famous tycoon shook the financial system. Stocks didn't trade from September 18 until September 30.

1914. The NYSE closed its doors for 4½ months at the onset of World War I. Officials figured if nervous investors had no place to sell their stocks, a bear market couldn't happen. In fact, a bear was already in progress when the shutdown was announced. A flea market for stocks, called the "gutter market," sprang up outside the exchange, and prices fell some more. When the NYSE reopened, stocks had a rally.

1963. Trading halted on the afternoon of November 22, when President Kennedy was assassinated in Dallas. The NYSE was closed the following Monday. When it reopened on Tuesday, stocks went up. There hasn't been a shutdown since 1963, although the Exchange considered the possibility in 1987, after the Dow dropped 508 points in a single day.

1997. Trading was halted briefly on the day the Wall Street caught the Asian flu, and the Dow dropped 554 points.

BULLING AND BEARING

When the markets were smaller and there was no SEC to play ringmaster, the bulls and bears didn't stand by idly and wait for stocks to go their way. A well-financed tycoon could wangle a favorable outcome by launching a bull raid or a bear raid, driving stock prices up or down by connivance and chicanery. A prominent speculator could put out misleading information about a company, good or bad, to cause others to buy or sell. Although this sort of tactic is far from unknown today, it was used more widely pre-SEC. Unscrupulous insiders could flood the market with new shares, depress the stock price, and make a profit on the short side.

Investors in those days were less inclined to analyze companies to guess next year's profits, or figure out whether sales and cash flow would come in ahead of Wall Street expectations. Such fundamental analysis was less relevant then. Who cared what Erie Railroad was doing, or U.S. Steel? It only mattered what a Cornelius Vanderbilt or a Daniel Drew was doing behind the scenes, to mention two prominent mugs in the bull and bear's gallery. Behind every big move in a stock, it was thought, some big bankroll was pushing in one direction or another.

Instead of going to malls to find a good stock, as Peter Lynch advises, the average investor looked for telltale signs of bulling and bearing on the tickertape that ran through the glass-covered machines in the brokerage houses. Tape reading was a popular pastime for neighborhood tycoons. Whenever the tape readers saw a sudden increase in the number of shares being traded, along with a noticeable swing in the price, they assumed a Vanderbilt or a Drew was behind it. Often, they bought a few shares to go along for the ride. Manipulators played to this audience, buying blocks of shares to "paint the tape" which caused the price to rise and convinced the public to buy. In the end, the "smart money" was selling to the dumbest.

You've Heard This One Before

What you've heard lately: Baby boomers will continue to pour money into stocks via mutual funds, thus insuring a profitable outcome. "Buttressing much of the buying is a feeling that the huge baby boom generation of Americans born after World War II is beginning to save in earnest for retirement. This theory holds that they have created a perpetual motion machine for rising markets by pumping so much money into stock mutual funds." (*Washington Post*, February 10, 1996.)

When last heard: 1968. Research study by prominent investment firm, Loomis-Sayles predicts stocks will continue to rise thanks to continuous buying from mutual funds, pension funds, and the rest of the "institutional sector."

What you've heard lately: The government is considering a plan to put Social Security money into stocks, and several states are thinking of doing the same for their pension plans. This official buying will make stocks a can't lose proposition and do wonders for my mutual funds.

When last heard: Japan, 1980s. United States, 1960s. "States are moving to put stocks in their retirement funds, another bullish development," an article in *U.S. News* reported in 1968, "and the average family has 45 percent of financial savings in stocks. As family incomes increase and the preference for stocks keeps growing . . . stock prices could rise 55 percent by 1978." They didn't! They fell!

What you've heard lately: Stocks deserve to sell for unusually high prices, because supplies are limited and demand is growing.

When last heard: 1920s, 1960s. "One reason prices of stocks were so high, it was explained, was that there weren't enough to go around, and accordingly, they had acquired a 'scarcity value'." (John Kenneth Galbraith, *The Great Crash*)

What you're heard lately: Wall Street can't have a severe bear market. The Federal Reserve won't let it happen.

When last heard: Japan, 1989. "They believed their money god, the Ministry of Finance would never let the market go down. Our mutual fund buyers fervently believe that our money god, Alan Greenspan will never let the market go down, says Seattle short-seller Bill Fleckenstein.

Self-professed experts were so convinced of Japanese superiority that two years after the Nikkei Crash, President Clinton suggested the United States reorganize along Japanese lines with industry developing a cozier relationship with government for the common good. Having suffered the effects of too many cozy relationships, Japan decided to reorganize along U.S. lines, with more separation between state and smokestack.

Meanwhile, the Dow of the late 1990s has imitated the Nikkei of the late 1980s, rising through benchmarks with scarcely a hitch as it, too, enters the realm of silly prices. What have the experts been saying? That the American economy is the strongest in the world, and that mean, lean American companies deserve to sell for 20, 30, or 40 times earnings like their Japanese counterparts.

Fleckenstein recalls, "Japan supposedly had triple merits: strong yen, low interest rates, low oil prices. We have a different set of triple merits: low inflation, stable rates and economy under control, courtesy of the Fed. Japanese investors had its $400 billion gorilla, Nomura Securities. We have our $400 billion gorilla, Fidelity Management."

Fleckenstein made a large profit for a client and for himself—betting against the overvalued Japanese market. Though shorting individual stocks was illegal in Japan, he found some "put options" trading in Amsterdam. He cashed his puts near the bottom of the decline and flew to Tokyo to celebrate.

MAJOR STOCK MARKET DECLINES IN THE UNITED STATES

1929–1932	Down 89 percent
1937–1938	Down 49 percent
1906–1907	Down 49 percent
1919–1921	Down 47 percent
1901–1903	Down 46 percent
1973–1974	Down 45 percent
1939–1942	Down 40 percent
1987–1987	Down 36 percent
1968–1970	Down 36 percent

Source: John Dennis Brown, *Panic Profits.*

THE FIVE LEAST PROFITABLE YEARS IN U.S. STOCKS

1931	Dow Down	52.7
1930	Dow Down	33.8
1937	Dow Down	32.8
1974	Dow Down	27.6
1932	Dow Down	21.3

Source: Ibbotson SBBI Yearbook.

THE FIVE BIGGEST DROPS SINCE 1929

1987 October 13–October 19. Dow loses 30.7 percent in four trading days, after falling 508 points on October 19.

1940 May 9–May 24. Dow loses 23.1 percent in thirteen trading days.

1938 March 15–March 31. Dow loses 22.2 percent in fourteen trading days.

1973 October 29–December 5. Dow loses 20 percent in twenty-six trading days.

1939 March 14–April 8. Dow loses 19.6 percent in twenty-one trading days.

BEAR'S DEFINITIONS

bear market. Stocks down 20 percent or more. Wall Street has experienced eight bear markets in past half-century, one approximately every six years.

blip. A decline of 5 percent or less in a stock market average.

correction. Popular euphemism for a decline in a stock market average of more than 10 percent and less than 20 percent. Makes a negative into a positive, as in: "My front fender had a correction when it hit a tree."

Bear's Favorite Reading Material

Wiped Out. Chronicle of an investor who managed to whittle a $62,000 portfolio down to $297.78 from May 1957 to May 1964—a period when stocks in general were doing well. This book is hard to find.

Getting Creamed on Wall Street. Pamphlet by "Horatio Alger" (pseudonym). The author decided to speculate in stocks to supplement his income. In spite of his MBA degree, his college major in finance, his stint as a stockbroker, and his training as a research analyst for a major oil company, his results were abysmal.

He opted for technical analysis, studied the chart books, and installed a tickertape machine. After making several profitable trades on the short side in early 1982, he quit his regular job. He then reports that he was "taking Valium and smoking more than at any other period in recollection." Several losing trades followed, and by year end he was out of a job and also out of money.

> So what have I learned from all my experiences? To you I say: Don't buy stock. Keep your hard-earned money in the bank and buy Treasury bills directly from your local Federal Reserve Bank." (Published by Fraser Publishing Company, Box 494, Burlington, VT 05402.)

Bears' Fondest Memory

Responding to pressure, in 1931, the New York Stock Exchange banned short selling altogether, then reversed the decision two days later when cooler heads prevailed. The NYSE also imposed the "uptick rule," still in effect today, which stipulates that a stock can only be sold short at a moment when the price is rising.

An inquisition, disguised as "hearings," was held in the Senate Banking and Currency Committee. The New York Stock Exchange, represented by the brash Richard Whitney, defended short selling, or at least the idea that Wall Street should be left alone to handle the problem.

Whitney said a market without shorts would be like a chair with one leg. He was on the witness stand when the committee released the names of 350 big-time short sellers who supposedly had brought the market down. This bombshell turned out to be a dud. The only name on the list anybody recognized was Sell 'Em All Ben Smith.

In one of the great moments in Wall Street history, the haughty and imperious Whitney, wearing his vested suit and sporting a gold pig on his watchfob, asked Smith for a loan. Smith detested Whitney and his snobbish airs, in spite of the fact that Whitney had defended short selling in his testimony to the senators.

Saying he "wanted to get this over quickly," Whitney requested a $250,000 loan "on my face."

"I remarked he was putting a pretty high value on his face," Smith later recounted. "So he told me that was his story and his back was to the wall and he had to have $250,000. I told him he had a lot of nerve to ask me for $250,000 when he didn't even bid me the time of day. I told him I frankly didn't like him—that I wouldn't loan him a dime."

Whitney was later sent to jail for stealing money from clients of his firm, the highly respected J. P. Morgan. This was Wall Street's greatest scandal, and Whitney's hitting up a bear for a loan was the bears' greatest moment.

THE MARCH OF BEARS

The following information is based on John Dennis Brown's *Panic Profits*.*

> *June–December 1890.* Result: Dow down 26 percent. Recession, bad year for crops, dollar loses support as Congress passes Sherman Silver Act, British investors stuck with losses from speculations in

---

* Adapted from *Panic Profits* by John Dennis Brown (1994). Reproduced with permission of McGraw-Hill Companies.

Argentina, Barings bank in trouble. "Bear raid" against the Northern Pacific drops price of that stock.

Sherman Anti-Trust law enacted, making large conglomerations such as the Standard Oil Trust illegal. This spooked investors. Congress authorizes Treasury to buy silver to support sagging price. Protective tariffs go into effect.

March 1892–July 1893. Dow down 43 percent. Railroads default en masse. One-third of the nation's track is owned by bankrupt companies. The Erie in receivership for the third time. Various rate agreements break down. Unnerved by the Sherman Silver Act, foreigners make a run on gold. This adds to gloom.

Stocks take dive after England's Barings Bank says it's crippled with bad loans in Argentina. Overexpansion of railroads (mostly with British money), ends in bust. Many railroads go bankrupt. Congress passes generous pension legislation, which threatens to sap U.S. Treasury. Foreign doubts about U.S. ability to maintain gold standard causes run on gold, draining U.S. supply.

September 1895–August 1896. Dow down 34 percent. London investors take bath in South African gold shares—"kaffirs"—as prices sink. Losses in South Africa causes Londoners to pull money from United States, causing losses in Dow. Squabble over Venezuela, fear of William Jennings Bryan silver candidacy add to panic.

William McKinley running for president on gold standard against Democrat William Jennings Bryan, supporting silver.

September 1899–September 1900. Dow down 32 percent. Boer war leads to huge losses in London's "Black Week." Again, British investors sell U.S. stocks to raise cash, causing decline over here. Glut in the iron market bad news for iron shares. U.S. troops fight Phillipine insurrection. Boxer rebellion in China.

John Hay, Secretary of State, sends "open door" note to European governments, urging them to keep ports in China open to all comers, and not to levy higher tariffs.

Congress passes Currency Act, making several types of currency redeemable in gold on demand, and reducing capital requirements for banks in small communities.

September 1901–November 1903. Dow down 46 percent. United States in recession until 1904, stocks hit bottom several months before economy falters. U.S. Steel shares drop from $40 to $10 after company cuts dividends, says it will close 25 percent of its factories. Heavy dose of antitrust legislation depresses Wall Street. Bigger trusts survive, but lesser trusts in witch hazel, caskets, bicycles, wallpaper, saws, etc., disband. Several underwriting deals fail. Well-financed attempts to nudge prices higher are foiled in this so-called "rich man's panic."

Teddy Roosevelt elected President. Congress authorizes Panama Canal. Coal miners' strike cripples coal industry, as workers lobby for right to form union. Roosevelt threatens to keep mines open with federal troops.

European countries block Venezuelan ports after that country reneges on foreign debts.

New legislation—the Elkins Act—strengthens the Interstate Commerce Commission, which has proven ineffective.

January 1906–November 1907. Dow down 49 percent. Copper boom ends in bust. Railroad stocks fall from perch that won't be reached again until 1920s. Tight money worldwide leads to economic depression. Fat cats stunned at Roosevelt's disloyal trust-busting.

Congress passes Pure Food and Drug Act.

November 1909–September 1911. Dow down 27 percent. Railroad stocks slump after Interstate Commerce Commission lowers freight charges, instead of raising them at companies' request. Various big businesses sued by antitrust factions. Europeans sell shares in United States on news of crisis in North Africa.

Ruling on cases involving the Sherman Anti-Trust Act, the Supreme Court orders the dissolution of Standard Oil Company and the American Tobacco Company. This is a huge blow to big business, Wall Street.

Business failures in Nicaragua and Honduras prompt U.S. banks to offer bailout loans. Henry Ford announces his company will produce only one chassis, the Model T variety. Mass production will keep prices low, so the average person can afford to buy a car.

September 1912–July 1914. Dow down 24 percent. War in Balkans, election of left-wing academic, Woodrow Wilson, spooks Wall Street. Recession follows. Scandals in railroad industry. World joins war in July 1914 and European markets sell off. New York Stock Exchange tries to avoid similar fate by going on vacation until mid-December. Official Dow loss for year doesn't include holiday period, when stocks trade at lower prices in "gutter market" that operates outdoors.

Passage of the sixteenth amendment gives Congress power to levy income tax, eliminates prior flaws in legislation that caused courts to declare income tax unconstitutional. Federal Reserve System established. In April 1914, U.S. Marines seize port of Veracruz, Mexico. Mexican guerilla Pancho Villa crosses border, attacks Columbus, New Mexico.

November 1916–December 1917. Dow down 40 percent. Investors have three worries: (1) Wilson's peace plan will keep United States out of profitable war; (2) United States will be dragged into unprofitable war; (3) without war to distract it, U.S. government will attack American business, impose new rules, levy new taxes. Railroads fall on rumors of government takeover. Stocks in car companies fall on rumors of government steel rationing.

German subs attack and sink American cargo ships, in violation of prior agreement. War declared on Germany.

November 1919–August 1921. Dow down 47 percent. Fed fights post-war inflation with higher interest rates. Europeans, suffering from deflation, stop buying U.S. stocks. Bear market in Liberty bonds, auto showrooms empty, General Motors in trouble. Pierce-Arrow Motors makes popular car, but stock falls from $83 to $9. In summer, 1921, Fed relents and drops interest rates. Market rallies.

Steelworkers strike against 12-hour day. Strike lasts for months; strikers eventually defeated. Volstead Act making liquor illegal is passed over Wilson's veto. Wilson signs Transportation Act, giving the Interstate Commerce Commission power to set rates on rail traffic. Prosperous railroads are obliged to share profits with their less fortunate rivals.

September 1929–July 1932. Dow down 89 percent. See page 240 for details.

March 1937–March 1938. Dow down 49 percent. Five years of prosperity on Wall Street come to sad end. Depression returns; two million names added to unemployment rolls. Industrial production sags. Japanese sink U.S. gunboat, Panay; Hitler cozies up to Austria. From this point forward, economy expands as United States prepares for war, with no letup until 1945.

Widespread labor troubles. CIO organizes auto and steel workers; sit-down strike makes its debut at a General Motors plant. Strikes contribute to business recession in October, 1937; stock market reacts badly.

Senate passes bill to set wages and hours for workers nation-wide—it goes into effect in October, 1938.

November 1938–April 1939. Dow down 23 percent. After rising on thoughts of a kinder, gentler Hitler, stocks fall as a meaner, harsher Hitler marches on Czechoslovakia. Steel stocks hardest hit, a perplexing result since war machine runs on steel.

Roosevelt asks Congress for $522 million for defense. Sends letter to Mussolini, Hitler, asking them to refrain from aggression.

September 1939–April 1942. Dow down 40 percent. Stocks register short-term gains as poorly-informed investors buy on sound of cannons. Sucker's rally gives way to three-year decline. Stocks meander between sharp drops, such as the Dunquerque drop of May 1940. Corporate earnings on rise, otherwise, this bear might have turned more vicious. Stocks hit bottom in early 1942, in delayed reaction to bombing of Pearl Harbor.

Hitler attacks Poland in 1939; Britain, France declare war and also place large orders with U.S. manufacturers. Roosevelt expands Navy, prods Congress to pass Lend Lease Act to supply more material to Allies. This has positive effect on business, adds 6 million workers to payroll. Auto manufacturers get so many new car orders from this new prosperity they're reluctant to convert to military production.

War is financed mostly by borrowing; total cost to United States is $350 billion, ten times the cost of World War I.

May 1946–June 1949. Dow down 24 percent. Prices so low many great companies sell for less than the amount of cash they have in bank. Stocks shunned by misguided investors who think every war leads to depression.

Pent-up demand from war leads to surge in consumer buying, enormous appetite for TV sets (now popular nationwide), dishwashers, electric stoves. Some commodities in short supply, prices rise dramatically, workers struck for higher wages in coal, automobile, steel and railroad industries. Financial crisis in Europe causes United States to come to rescue with Marshall Plan.

April 1956–October 1957. Dow down 19 percent. Auto stocks sunk by lousy car sales as Detroit cuts production almost in half. Country suffers from inflation and recession at same time. Suez war, Russian tanks in Budapest, and Sputnik in space add to gloom.

Eisenhower sends to troops to Little Rock to enforce school desegregation. During this period, 135 large companies owned 45 percent of U.S. industrial output. Recession of 1957 was first in which commodity prices didn't drop. That's because the conglomerates cut production to reduce supply, rather than risk lower prices from oversupply.

January 1960–October 1960. Dow down 17 percent. Pennsylvania Railroad shuts doors for first time in 118-year history. Cyclical companies hard hit; office equipment companies do OK.

December 1961–June 1962. Dow down 27 percent. Shortest bear since World War II. Stocks very expensive going into drop, with p/e ratios highest since 1929. Small stocks pricier than big stocks, thanks to new issue craze. Market sobers up in spring, when President Kennedy slaps price controls on steel industry.

February 1966–October 1966. Dow down 25 percent. Dow advances to 1,000, beats hasty retreat. Stocks bedeviled by Vietnam, inflation. Prime lending rate hiked four times in eight months, reaching highest level in 45 years: 6 percent. Banks caught in credit squeeze. Fed chairman calls for higher taxes.

December 1968–May 1970. Dow down 36 percent. High inflation makes for higher interest rates, as prime hits 8.5 percent. More troops sent to Vietnam, Cambodia makes round trip in body bags. Penn Central goes bankrupt. Ross Perot loses $1 billion on paper as his Electronic Data Systems stocks fall from $164 to $29 in a few weeks. Four students shot at Kent State.

January 1973–December 1974. Dow down 45 percent. Watergate, Spiro Agnew, Arab Oil embargo, Yom Kippur War, Nixon's resignation combine with recession to knock stocks off cliff. Consumer confidence at lowest level since 1946. Overpriced "Nifty Fifty" companies fall hardest; Disney (a typical case) drops from $110 to $16. At bottom, Dow sells for less than six times record earnings of 1974.

September 1976–February 1978. Dow down 27 percent. Rising interest rates, inflation, threat of tax hike, and weak dollar (even against the lowly Mexican peso) cause decline, mostly in large stocks. As Dow falters, small stocks reach new highs. Newer cable TV issues do well; chemicals, steels falter.

April 1981–August 1982. Dow down 24 percent. Fed raises interest rates to fight high inflation. Prime rate hits ozone of 20½ percent and government bonds yield 15 percent. Argentina invades Falklands; Israel marches on Lebanon. Inflation turns to deflation; commodity prices, oil stocks take tumble, Standard Oil of Ohio down to $28 from $92. Each of four prominent Dow Industrials (Chrysler, Inco, International Harvester, and Manville) sell for less than $10 a share, the cheapest prices they're fetched since 1932. Scandal at the Penn Square bank.

In July 1982, Fed lowers rates. In August, economist Dr. Henry Kaufman, a.k.a. Dr. Doom, says he sees lower rates ahead.

August 1987–October 1987. Dow down 36 percent. Stocks give back huge gains from earlier extravagant market. Along the way, the Dow falls 500 points in single traumatic session: Black Monday. Program traders and "portfolio insurance" blamed for Crash, but various blue-ribbon panels and study groups can't identify any particular culprit.

July 1990–October 1990. Dow down 20 percent. Saddam Hussein invades Kuwait. After reaching 2999.75 in July, Dow rattled by $40 a barrel oil, Congressional buffoonery, rising interest rates, unemployment, and fuel bills. Retail stocks catch the brunt: the Limited has its own 50 percent correction; Wal-Mart down 32 percent. Japanese Nikkei falls 48 percent from its high near 39,000 yen.

INDEX

INDEX

INDEX